MW00809964

Smedley D. Butler, USMC

Smedley D. Butler, USMC

A Biography

MARK STRECKER

McFarland & Company, Inc., Publishers
Jefferson, North Carolina, and London

LIBRARY OF CONGRESS CATALOGUING-IN-PUBLICATION DATA

Strecker, Mark, 1970–
   Smedley D. Butler, USMC : a biography / Mark Strecker.
      p.   cm.
   Includes bibliographical references and index.

   ISBN 978-0-7864-4807-4
   softcover : 50# alkaline paper ∞

   1. Butler, Smedley D. (Smedley Darlington), 1881–1940.
2. Generals—United States—Biography. 3. United States.
Marine Corps—Officers—Biography. 4. United States—
Politics and government—1933–1945. 5. Fascism—United
States. 6. Subversive activities—United States. I. Title.
VE25.B88S77 2011
359.9'6092—dc22 [B]   2010054473

BRITISH LIBRARY CATALOGUING DATA ARE AVAILABLE

Front Cover: United States Marine Corp insignia; Butler at Quantico
packing personal effects upon retirement from the Marines in 1931.
From the Smedley D. Butler Collection, courtesy of the Marine
Corps Archives and Special Collections Department at the Gray
Research Center, Quantico.

Manufactured in the United States of America

McFarland & Company, Inc., Publishers
  Box 611, Jefferson, North Carolina 28640
  www.mcfarlandpub.com

To the memory of
my loving sister,
Tamera S. Keller, 1968–2010

Acknowledgments

A number of people gave me invaluable help during the research and writing of this book. The entire library staff in the Special Collections Department at the Gray Research Center in particular withstood my constant requests and questions for four days without a complaint, offering inestimable help. I wish to thank J. Michael Miller, the head of the Archives and Special Collections at the Marine Corps University. When I wrote to that university's library asking for a copy of a book unique to its collections, I figured I would receive a looseleaf duplicate if I could get anything at all. To my surprise and delight, one day I found a bound copy of it in my mailbox. Better still, Mr. Miller, the book's editor, wrote a nice cover letter to me as well. This went above and beyond the call of duty!

Two of Smedley Butler's granddaughters, Molly Swanton and Edith Wehle, gave me a treasure trove of anecdotes, insights, and corrections. They kindly offered to read the manuscript before its completion, and for this they have my immense gratitude. I also need to thank Jessica Little, librarian extraordinaire, who read one of my later drafts. Her amazing editorial suggestions helped me to keep my facts and timeline straight. Finally, I need to add a blanket thanks to all those countless others at libraries and museums who assisted me in so many different ways.

Contents

A Note on Names
and Quotations

Many of the geographic names that appear in this book have changed since Butler's time, especially those in China. Peking, for example, is now Beijing. For the sake of consistency I have used the geographic names as Butler and his contemporaries knew them rather than their modern variations. In that same vein, when reproducing quotations, I have retained the spelling, capitalization (or lack thereof), and grammar found in the originals except for minor tweaks to get them to fit smoothly into a sentence.

Preface

When people asked me about the subject of this book, I often replied, "I'm writing a biography of a Marine general you've never heard of." This, alas, satisfied them, especially when I told them his name. Few people today, save for Marine historians and conspiracy theory devotees, have heard of Major General Smedley Darlington Butler. In all honesty, until I read Joel Bakan's *The Corporation: The Pathological Pursuit of Profit and Power* (a companion to the documentary *The Corporation*), I did not know of him either. Bakan outlined the story of how Butler exposed an alleged fascist plot to remove President Franklin D. Roosevelt from office. This incident sparked my interest, and I thought I would like to write something about this if enough material existed to do so.

As I delved into its details, I discovered a booklet written by Butler published in 1935 titled *War Is a Racket*. It made the case that big business promoted wars because of the obscene profits made from them. In a complementary article Butler penned for the November 1935 issue of the socialist magazine *Common Sense*, he wrote, "I was a racketeer for capitalism…. I feel I might have given Al Capone a few hints. The best *he* could do was to operate his racket in three city districts. We Marines operated on three *continents*."[1]

Inspired by these words as well as the story of the conspiracy, I started research in 2005 for a book examining the history of the American government's use of its military to further the foreign interests of large American corporations. I soon realized I could best accomplish this by writing a biography of Butler himself, since telling the story of his life presents a poignant history of this very subject. Butler interacted with or fought against a number of dictators in the Americas for the benefit of U.S. corporations — events that deeply shaped his politics. His experiences transformed him from a conservative Republican into an anti–corporate left-wing populist.

Butler merits a biography for several reasons. He not only participated in historically significant events, he helped to shape them. The modern Marine Corps owes much to his influence. He lived in a transformative era that began with the age of the horse and buggy and ended with World War II; a study of his life offers an excellent personal snapshot of that time period. Best of all, Butler's life reads like an adventure novel, making it an almost guaranteed page turner. Yet make no mistake: this biography will not place Butler upon a pedestal nor attempt to tear him down. It will present him as honestly as possible, warts and all.

1

The Fighting Quaker

Imagine for a moment living in southeastern Pennsylvania in 1881. Here flowed the Delaware River, and along its banks stood the mighty city of Philadelphia. Nearby one would find Chester County, an area blessed with gentle hills, unburdened by mountains, and watered by creeks and streams. It offered a pleasant place to live[1]—so far as that went. In 1881, even in the well-settled East, danger lurked everywhere. Take a typical week as reported by the July 30 issue of the *Chester Daily Times*: John Roach died while trying to board a passing train; a "fall of coal" crushed Joseph Vallance to death; John Beutley's life ended in a somewhat horrid way when he got "caught in the machinery while repairing some leathern belting at the Central Foundry" in Lewisburg; and lightning struck and killed Patrick Lavelle, Mrs. Jogenski, and the wife of Henry Van Vorst during a thunderstorm, while several others suffered injuries.[2]

In contrast, the *Chester Daily Times* offered no mention of any births on this day, such as that of a boy in West Chester born to Maud Mary and Thomas Stalker Butler on July 30, 1881. Christened Smedley Darlington, he arrived as a "blue baby," making him the runt of his family and leading to his suffering from ill health all his life. Baby Smedley would defy all the odds against surviving to adulthood in this era, then flout them again as a professional soldier who put his life in danger countless times.[3] The unusual name "Smedley" originated in the Nottinghamshire region of England around 1591 as a surname. It may have derived from the Old English words for "smooth" and "wood" or for "clearing."[4] The Butlers chose "Smedley" in honor of Maud's maternal grandparents and "Darlington" after her maiden name.[5] Smedley Darlington's closest friends often called him "Smed."[6]

Maud and Thomas married in February 1879.[7] They lived on South High Street in West Chester until 1885, when they bought a house on Miner Street.[8] West Chester itself stood roughly in the center of Chester County and served as the county seat.[9] Maud and Thomas produced two younger brothers for Smedley: Samuel on April 20, 1884, and Horace on April 3, 1893. In one of

3

life's little ironies, Smedley, the career soldier who saw his share of combat, died peacefully in bed. His brothers had less fortunate ends. Although Horace, the youngest, served as an officer in the U.S. Navy during World War I,[10] for most of his life he worked in the oil industry. He met his end on February 14, 1930, near Mineral Wells, Texas. As he rode in a car driven by his brother Sam, a child ran out in front of it. Sam swerved to miss, hitting another vehicle in which rode a husband and wife as well as their four-year-old daughter. Horace and the girl died instantly, while the girl's parents died later at a hospital.[11]

Sam suffered a more gruesome end. On October 15, 1947, a pair of fishermen discovered two bodies at the head of Ringling Lake, located about two miles north of Eastland, Texas. Authorities identified one man as Frank Dwyer and the other as Samuel Butler. Both men had died from shots to the head from a .32 caliber gun, found at the scene. At that time Sam lived in Denver and worked for the Sharples Oil Company, a corporation in which his brother-in-law had a "controlling interest." Before taking this job, Sam had owned his own business, the Arab Oil Company, but during World War II he dissolved it and went to work for Sharples.[12] Sam had employed Dwyer as a superintendent for his company before it shut down.[13] Two days after the discovery of the bodies, Justice of the Peace E.E. Wood ruled that Dwyer had murdered Butler, then shot himself. No one knew Dwyer's motive, but one newspaper account hinted it had something to do with the fact that Dwyer lost his job when the Arab Oil Company closed.[14]

Thomas Butler supported his family the first few years of his married life by practicing law. He became a judge of the Fifteenth Judicial District of Pennsylvania "for several years," then left that job in favor of a run for the U.S. House of Representatives as a Republican. He won a seat in 1896 as representative of the Sixth Congressional District, one that encompassed Delaware and Chester counties. He would hold it until his death.[15]

Thomas and Maud raised their boys in a community dominated by members of the Society of Friends, known to non–practitioners as Quakers. The Butler family belonged to an offshoot faction called the Hicksites, a group that had splintered from the mainstream in early 1827 in an event called the Great Separation. The Hicksites derived their name from their founder, Elias Hicks,[16] whose theological differences with the mainstream amounted to a debate we need not get into here. The Hicksites tended to focus more on helping the less fortunate than their orthodox brethren. After the Civil War, for example, they set up schools for former slaves.[17] Smedley remembered his earliest religious vocation as such: "I was vigorously brushed and combed and soaped to acquire the cleanliness next to godliness before going to the Friends' Meeting twice a week. Dozing off on a hard bench to the drone of words that meant nothing to me and being poked awake and upright again are all I remember of those early services."[18]

While this upbringing would shape Smedley's personality, it did not mean he adhered to all of the Friends' teachings. Friends, for example, avoided alcohol or at least drank little, refused to swear or to give oaths, and practiced pacifism. Smedley did the opposite of all three.[19] The Friends spoke the so-called Plain Language. This speech, based on the idiom found in the King James Bible, involved a good supply of "thee's" and "thy's," but no "thou's" or "wilt's." By the time of Butler's birth, most Friends confined the Plain Language to their homes and meetings, using the vernacular in public.[20] Although Smedley recalled that his father used the Plain Language in his public life,[21] a sampling of his discussions on the floor of Congress in 1916 shows that he did not do so there.[22] After his marriage, Smedley and his family spoke the Plain Language among themselves at home.[23]

Despite the fact that George Fox, the founder of the Society of Friends, proclaimed to no less a figure than King Charles II of England in 1660 that his brethren refused to participate in war because it went against the precepts of their religion,[24] some members of the Butler family had earned the appellation "Fighting Quakers" because of their participation in the Civil War. Both of Smedley's grandfathers had served in this conflict. Their war stories conferred upon Smedley a love of all things military.[25] Thomas Butler himself became a member of the House Naval Affairs Committee and chaired it throughout the Harding and Coolidge administrations.[26] In this position he strove to ensure that the United States had the world's most "efficient" navy, one "on a parity with Great Britain's," although in his later years he tried and failed to initiate a reduction in the size of all of the world's navies.[27]

Smedley and his brothers attended Society schools. Smedley in particular went to the Friends' School and, later, Haverford College Grammar School near Philadelphia.[28] About school, he noted, "Studying was not my specialty."[29] Athletic, he served as the captain of Haverford's football and baseball teams.[30] While he would never attend college, his brothers did. Since his father had not paid for Smedley's higher education, he instead gave him $4,000 years later.[31]

Smedley learned one skill at school that would serve him well in his later years: elocution. Because he did so well at it, a teacher entered him into a public speaking contest. He pledged to recite a speech by oratory giant William Cullen Bryant. When the time came to give it, he instead delivered a passage from Mark Twain's autobiographical book *Roughing It*. Although Butler recalled in his memoir that he performed "Storm on the Erie Canal," he had in fact recited a poem *about* a storm on the Erie Canal called "The Aged Pilot Man." It told the tale of how the crew of a boat on this canal reacted to a storm. To save themselves from sinking into the four feet of water below them, they dumped over the side of their barge three anvils, a keg of nails, four bales of gunnysacks, 200 pounds of glue, two sacks of corn, four sacks of wheat, a box of books, a cow, a violin, Lord Byron's complete works, and a ripsaw. As Butler spoke, the boys in the crowd went wild, but the teachers judging the contest did not find Butler's surprise amusing. He did not even receive an honorable mention.[32]

The direction of Butler's life changed profoundly on February 15, 1898. On this day the USS *Maine* blew up in Havana Harbor, Cuba. While no one at the time could decide whether the ship's end had come from accident or attack,[33] many American newspapers had a field day with the subject. Those papers that expounded the belief that the Spanish had caused the ship's destruction created a slew of jingoistic phrases and propaganda to whip up support for a war against Spain. The *New York Journal,* for example, dedicated "an average of eight and a half pages of news, editorials, and pictures to the *Maine.*"[34] William Randolph Hearst, the newspaper mogul, offered a $50,000 reward for the arrest and conviction of those responsible. On February 17, 1898, Hearst's *New York Journal* ran this headline: "THE WARSHIP *Maine* WAS SPLIT IN TWO BY AN ENEMY'S SECRET INFERNAL MACHINE." Joseph Pulitzer's *The World* soon added to this speculation with "THE *Maine* EXPLOSION WAS CAUSED BY A BOMB — SUSPICION OF A TORPEDO." Hearst outdid his professional rival on February 18 with this now infamous rallying cry: "REMEMBER THE *Maine!* TO HELL WITH SPAIN!"[35]

Not all major newspapers held these opinions. The *New York Times,* for example, editorialized, "Of course, nobody is so foolish as to believe that the Maine was destroyed by Spaniards with the knowledge and connivance of their Government…. Spain has just now too many reasons for avoiding cause of offense to us to make it permissible to suppose that she would not exercise due diligence to protect a ship of our navy visiting her waters."[36] Such a sober assessment failed to affect the masses. More people enlisted in America's armed forces than they needed or ever used during this conflict.[37] Thirty-five years after this event, Butler still thought the Spanish guilty, for he recalled without a mention of doubt: "I clenched my fists when I thought of those poor Cuban devils being starved and murdered by the beastly Spanish tyrants. I was determined to shoulder a rifle and help free little Cuba."[38]

President McKinley balked at the idea. Both he and his secretary of the Navy, John D. Long, suspected the *Maine* had exploded by accident. They knew that since 1895 thirteen American naval ships had experienced similar, if not such fatal, occurrences started by spontaneous combustion in the ships' magazines. McKinley would wait for an inquiry. This faced difficulties because Havana Harbor contained muddy waters that made it hard to explore, leading investigators to conclude a Spanish mine had set off the *Maine's* magazine which, upon exploding, destroyed the ship.[39] Since then theories have abounded as to the real cause, but no consensus exists.[40] When the report became public on March 28, public anger against Spain swelled.[41] On April 20 "McKinley signed a joint resolution of Congress" that recognized Cuba's independence, demanded Spain leave the island, and authorized the president to use military force if necessary to extricate the Spanish from the island.[42] Spain reacted by declaring war on the United States on April 24. The United States in turn declared war on Spain on April 25, making it retroactive to April 21.[43]

The war with Spain had roots far deeper than just the explosion of a battleship. In the early 1890s American investments in Cuban sugar and mining interests amounted to $50 million. By 1893 American trade with the island exceeded $100 million.[44] Sugar more than anything else had made Cuba rich in the last two decades of the nineteenth century, thanks in no small part to American money invested for the purchase of modern mills and transport systems.[45] In 1895 a terrible sugar depression ensued. The passage of an unnecessary tariff by the U.S. Congress that imposed a forty percent duty on sugar imports caused the market to collapse. Sugar's price dropped from eight cents a pound to two cents. Cuban sugar plantations closed and workers lost their jobs.[46]

This drove the former Cuban slave population, only emancipated in 1886, to rebel. Cuban independence leaders exiled abroad returned to the island to lead the fight.[47] One such principal, José Julián Martí y Perez, a poet and essayist, came to the island in 1895 to lead his people to freedom. Although killed in a skirmish with Spanish troops, he left a telling legacy in the United States. In 1892 he had set up a movement based in Manhattan to marshal the American public to his cause. This had popularized the rallying cry "*¡Cuba libre!*"— one that the American people and press soon embraced.[48]

The American business community had mixed feelings about military intervention in Cuba. On one hand, some wanted to make Cuba an American colony, while on the other, Wall Street stock prices dropped every time it appeared war in Cuba might occur, then went up when it looked like peace would prevail.[49] When the *Maine* exploded, a majority of American businessmen still opposed war with Spain over Cuba. Nonetheless, the minority opinion that war would benefit American business won out. In May 1897, a group of businessmen presented "a memorial on the subject" of American financial losses in Cuba "bearing over three hundred signatures ... presented to John Sherman, Secretary of State."[50]

At the same time, a group of Cuban-American businessmen, all U.S. citizens and many associated with the Cuban Revolutionary Party, formed a "junta" to do everything possible to fan the flames of tension between Spain and America. In December 1897, Dupuy de Lôme, Cuba's Spanish minister, wrote a private letter to José Canalejas, a liberal politician and newspaper editor in Havana. In it Lôme criticized President McKinley and the ongoing trade negotiations between Spain and America. Somehow this letter got into the hands of the junta. Horatio Rubens, its legal counsel, decided to do a creative translation from Spanish to English before releasing it to the American press. Since no one who received it had access to the original, the media never realized Rubens had produced a tone that made Lôme's insults seem much worse. Published on February 9, 1898, it did its job well: newspaper editors across the country called for war with Spain.[51]

When the war came, Butler tried to join the National Guard's Sixth Regiment, First Company, to whom he "lied glibly about his age, but the recruiting officers … would not believe him."[52] He heard his father say Congress had authorized an expansion of the Marine Corps. Only a year earlier it had had a mere 3,806 officers and men on duty. Butler did not know much about that military branch of service at the time, but had seen several Marines marching in the streets and decided he would not mind wearing their uniform. The next day he told his mother in private if she did not give her consent for him to join the Corps, he would run away and sign up anyway. Resigned, she agreed.[53]

The two went to a recruiting office in Washington, D.C. Butler gave his age as eighteen, then successfully took a test to qualify as an officer. As the recruiting sergeant asked him questions, Butler could see his father outside the window.[54] He received an appointment as a second lieutenant on May 20, 1898.[55] When the Friends threatened to read him out of their meetings for joining the military, his mother intimated she would start her own branch if they did. He stayed.[56]

Butler joined at just the right time in the Marine Corps' history. Earlier in the decade it had nearly disappeared. In 1890 a group of naval officers, spearheaded by a paper written by a young lieutenant named William F. Fullam, tried to transfer the Marines to the Army so as to give the Navy a chance to create its own amphibious force composed of bluejackets (enlisted seamen). In 1894 this naval cabal convinced the Senate to introduce a bill that would have combined the Marines with five U.S. Army regiments of artillery. It failed in a committee, but certain officers in the Navy worked hard to reduce the role of the Marines over the next few years. This trend finally reversed with the outbreak of hostilities with Spain; the upcoming conflict prompted Congress to expand the Corps for the first time in years.[57]

Out of this came the newly formed First Battalion of Marines, which the Navy transported to Key West for deployment to Cuba in early April 1898.

Lieutenant Colonel Robert W. Huntington, a veteran of the First Battle of Bull Run, commanded. Although he picked Major Percival C. Pope as his second-in-command, Pope could not go due to illness, so Huntington reluctantly named Major Henry Clay Cochrane instead. The two men had, years earlier, come to blows while serving together on a promotion board.[58]

At Cuba itself, Captain Charles Sigsbee, who had served as the commander of the *Maine* when it exploded, proposed the conquest of a bay called Guantánamo. He believed it could provide an excellent coal depot as well as a good shelter for ships during a hurricane. On June 7, as two Navy ships bombarded Guantánamo's fortifications, the transport *Panther* deposited 650 of the newly arrived Marines on shore as well as a number of war correspondents, including Stephen Crane of *The Red Badge of Courage* fame. The Marine force, commanded by Huntington, headed to Crest Heights, the area's high point. Although the Marines went unmolested the first day, a corps of 3,000 Spaniards attacked the next. Armed with one-shot Winchester-Lee straight-pull bolt-action rifles, the Marines held them off for three days. Huntington knew they could not maintain this position forever, so he moved his men down to the beach. When Cuban reinforcements came, they told him destroying Cuzco Well, the only source of water the Spaniards had access to, would drive them back. Huntington sent Captain George F. Elliott to accomplish this, which he and his Cuban allies did. Although around 6,000 Spaniards remained in the area, they did not harass the Marines,[59] who have a base there to this day.

As the war progressed, Butler learned the trade of a Marine officer in Washington, D.C., under the tutelage of Sergeant Major Hayes. Butler, along with two other second lieutenants, George Reid and Peter Wynne, shipped out to Cuba from New York Harbor on the steamer *St. Paul.* They arrived at Santiago on July 10, 1898, then transferred to the cruiser *Vesuvius*, upon which they suffered from terrible sea sickness. This vessel took them to Guatemala, where they boarded the USS *New York*, Admiral William Sampson's flagship and Butler's official posting with the North Atlantic Marine Battalion. From this they took a transport to the Cuban shore at the secured Guantánamo Bay.[60]

They asked a corporal where they could find Colonel Huntington, the man to whom they had to report. The corporal pointed them to his headquarters, at which a "bow-legged" old soldier with a white beard sat in a canvas chair. They asked him for the colonel's whereabouts. What did they want him for? They told him. He asked, "'Going to help him win the war, are you?'" The three young officers did not like his attitude. Butler dressed him down. Upon seeing this, another old fellow in the room laughed so hard he fell off the crate upon which he sat. Lieutenant Wynne threatened to report him. A moment later a private came in and saluted the old man in the canvas chair, stunning the three lieutenants by addressing him as Colonel Huntington. Butler learned he would serve directly under the fellow who had laughed, Captain Mancil C. Goodrell, the company commander.[61]

Butler found that despite his rank, the enlisted men did not respect him or his fellow second lieutenants because of their lack of experience. Luckily for Butler, Goodrell took him under his wing. Butler's first time in command came one night when he took charge of the thirty-man Salt March Picket. Terrified, he gave no orders and later admitted he had no idea what he would have told the men in any case. A Sergeant Slater kept them in order for him. He saw no combat that night. On another evening, Captain Goodrell took him on a walk near the front lines. Along the way, a bullet whizzed past his head. He hit the ground, but the captain stood firm. Embarrassed, he got back to his feet. His self-esteem failed to improve when he tried to drill his men. He had no idea what orders to give and made a mess of it. He credited Captain Goodrell for teaching him much about this process.[62]

His battalion boarded the *Resolute* to head with a flotilla to the port city of Manzanillo, the target of an American bombardment and invasion.[63] This city had already suffered from periodic attacks by the U.S. Navy. On the first occasion, a naval skirmish, and later a brief but intense naval battle, had erupted. This and the following assaults failed to neutralize the harbor's defenses or completely stop blockade runners from escaping. The latest American flotilla arrived on August 12, 1898, to make the last and most massive attempt at conquest.[64] Butler's battalion received orders to land the next day — quite possibly a bloody affair. Before deploying, word of the Spanish surrender reached them, so the planned bombardment and amphibious assault did not take place.[65]

Butler returned home in September on the USS *New York*, which docked at the Brooklyn Navy Yard. On board he learned all about ships and sailing.[66] In October he participated in a Peace Jubilee parade held on League Island,[67] located in the Delaware River, the home of a navy yard. Butler did not stay here long. The Corps abruptly mustered him out on February 16, 1899,[68] because it lacked the authorization to keep its wartime size. Shortly thereafter, Congress tripled its numbers because it had demonstrated its usefulness during the recent war.[69] This gave Butler the opportunity to rejoin on April 8, 1899, as a first lieutenant.[70]

Now other events about which Butler had little knowledge conspired to drag him to the Philippine Islands. While the Spanish-American War had given the United States an easy military victory, it had left the U.S. with an unsettling legacy: possession of the Philippines and its people, a populace disinclined to exchange one master for another. Like the Cubans, the Filipinos had suffered from Spanish rule and wanted independence. Unlike Cuba, where the U.S. worked with resistance leaders, America failed to embrace the Filipino revolutionaries.[71]

Composed of several factions and leaders, the Filipino revolutionary movement elected Emilio Aguinaldo y Famy as its president in early 1897, the same year the revolutionaries asked for an agreement to end hostilities. The Spanish offered them one: they would provide Aguinaldo and his revolutionary cohorts with 800,000 pesos, give amnesty to all revolutionaries, and implement reforms as to how they administered the Philippines. In exchange, Aguinaldo and the other leaders would go into exile. The Treaty of Biak-na-Bato, signed on December 14, 1897, made this official.[72]

After receiving the first 400,000 pesos, the revolutionary leaders went to Hong Kong. They put their money into a British bank and lived off the interest. They planned to use the principal to pay for renewed hostilities in case the Spanish went back on their word, which they did.[73] (Spanish officials, for example, failed to stop the persecution of natives who did not wish to convert to Christianity.[74]) At this time Admiral George Dewey commanded the U.S. Asiatic Squadron. One of his subordinates, Lieutenant R.V. Hall of the gunboat *Petrel,* sought out Aguinaldo to offer him a deal. The Americans would arm his men and transport them back to the Philippines if he agreed to help fight the Spanish. Hall assured Aguinaldo that America had no interest in possessing the Philippines for itself.[75]

Out of the blue, Isabelo Artacho, a former Filipino politician who had served in the revolutionary government for only two months, appeared before Aguinaldo and the other exiles and demanded they give him 200,000 pesos. If they refused, he would take legal action. The exiles decided upon a bold course to stop this: Aguinaldo and two aides withdrew the money from the bank and, using false identities, took it Singapore, where they would go into hiding. There the U.S. consul, E. Spencer Pratt, somehow learned of Aguinaldo's presence and, in a "cloak-and-dagger" effort, met secretly with him. Pratt assured Aguinaldo that Dewey himself guaranteed America would recognize the Philippines' independence if the exiled president would lead his rebels against the Spanish, pointing out that since the Spaniards had reneged on their pledge to implement promised reforms, Aguinaldo had every right to rebel once more.[76] When Secretary of State William Day heard of this deal, he told Pratt not to negotiate with the insurrectionists.[77]

Aguinaldo and two aides returned to Hong Kong to sail with Dewey to the Philippines, only to find that the admiral and his fleet already departed, although Dewey sent a ship back to retrieve them. Once home, Aguinaldo met with Dewey face to face for the first time. Dewey twice assured Aguinaldo he would guarantee the Philippines' independence. Dewey and all other American officials who had negotiated with the Filipino rebel leader later denied having ever made any such promise. To his regret, Aguinaldo had never convinced any American representative to put anything into writing.[78]

During the planning stages of the U.S.-Filipino joint attack on Manila, Aguinaldo came to the realization the U.S. would not keep its word when he learned that American officials had made a separate deal with the Spanish living in the city, the latter agreeing to surrender peacefully if the Americans pledged to exclude the Filipinos from the occupation of the walled section of Manila. They would.[79] Filipino forces nonetheless controlled the rest of the city. When President McKinley decided to make the Philippines an American territory, the Filipinos rebelled. They started their new war on February 4, 1899, two days before the signing of the treaty in which the Spanish gave the Philippines to America.[80]

The revolutionary forces, known locally as *insurrectos,* tried to wage a conventional campaign. On November 12, 1900, with the Filipino rebels nearly out of ammunition, Aguinaldo ordered a switch from conventional to guerrilla warfare.[81] The rebels set up shadow governments in towns, often intimidating and sometimes getting the cooperation of their mayors. They also frightened the population at large, making it unwilling to assist American forces.[82]

Butler landed in Manila in April 1899.[83] At this point the rebels had just begun the conventional phase of their rebellion; he would leave the country long before the guerrilla stage. Stationed at Cavite Naval Base, about ten miles from Manila, he commanded Company A and served directly under Captain H.C. Haines. He "quartered in the former Spanish Commandant's palace." There each officer had a Chinese servant, "whose chief occupation was to see that the supply of whiskey, ice and mineral water didn't run low."[84] Butler might have found life easy here, but it did not satisfy him. Despite the terror he had felt during his brief time walking the Cuban battle lines, he nonetheless wanted to see combat. Frustrated at a lack of opportunity for this, he wrote to his mother and asked her to request that his father use his influence to get him into combat. How else, he asked, would he ever prove himself?[85]

One of Smedley's earliest forays into action failed to fulfill that need. His company participated in an attack on the small town of Orani on the north shore of Manila Bay. The eccentric Colonel Percival Pope commanded this venture. Butler remembered him as a man who lacked any hair on his head "but he thought none of us knew it." Colonel Pope had "two wigs, one long-haired and the other, closely clipped. On the first of each month he stirred up a great commotion about sending for the barber. That evening he appeared at dinner in his short wig and explained most elaborately that he had just had a hair-cut. About the middle of the month he changed to the long-haired wig and began to talk about needing the barber again."[86]

In his honor, the Marines christened their transport — a fortified ten-foot-wide, fifty-foot-long shallow-draft barge — the *Pope.* They hid in its bottom as it skimmed its way toward the town, two steam launches pulling it. Lined with boilerplates to repel bullets, it had two three-inch landing guns tied down with ropes. When fired, one broke free and fell into the ocean, taking part of the barge with it. The force of the other swung the barge around, prompting the concealed Marines to yell and stand up for fear of drowning, ruining the "Trojan Horse strategy." It did not matter because the townspeople had already abandoned the settlement. Two pigs died.[87]

When rebels raided several towns south of the U.S. naval base at Cavite, the U.S. Army decided it needed to force them out with Marine support.[88] On October 8 the combined American military forces attacked the area from unexpected points, an assault the rebels did not anticipate because the annual October rains had flooded the whole area, making an intrusion difficult.[89] As the Army attacked its real objective, Cavite Viejo (modern Kawit), the Marines provided a diversionary attack on the town of Noveleta.[90] Two U.S. gunboats, the *Wheeling* and *Petrel,* bombarded the shore to provide cover as the Marines crossed a nearby causeway. These men, Butler among them, made their way down the peninsula, traveling on "a narrow road through swamps." About a mile into the march, the enemy, lodged in trenches across the road, opened fire. Flanking the Filipino rebels, the Marines drove them out. The rebels retreated across a creek, destroying the bridge upon which they had traversed, then made their way into sand forts. The Marines followed, wading through rice paddies and the creek, its water going up to about their shoulders. They took the forts, then headed into Noveleta proper. There *insurrectos* fired at them from the cover of houses and huts along the road, so the Marines burned them out.[91]

Butler's company contained fifty-six men. It pushed ahead up the road. After Captain Haines lost sight of it,[92] the company made its way up a sandy road and, turning "a sharp corner," nearly ran into an enemy entrenchment. Taking fire, everyone dropped to the ground save for one Irish sergeant who suffered a crippling wound as a result. When Butler realized his men awaited his orders, he shook off his panic, stood up, then told them to "commence firing." Moving ahead, they drove the *insurrectos* forward. By the time he and the other Marines met up with the Army, the fighting had ceased.[93]

Well over a thousand miles away at Fen Cho Fu, a settlement found in Shanshi Province in northeastern China, an American missionary named Eva Jane Price and her family faced a gathering danger. They and the other Christian missionaries found themselves threatened by a sect of Chinese fanatics called the "Boxers," a cult that desired the eviction of all Christians from China. In early February 1900, Price wrote home reporting that these so-called Boxers had already killed several European missionaries and molested people she knew. In late July 1900, the governor of the province ordered all foreigners out. In a later letter, Price complained that this "wicked" governor had recently orchestrated the beheading of thirty-three of her friends on July 8, including two pregnant women and twelve children. The missionaries planned to escape into the nearby mountains. Eva wrote, "If only foreign soldiers could soon come into the province we would probably be saved."[94] When the missionaries departed on August 15, 1900, the local district magistrate assigned twenty soldiers to escort them.[95] But could the missionaries trust them? Would Western soldiers come to their rescue?

Upon his return to Cavite, Butler went to a Japanese tattoo artist and had him emblazon the Marine Corps emblem across his chest. (This he received while drunk and not only did he find he could not remove it, it caused an acute illness, probably an infection.[96]) He spent his spare time enjoying life to its fullest. On Saturday nights, for example, he and his friends went to cockfights held by the tailor who made Marine uniforms on their base. One night several men burst into Butler's room, which he shared with his friend Pete Wynne. These fellows introduced alcohol, starting an impromptu party. They made so much racket they kept the man in charge of all Marines in Manila, Colonel Robert L. Meade, awake. Irritated, the next morning Meade relieved Butler of his command, then asked him if he would like a transfer to avoid humiliation. Butler stayed.[97]

In December 1898, a new major, Littleton Waller Tazewell Waller — "Tony" to his friends — arrived in the country to command the Marines' First Battalion. He soon became one of Butler's best friends as well as his mentor. About him Butler wrote in his memoir: "I can say without reservation that Littleton Tazewell Waller was the greatest soldier I have ever known."[98] Waller influenced the impressionable Butler and taught him more about becoming a Marine officer than anyone else he fought with.

Born on September 26, 1856, in York County, Virginia, Waller saw his first battle as a boy during the Civil War when he climbed up a tree to witness the historic naval battle of the *Merrimack* and *Monitor*. He joined the Marines in 1880 as a second lieutenant, serving in a variety of places including a naval siege of Alexandria, Egypt. In 1884 he made his name not in combat but rather as a judge advocate general, serving in that position in August and September. Despite having no formal training as a lawyer, he entrenched his reputation by winning the court-martial of David B. Sayre, a paymaster's clerk charged with embezzlement. Sayre appealed this conviction on the grounds that the military had no jurisdiction over him. The case went all the way to the Supreme Court. Waller joined Virginia's Eastern Circuit bar, then successfully argued the case before the justices.[99]

In June 1900, Waller received orders to report to the backwater post of

Guam. He could take five officers with him, so he asked Butler to come. Because of his friendship with Waller and not of out a desire to see that "God-forsaken island," Butler agreed. Right before departing, Waller and his men received new orders to head for China instead. Waller also gave Butler some good news: he would regain command of his company.[100]

2

An Imperial Action

Waller's Marine detachment sailed out of Manila at midnight on June 13, 1900, bound for Taku, China, upon a hospital ship called the *Solace*.[1] This force, consisting of seven officers and 106 enlisted men, arrived on July 2, 1900, at three-thirty in the morning.[2] Taku stood at the mouth of the Pei-Ho River on the western shore of the Gulf of Pe-Chi-Lo. The gulf's shoal water and a series of steep sand bars prevented deep-water vessels such as the *Solace* from getting too near, forcing those disembarking to take shallow-draft transport boats. A sandbar at the Pei-Ho's mouth limited traffic into this river — only boats drawing less than eleven feet of water could cross it at high tide.[3]

Filled with corpses and stinking of sewage, the Pei-Ho River flowed through Chihli Province, the one in which all the events chronicled in this chapter take place. An embedded journalist named Thomas F. Millard considered the Pei-Ho nothing more than a "ditch," although it had enough width to accommodate "endless double lines of junks." It served as a breeding ground for "mosquitoes by the million" that allowed for the spread of "disease in many forms, and death multiplied for friend and foe alike."[4]

Three Chinese-built and -manned fortresses, the Taku forts, stood at the river's mouth, each one outfitted with modern artillery, and each possessing the equipment needed to bar entry to the river should it become necessary.[5] Despite such defenses, the invading Europeans managed to take them on June 17, 1900, in preparation for a full-scale invasion.[6] This roused the ire of China's Qing Dynasty, or Manchus, prompting its de facto ruler, Empress-Dowager Cixi, to side with the Boxers. After issuing an edict blaming the Boxer uprising on the foreigners' own actions, she declared war on June 21.[7] The foreign troops flooding into the country would therefore face both Boxers and Imperial Chinese soldiers, the latter of whom had modern weapons but little training using them.[8]

Waller and his men expected to face hordes of Boxers at Taku. Their ignorance of the Boxers' ethos and purpose fueled their fears.[9] Knowing more about the Boxers' origins would not have eased their minds. The Boxers called themselves the *I Ho Ch'üan,* or Righteous Harmonious Fists, but Westerners used the term "Boxers" because of this group's dedication to martial arts.[10] About seventy percent of the Boxers, all male, came from the peasant class. A female version, the Red Lanterns Shining, composed mainly of girls aged twelve to eighteen, targeted Chinese Christian women. The Boxer religion contained elements of Taoism, Buddhism and Confucianism. The Westerners' lack of respect for Chinese gods or the Buddha angered them, and they considered conversion to Christianity a form of heresy. The Boxers originated in Shantung Province,[11] a place that for millennia had little to no contact with foreigners in general and Westerners in particular. When a treaty allowed Western missionaries to go there in 1858, their presence changed the province's dynamics with the introduction of Christianity.[12] Making matters worse, a number of the white Christian missionaries who came to do the converting considered theirs a superior race, one with a duty to help civilize "lesser races" such as the Chinese. The Chinese, too, had delusions of racial superiority with equal conviction. They considered the white men barbarians.[13]

In addition to tense race relations, the encroachment of Western imperial powers into China had caused its people much pain and suffering. Not only did the Western powers skim money from the Chinese government's treasury by taking a percentage of its customs' duties, their presence forced the Chinese government to modernize at an accelerated pace, compelling it to borrow large sums of money from Western governments. To pay its debts, the Chinese central government demanded increased revenue from the viceroys of its provinces, who in turn tried to squeeze more out of the common people. But they had nothing more to give. This hardship came to a head in 1898 and 1899 when "famine, flood, and banditry" created the perfect circumstances in which a movement like the Boxers could rise.[14] The Boxers had no central leadership. They initially opposed the Chinese government but soon took to supporting it, although they did not trust it.[15] In their first act of aggression in October 1898, they chased a family of Chinese Christians out of their house. Soon enough they escalated to killing Chinese Christians, then the missionaries themselves, and finally went after symbols of foreign imperialism by destroying their telegraph and railroad lines.[16]

In June and July 1900 the Boxers made their way north into Peking and Tientsin. Dressed in their "motley uniforms of red, black, or yellow turbans and red leggings, and with white charms on their wrists [to protect them from bullets]," they patrolled the streets in search of foreigners and Chinese Christians alike.[17] Peking served as China's capital, so all nations with diplomats in the country had their legations set up there. When the Boxers began their rampage, legation diplomats expected a liberation force to come any day. A Japanese diplomat went to the railway station to look for it, whereupon Chinese

Imperial troops shot him dead. The German minister, traveling on a sedan chair to meet with Chinese officials, suffered a similar fate.[18] Rather than help the foreigners, the Chinese government demanded everyone in the Legation Quarter leave the city within twenty-four hours, and that they head east to the coast. When the deadline passed, 4,000 people from eighteen nations still crowded the Legation Quarter, 3,000 of them Chinese Christians. They would live through fifty-five days of hell — an apt metaphor for at the time a massive heat wave baked the city, causing the dead bodies littering the streets just outside the Legation Quarter to decompose even faster than usual, which in turn attracted a plague of flies. A scarcity of food forced people to eat carrion, shoot dogs, and forage for roots and leaves.[19]

When a British vice-admiral, Sir Edward Seymour, stationed in the country received word of the danger to the British Legation in Peking, he took it upon himself to do something about it. He gathered a force of about 2,000 men that arrived in Tientsin on June 10.[20] Here the admiral tasked a Royal Navy captain named Edward H. Bayly to get the railroad to Peking running again. Bayly found the station's director obstinate and unwilling to release an engine from storage, so he threatened to hang the fellow if he failed to cooperate. The director concurred. A mob of irate locals then tried to stop Bayly from commandeering an engine, but twenty of his men, all well-armed, put a stop to that.[21] Seymour figured it would take a matter of three or four hours to reach his destination. He loaded his force onto a train and headed northwest toward Peking on the same day as his arrival in Tientsin.[22]

Seymour's expedition met heavy resistance from the Boxers, turning the expected hours into days. Boxers lurked in each village through which the train passed, and they attacked at every chance. Seymour sent an advance force ahead to try to clear the way. On June 13 this detachment faced a major attack, bogging it down. The Chinese assaulted the train itself as well as a detachment Seymour had sent to protect his rear, forcing him to send reinforcements to it. When the train reached Anting, a settlement about halfway to Peking, it encountered track so torn up that Seymour had to admit the train would go no farther. He ordered a return to Tientsin. The Boxers destroyed the track in this direction as well, so the train made it no farther than Yang-Tsun. From here Seymour's force had to dash to Tientsin on foot alongside the Pei-Ho River, placing the wounded on board a boat sailing upon that waterway.[23]

Enduring attacks on all sides, the expeditionary force captured the Hsiku Imperial Arsenal, located about eight miles north of Tientsin alongside the Pei-Ho. Burdened with his wounded, who had not escaped down the river as planned, Seymour knew he could not hold out for long here. He needed relief and soon. He sent a Chinese servant named Chao Yin-ho to Tientsin for help.[24] At this point no foreign forces in the country knew the fate of the expedition nor of its dire situation. If Yin-ho could not reach Tientsin, Seymour's force could well face annihilation.

Upon landing at Taku, Waller and his men faced no hordes of Chinese fanatics despite stories to the contrary. This did not calm one frightened Marine, a fellow no "more than eighteen." He "raced from one native to another, seeking all the details of the reports said to have come from the Boxers." He learned, for example, that the Boxers had mined the railroad to Tientsin and blown up bridges. Not long afterward, he panicked upon hearing a single gunshot and accidentally killed himself with his own rifle.[25] Waller received orders to take his Marines to the besieged city of Tientsin to help in the defense of the Americans there.[26]

To get to this destination, they climbed on board a steamer, the *Monocacy,* and sailed up the Pei-Ho River to Tangu, the terminus of a railroad to Tientsin, a city whose name means "The Heavenly Ferry." It stood about thirty-three miles west of Taku. One could unerringly find it by following the Pei-Ho River, although sailing up that waterway made the trip twice as long because of its erratic meandering. As the second largest city in northern China, Tientsin had just over one million residents. "An important center of trade," it served as "the terminus of the imperial canal and of a railroad, Tung-Chau ... which [had] opened a dozen years" earlier. Its filthy, unpaved streets contained garbage that no one ever "carried away." The poor lived in houses "constructed of sun-dried brick," although businesses used structures built with superior materials and more aesthetically pleasing designs. In contrast to the neglect of its streets, the city maintained "a public garden" which received "very good care."[27]

Nestled within a massive defensive wall stood the original part of the city, better known as the Walled City. Around this had grown a newer section and within that one could find the Foreign Concessions, an area south and southwest of the Walled City controlled by European and Japanese businessmen. Here lived their foreign personnel,[28] such as an American named Herbert Hoover, who worked as the chief engineer for the Chinese Engineering and Mining Company. He had arrived in the city a year before the Boxer Uprising to oversee the construction of a new harbor and train system for his employer.[29]

On June 10, the day Seymour's expedition had passed through the city, Hoover and his wife, Lou, found themselves in the middle of a war zone. Using the Walled City as their base of operation, Chinese forces began shelling the Foreign Concessions, an area protected by a mud wall on all sides except the east, along which flowed the Pei-Ho. A mere 1,100 marines and seamen stood ready to defend it, a force that had originally planned to just go through the city on its way to relieve Peking. Save for the British, who refused to obey a foreign commander, these soldiers served under a Colonel Wogak.[30]

Armed with a dozen machine guns and two small cannon, they faced 25,000 well-armed Chinese. Despite such odds, this little force managed to stop the Chinese when they attempted to invade. This happy result came in no small part from the efforts of Hoover and his engineers. They had raided the local warehouses of anything with which they could use to construct barricades.[31] At night they stacked bales of camel wool two high stretching for two miles along the river's west bank to prevent the Chinese from firing at them from that direction. They barricaded the streets with bags filled with sand, silk and cotton.[32] Still, they could not hold out forever — they needed relief soon.

Waller and his Marines, armed with Krag-Jorgesen rifles, a Colt M1895 machine gun, and a three-inch field gun, planned to do just that. The Marines captured a railroad engine at Tangu with which they planned to travel to Tientsin. They put together a train filled with material to repair the destroyed tracks ahead. Roughly eight miles out they "picked up" a Russian column of about 450 men. The train came to a halt when it reached a destroyed bridge, so the Marines sent it back to Tangu for reinforcements. Placing their three-inch gun on the tracks, the Marines bivouacked on the spot with plans to move forward when the fresh troops arrived. The Russians decided not to wait, so Waller, who had not planned to move out, resolved to march with his new allies anyway. Before departing, the Marines discovered their three-inch gun did not work, so they disassembled it, then dumped the pieces into the river.[33]

The combined American and Russian force marched as far as outer Tientsin near the East Arsenal[34] when 5,000 "well-armed" Imperial troops halted them.[35] At first the American and Russian soldiers held their ground. The Marines' Colt machine gun suppressed an advance by the Chinese. One by one, the machine gun's crew fell to enemy fire. When the gun jammed, its remaining members disabled it, then joined the ongoing retreat around them. During the four-hour running battle to get to the safety of the Russians' base to the east, someone realized that a Marine private, C.H. Carter, had gone missing. Lieutenants Butler and A.E. Harding took four enlisted men, W. Kates, Albert R. Campbell, Charles R. Francis and Clarence E. Mathias, back to look for him.[36]

They found Carter lying wounded in a ditch beside a railroad track. He had a broken leg — a compound fracture in which a bone stuck through his skin. Suffering from terrible pain, he told Butler and the others to leave him behind. Having none of that, they carried him without a stretcher, all the while taking fire.[37] Waller and a few Marines met up with them. They provided protective fire to keep the Chinese from encircling them. Of the men carrying Carter, one suffered a leg wound and another a head wound, yet they kept going as if nothing had occurred. After they had traveled as such for about six or seven miles, Lieutenant Henry L. Leonard, a close friend of Butler's who had fought beside him at Noveleta in the Philippines, appeared with twenty-five men. Leonard's men constructed a makeshift stretcher out of two rifles and a poncho with which they carried Carter to safety.[38] The two enlisted men wounded during Carter's rescue received Medals of Honor for their bravery. No one awarded Butler or the other officers this citation because officers did not become eligible recipients for it until 1914.[39]

The retreating force marched a total of seventeen miles to reach the Russian base. There the commanders had a conference and decided to stay put until British and Russian reinforcements, currently landing at Taku, arrived. They waited for two days. A 500-man British force headed by Commander Christopher Cradock of the Royal Navy appeared.[40] The arrival of Russian reinforcements swelled the force to about 2,200 men. Craddock took command and marched it along the railroad line straight to Tientsin. Facing a dust storm and heavy fire, it pushed its way into the outer city, then into the Foreign Concessions.[41]

During this march Butler learned much about soldiering and, from Waller, how a good officer commands. Waller woke his Marines up at two-thirty every morning, a routine he continued for two months. He motivated his men with pep talks "on the honor and glory of the Corps." Butler underwent many hardships, including constant hunger, a dust storm that caused "barber's itch" on his face, sores on his heels from marching, and a "howling toothache." A Russian soldier taught him that on long marches he could keep his feet from chafing by rubbing bacon grease on them.[42]

When the enlisted men told Butler they wanted to return to the *Monocacy* for a rest and good bath, he suggested this to Waller. The major curtly replied, "You ought to be ashamed of yourself to make such a proposition to me. As long as you serve in this Corps, never express an idea like that again, let alone think it." Butler dressed his men down for making him look like a fool. Here he learned the true meaning of the life of a Marine: soldiers in this service would put up with anything and never utter a word of complaint about it.[43] During this march, and his time in China overall, Butler developed into more than just a soldier who had seen some combat. He became a professional officer.

Upon entering Tientsin, the Marines heard rumors that Seymour's expeditionary force had secured itself near Peking and faced 300,000 Imperial Chinese troops and Boxers.[44] Only when Seymour's servant arrived in the city did anyone learn definitive news of the expedition's fate. This brave fellow had faced many obstacles and hardships during his trek to Tientsin. He suffered from interrogations by Boxers and Imperial troops ("who tied him to a tree"), and had to dodge rifle fire from French soldiers. At one point he ate the ciphered message he carried upon his person but nonetheless made it to the British Consulate, where he made a verbal report.[45]

Waller itched to go to Seymour's assistance, so he joined his Marines up with the planned relief force. Leaving at night, it found Seymour and his men at noon the next day holed up at Hsiku Arsenal. The newly combined military forces broke out on the morning of June 28, blowing up this weapons store after departing.[46] They did this not out of spite but military necessity. Hsiku had the capability of making shells for German Krupp guns as well as Remington rifles and the ammunition needed for them. The foreign invaders had no desire to see the Chinese use such arms against them.[47]

Upon his return to Tientsin, Butler had no time to rest. He, Lieutenant Leonard and a Captain Grant took a detachment of fifty Marines to join a force of about 600 Japanese and British troops with the mission of clearing the Chinese out of the destroyed northwestern section of the Foreign Concessions. As rain drenched them, Butler received orders to protect the main force's left flank. The Marines made their way into a marsh that provided them with ample cover, and here they remained under fire for one and a half hours. When the main force finished its business, the Marines guarded its rear as it made its way south to safety.[48]

While waiting for the assault by the allied forces on the Walled City to commence, Butler had to deal with a more personal and, to him, immediate problem. He still had a bad toothache and needed the offending tooth removed. He tracked down a European dentist who, with some reluctance, agreed to take care of the problem. Before the dentist could start the procedure, a shell burst through the walls of the house in which he lived and practiced. This fellow dropped everything and ran for his life. Butler never saw him again. The toothache soon went away on its own.[49] This incident foreshadowed Butler's future dental health, which only worsened in the years to come.

The offensive to oust the Boxers and Imperial troops from the Walled City began on June 13. A mud wall surrounded the outer city. To help repel attacks, the Chinese flooded the area in between it and the inner city's walls to create a quagmire, one already crisscrossed with "canals, irrigation channels, and lagoons." Within this killing ground, only Chinese graves, low dikes, and piles of salt provided cover.[50] Waller found an American engineer who knew the area into which the Marines would move. He asked this man to accompany them as a guide. He agreed. Thus a future president of the United States, Herbert Hoover, would stand alongside Butler during the first day's offensive, although Hoover never fired a shot and admitted to suffering from extreme fear during the venture.[51]

The allied force of 6,000 faced about 30,000 Boxers and Imperial troops. The British, Americans, Japanese and French moved from the south "in three columns," while the Russians and Germans came from the northeast with the goal of taking the East Gate.[52] To get there, allied soldiers had to negotiate the mud wall, trudge through mud and water, and dodge enemy fire by taking cover behind graves and in ditches. They found their return fire ineffective because Tientsin's inner wall provided the Chinese with excellent cover. The Marines attacked from the south at six-thirty in the morning. They made their way forward until they reached a water-filled ditch about six feet deep. Although this gave them shelter, they could go no farther. To their discomfort, by noon the temperature had risen to 100 degrees Fahrenheit.[53]

As evening came, the Chinese launched a counteroffensive. They poured out of the West Gate. Seeing this, Butler and about seventy-five men charged them. Either confused or intimidated, the Chinese wavered and retreated. Before the Marines could advance, Colonel Robert Meade, who had recently arrived in the country from the Philippines, ordered them to return to their previous position.[54] As Butler made his way to the safety of the ditch, he saw a private named Partridge take a bullet and fall. He headed to retrieve his fallen man, but a bullet pierced his right thigh, knocking him down.[55] Lieutenant Leonard chased after his friend, but while pulling him back to the ditch, he suffered a bullet wound to his arm,[56] which he would soon lose to infection. Despite this, Leonard stayed in the Marines for many years thereafter. At Quantico he taught officers' classes and took the men on fifteen- to twenty-mile hikes during which he showed no fatigue.[57] In civilian life he became a lawyer.

Butler's account of this story differs from official reports. According to him, when he saw Private Partridge fall as they climbed over a rice dike to repel the oncoming Chinese pouring out of the West Gate, he did not consider the man's wound serious, so he waited until the routing of the Chinese to retrieve him. He and several others carried the unconscious Partridge to safety. While doing this, Butler received a gunshot wound to his thigh. Butler made no mention of Leonard's risking his own life to pull him to safety and in doing so suffering a arm wound that would result in that limb's amputation; he only wrote that Leonard had suffered the wound and lost his arm to an infection.[58]

The Marines could not hold their position for much longer due to a lack of food, water and ammunition. When night fell, they retreated.[59] Butler hobbled along as best he could. A peculiar and probably apocryphal story has emerged about this incident, a tale Butler repeated in his autobiography. While it has many variations, it goes something like this. Right after Butler suffered the wound to his thigh, either a Lieutenant Bill Lemly or an unnamed Royal Welsh Fusilier came to his aid. This fellow had suffered a wound to his *left* leg. Undaunted, he and Butler tied their bad legs "together and, like contestants at a village fair in a three-legged race," made their way to safety. Another account placed the incident at Peking, but Butler did not receive a leg wound there.[60] For his earlier bravery in saving Private Carter, and his attempt to save Private Partridge, who died, Butler received the brevet rank of captain, which became permanent on June 23, 1900. He also earned an advance of two numbers on the captain's seniority list.[61]

At around three in the morning the Japanese blew the South Gate of Tientsin's inner wall. The Japanese had made several attempts at this already, but the Chinese kept cutting the explosive's fuse. Tired of this, one Japanese soldier went to the wall and blew himself up to accomplish the deed! His fellow countrymen streamed into the city, the British following. The Russians stormed the East Gate later in the morning.[62] Just outside the wall the allies found the beheaded bodies of those Chinese citizens who had refused to fight, tossed there by those who did. Within the Walled City allied soldiers discovered the maimed corpses of Boxers, complete with their bullet-repelling charms, littering the streets. To get anywhere, one had to climb over the rubble of the buildings destroyed by allied artillery.[63] It had taken 800 allied lives to make this conquest.[64]

The Chinese survivors ignored the bodies of their brethren, probably out of pure shock. They just walked over them as if they were nothing more than common garbage. A looting frenzy started by Chinese locals soon infected the allied soldiers. The British, for example, raided a large pawn shop, and the Americans stormed an arsenal and stole its supply of small arms. For three days foreign looters poured out of the city with their booty. Save for the French, the allies decided not to stop this, although British provosts seized what they could, then pledged to sell the plunder and distribute it as prize money (which the enlisted men doubted they would ever see).[65] Butler did not participate due to his convalescence.

Now all the foreign forces gathered in Tientsin made plans for an attack on Peking. Although they had collectively come into China to liberate their citizens under siege in Peking, each nation had its own hidden agenda as well. American military forces, for example, had headed to China because President McKinley believed U.S. commercial interests would benefit by keeping the Manchus in power and stabilizing their rule. Moreover, sending American soldiers into the country to fight would give McKinley a better negotiating position when the international relief force defeated the Boxers.[66] The Russians used the uprising as an excuse to take Chinese territory and integrate it into their empire, while the British, like the Americans, wanted to keep the current Chinese government in power. The Japanese, contrary to their later policies, sought to prop up the Manchus as well because they wished to prevent the dismemberment of China. To further this end, they, too, sent troops into the country.[67]

The allied army of Europeans, Asians and Americans left Tientsin on August 4. Although not recovered from his wound, Butler nonetheless managed to get himself declared fit for duty so he could march with it. Estimates of its size vary from source to source; Butler guessed it had between 17,000 and 20,000 men. He reckoned the multinational force would face about 30,000 Chinese enemies in Peking. The summer heat, which often reached temperatures of 115 degrees Fahrenheit, made the march to Peking deadly in and of itself. To add to the misery of the soldiers, rain poured upon them every night.[68]

Between the two cities stood a daunting landscape. Millard, the journalist who gave us the description of the Pei-Ho River, offered this bleak yet lively description of what those who traveled this route found:

> A more monotonous tramp, or one better calculated to take the life and energy out of troops, can scarcely be conceived. The landscape never varies. From the coast to Peking is one endless plain, unruffled by a single mound or gentle elevation. Dull-colored clay embankments, marking the course of roads, canals, or irrigation ditches ridge the flats in all directions, like welts laid with an enormous knout on a tortured country by some supernatural avenger. Uncultivated wastes of mud stretch everywhere, tainted by putrid ponds, and filling the spaces between the vast fields of millet, which cover the greater part of the land in North China. Thousands of big and little mounds dot the country, giving it the appearance, where not concealed by vegetation, of some vast prairie-dog village.... Yonder, now in touch with the crawling column, now reaching away as if to relieve the troops of it nauseous contact, only to come creeping, snake-like, back again, after having made a wide detour, is the sluggish Pei-ho.[69]

During the day dust permeated the air. It mixed with perspiration and caused eyes to gum up and sting. Flies by the thousands swarmed around them, replaced at night by just as many mosquitoes. Desperate for water, American soldiers drew it from wells and drank without first boiling it despite orders to the contrary. The American military failed to provide adequate support for the transportation of supplies. Worse for them, American soldiers carried more weight in supplies and equipment than any of their counterparts, and more Americans fell from heat fatigue than any other nationality. Butler barely made it himself; at one point he had to hold onto a mounted officer's horse to keep walking.[70]

In contrast to the Americans' water supply difficulties, Japanese soldiers carried portable filters and received daily rations of fresh water. The Japanese bested all other forces in terms of supply and training, and without their assistance, the battle against the Boxers would have gone much harder. They provided, for example, the only accurate maps of the area. When things went wrong, the other forces turned to them for possible solutions, advice the Europeans and Americans often took. The Japanese also had a superior telegraph system, better equipment, and an unrivaled medical corps.[71]

The allied army made its first contact with hostile Chinese forces at a place called Pei-tsang, a settlement just north of the Hsiku Arsenal. The Americans did not participate in this skirmish because they marched at the end of the column; by the time they reached the area, the fighting had already ended. Indeed, this scenario recurred over and over during the trek to Peking, harming American morale.[72] Most Chinese civilians had fled the region, and those who could not — the old, enfeebled, and abandoned — suffered the brunt of the foreigners' retribution. The trailing Americans found the human remains of these unfortunates as they passed through the ruins of towns and villages freshly destroyed by the passing Russians and Japanese — a trail of destruction about ten miles wide. The British and Americans tended not to participate in such wholesale slaughter, although exceptions existed.[73]

Upon reaching Peking proper, those who had never before seen the city discovered it emitted a foul odor, partly because of its filthy streets and the mass of over a million people who lived within, and certainly from all the decaying bodies courtesy of the Boxers. As a military target, Peking presented a daunting objective. A wall thirty feet high and twenty feet thick protected the southern portion, known as Chinese City. North of this stood Tartar City. This contained a city within a city within a city, each with its own defensive walls. At its core stood the Forbidden City, in which lived the emperor in a series of palaces. Imperial City enclosed this, and Tartar City completely surrounded that. Tartar City's walls spanned sixty feet in thickness at their base and fifty at their top; they climbed forty feet high. The besieged Legation Quarter stood in Tartar City's southwestern corner.[74]

The generals of the allied armies decided upon a plan of attack and determined they would launch their offensive on August 14. They intended to take the city in parallel columns, each aiming for a specific gate on the eastern side of the Tartar Wall. On the thirteenth a scouting party of cavalry galloped to within three miles of the wall to investigate its defenses. When the Russians among them saw a lightly defended gate, they stormed through it, throwing the whole allied plan into chaos because it forced the rest of the foreign armies to move ahead of schedule.[75]

When the Americans, led by the Fourteenth U.S. Infantry, reached the Tartar Wall the next day, they found the ambitious Russians pinned down by Chinese soldiers and artillery positioned on top of that wall.[76] At twelve-thirty in the afternoon Waller received the order to do something about it. The Marines planned to scale to the top of the wall and rush the Chinese upon it.[77] As Butler scrambled to its base, a bullet hit his chest, knocking him down and unconscious. When he awoke about half an hour later, he discovered the bullet had not penetrated his flesh. Rather it had flattened one of his shirt's buttons, taking a chunk out of his chest that removed part of South America from his Marine Corps tattoo. He found breathing difficult, suffered from pain and bruises such as he had never before known, and spat blood for the next two weeks. Despite this, he went into action the next day. For many years hereafter he carried the button that had saved him.[78]

The Marines entered Tartar City proper the next day to clear the way for allied artillery to move into position. At the Chien-men Gate of the Forbidden City, they received heavy fire. Butler's company returned it to good effect. The allies turned their artillery onto the gate to silence the Chinese for good.[79] On the move again, they made their way to the Legation Quarter. Upon seeing all the women and children they had saved, Butler felt vindicated for participating in such wholesale destruction.[80]

Many other foreign civilians living in China at this time did not survive. Eva Jane Price, the American missionary living in Shanshi Province who had hoped for liberation at the hands of foreign soldiers, did not receive it. Although she and her fellow missionaries had received an escort of Chinese soldiers for their trip to the mountains, a second set of soldiers followed and killed them all at a village called Nan-an shih.[81] Empress-Dowager Cixi and her court, in contrast, escaped the confines of the Forbidden City and made their way west to the relative safety *of* Shanshi Province.[82]

The victorious allies effected looting on an industrial scale. The Russians, for example, stripped the Summer Palace in the Forbidden City of its valuables, then packed and shipped this booty home.[83] Although the *New York Times* reported that Americans had refrained from such activity and suffered "ridicule" by their allies for doing so,[84] they in fact *had* participated. Butler admitted years later he and his men had personally helped themselves to that which they had no right to claim. He felt no remorse for doing so, justifying his actions thus: "But some allowance should be made for the fact that during the excitement of a campaign you do things that you yourself would be the first to criticize in the tranquil security of home."[85] One of his contemporaries, editorializing on this event, did not accept this weak and unjustified excuse: "Nothing could be more utterly stupid than the permission of such stealing by the common soldiery unrestrained by their officers, unless it be the practice of it by the order and under the direction of those officers."[86]

Butler and his company stayed in Peking until October 10. Before going home, he had a chance to sail around Japan on the USS *Brooklyn*. Two days into the trip, he came down with typhoid fever, so another vessel took him to the naval hospital at Cavite in the Philippines to recover.[87] This terrible infection, caught most often by drinking contaminated water, induces a high fever that can last up to four to eight weeks if untreated. Extreme fatigue, headaches, and "a rash across the abdomen known as rose spots" can also manifest themselves. In the more extreme cases the liver or spleen enlarges, and sometimes the latter of these two bursts.[88]

As Butler returned home, his parents erroneously received word of his death. They left immediately from West Chester and headed to San Francisco to recover his body. As they stood at the docks of San Francisco on December 31, 1900, to receive their son's coffin, they watched him hobble down the gangplank, a mere shadow of a person at ninety pounds, but still alive. West Chester gave him a hero's welcome. He gained thirty pounds during his convalescence, suffering pressure from his parents to quit the Marines and pursue his desire to become a civil engineer. He decided to continue his career in the Marine Corps.[89]

3

Coming of Age in the Marines

By the time Butler reached the age of twenty, he had grown to his full height of five foot eight inches, his slender frame masking strong muscles. He kept his brown hair cut short, military style, all his life. Caricaturists had a field day with his prominent nose and protruding eyes, but neither feature ever affected his presence or the love his men had for him.[1] He took up smoking and enjoyed good Dominican cigarettes or a fine box of cigars.[2] He always used nicknames for his loved ones, both friends and family, apparently having an aversion to using anyone's given name.[3] He belonged to the Shriners in Philadelphia, Oriental Lodge 289, and, while he never missed paying his dues, one of his fellow members complained that he failed to attend the meetings.[4] Butler wrote to one admirer that he considered *Ivanhoe* his favorite book, Shakespeare's *The Merchant of Venice* his favorite play, and Joyce Kilmer's "Trees" his favorite poem.[5]

After his recovery from typhoid fever, he took up a post at the Philadelphia Naval Yard in the Marine Barracks. When his initial commanding officer, Colonel James Forney, left, Colonel Henry Clay Cochrane came to replace him. Cochrane qualifies as one of the most peculiar and eccentric officers the Marine Corps has ever produced.[6] A by-the-book sort of fellow, he took his duties to extremes. Once, for example, he had a Marine returning to a ship charged with drunkenness. He then accused this fellow of trying to smuggle alcohol on board the ship using his (the drunken sailor's) own body as a container![7] On the same theme, after getting into an argument with his old nemesis Lieutenant Colonel Mancil Goodrell, Cochrane had him arrested for drunkenness. Their commanding officer gave both of them a "severe reprimand" for that debacle.[8]

According to Butler's own recollection of Cochrane, one no doubt filled with exaggerations, Cochrane had a habit of holding mock battles. Unlike the sort of war games that Butler would oversee years later, Cochrane issued little equipment and left nearly everything up to the ingenuity of the combatants. This might have worked had he bothered to tell his men just what he had dreamed up. Butler first witnessed such an event during his recovery from typhoid fever in Cavite. There Cochrane arranged for the Marines to perform a mock battle at San Felipe, an old Spanish fort. The defenders rammed rags down their muzzle-loading artillery pieces, which then spewed "shirts, under-clothes and socks." Anyone hit by such a garment suffered "death." When one attacking officer complained to Cochrane that his men had suffered from extraordinary losses, Cochrane ordered several of them to stuff straw down their shirts and act as bushes for the cover of the others. As the attackers scaled the fortress walls with bamboo ladders, its defenders poured hot water and garbage on their heads. When the escaladers got over the wall, a fist fight ensued.[9]

In Philadelphia, Captain Butler, who commanded Company B, suffered no end of indignities at the hand of Cochrane's peculiar behavior. Once Cochrane held a review but, lacking any senior officers, pounded a peg into the ground and had the Marines salute it as they passed by. Cochrane made Butler pretend he commanded two ranks when he only had one, then pro-ceeded to dress down one of the imaginary men. Another time Cochrane ordered Butler's men to present fantasy knapsacks for inspection, which he then criticized. Later, Cochrane made one poor captain pick up all the imag-inary knapsacks the men had left behind after their parade.[10]

At the end of 1901, Butler took a detachment of Marines to South Carolina to set up an exhibit at the Inter-State and West Indian Exposition in Charleston, where they established Camp Heywood.[11] Located on the banks of the Ashley River, the exposition covered over 160 acres with 2,000 feet of river frontage. It opened on December 1, 1901, and closed June 1, 1902. Set up to promote American industrial expansion into the islands of the West Indies, it included a women's building, a lover's lane along Lake Juanita, an art section, a nature section, and a court of palaces in which one could find the palaces of cotton, commerce and agriculture, all built to look like Spanish Renaissance buildings.[12] Upon the exposition's closure, Butler and his men stayed to pack up and guard the buildings.[13]

In September he went with his battalion to a small island twenty miles east of Puerto Rico called Culebra, or the Isla de Culebra, a desolate place about seven miles long and two miles wide that offered nothing but limestone hills and spotty vegetation. It even lacked a supply of fresh water, which the Navy had to ship in. Culebra's only attraction came in the form of a well-sheltered natural deep-water harbor at its southeastern end, the Great Harbor, at which the Navy had a established a base. The Navy shipped the Marines here under the pretext of using them for practice maneuvers, but really brought them in case it received orders to attack Panama.[14]

Not long after his arrival, Butler learned he had not, as promised, moved up two positions on the captain's seniority list. In a letter to his mother, he asked her to get his father to introduce a provision in the forthcoming Marine Corps Bill to remedy this situation. Butler often used his father's influence in Congress to further his own career or needs.[15] While his father did not always heed such requests, his presence on the House Naval Affairs Committee gave his son a powerful weapon to use against the enemies that his bombastic persona made him in the Corps and Navy.

Butler and his Marines bivouacked at Camp Dewey, where they had to put up with scorpions, centipedes, and other poisonous vermin. The Navy kept the Marines busy with one backbreaking task after another. It ordered them to drag guns weighing over a ton each up hills 400 feet high, then insisted they also build docks. This latter task kept them from doing the former, and when they failed to get the guns emplaced on time, an infuriated Admiral Joe Coghlan, the man in charge of the fleet, gathered up 125 naval gunnery men and held a contest. Bluejackets would compete against Butler and his sixty Marines to see who could mount their guns first. Admiral Dewey himself took an interest in this, ordering that whoever mounted their gun first should fire it. The Marines won and let loose a shot. It sped about a mile past Dewey's ship. Angered by its proximity, he reprimanded Butler for it.[16]

On another part of the island, the Navy directed its bluejackets to dig a canal from Great Harbor to Target Bay, one planned to span 1,300 feet in length and four and a half feet deep at low water. After six weeks of work, they had managed to dig a meager 300 feet. This task became so onerous those working on it mutinied, so Butler led a detachment of Marines to arrest them. The Navy then forced the project upon the Marines. Butler became its chief engineer and, along with 140 men, went to work. They excavated 300 feet of this marsh in just three and a half days, cutting through solid rock without explosives. Butler deemed the original survey worthless, so he made a new one himself.[17]

Shortly after Christmas, a holiday that everyone but the Marines had off, Chagres (Panama) fever broke out. Butler caught it. Transmitted by the bite of the sand fly, the disease has symptoms that include fevers, nausea, muscle aches, vomiting, and weakness.[18] Butler's fever rose so high his men feared he would die. They tried to get some ice for him from the Navy, which had an ice-making machine on board one of its ships, but it refused to give them any. This incident soured Butler's opinion of that arm of the military for the rest of his life. As he lay delirious, another Marine wrote to Butler's father and complained about Smedley's treatment and the Marines' task of digging the canal. Butler's father "raised hell with the Navy Department."[19] Admiral Dewey himself came ashore to relieve the Marines of this duty. He hired locals to do it instead. Impressed with what Butler had done thus far, he made him superintendent.[20] Here Butler demonstrated for the first time his genius for engineering, a talent that left a bigger mark on the Marine Corps than his actions during any military engagement in which he ever participated.

In February 1903 Butler and his men climbed on board an old banana transport, the *Panther,* as part of a flotilla of naval vessels embarked on a ten-day voyage to Honduras, where a revolution had recently broken out.[21] This started the previous year at the conclusion of a fall election in which General Manuel Bonilla defeated the incumbent, General Terencio Sierra. When the latter refused to acquiesce, Bonilla rebelled, and a war broke out. Both the American minister and the American consul requested protection for Americans and their property.[22] One such person, a Kansas City native named Doctor Eliot, certainly needed it. He owned "a large banana and rubber plantation at San Pedro Sula, thirty-seven miles from Puerto Cortez," upon which he ran into trouble with government troops. They accused him of harboring two rebels and demanded he turn them over. He knew nothing of them, but the government forces did not believe him and threatened arrest. They sent a search party into his plantation to ferret out the rebels. When they found the poor souls, they shot them, and then disfigured them beyond recognition, placing their maimed bodies on posts in front of Eliot's house.[23]

On March 21 the *Panther* took Butler and his men east to small place called La Ceiba, where, he told his mother in a letter, "we may find some American interests that need protecting."[24] By the time he and his men reached it, things had sorted themselves out: four towns along the Atlantic coast had declared themselves in favor of Bonilla, and one of Sierra's generals had surrendered.[25] Finding no American interests to defend in La Ceiba, the Marines sailed east to Trujillo. As they approached, they heard rifle fire. When they learned that an American consular agent faced imminent danger, they landed. Here they found the American Consulate building standing between the battling rebels and government forces. When the Marines approached, the fighting ceased. They found the consul agent hiding underneath the Consulate dressed in a costume made out of an American flag. The government troops soon changed sides, indicating their decision to do so by shooting their officer. When Bonilla became president, the Marines left the country.[26]

After his retirement, Butler wrote that he had gone to Honduras to help make it "'right' for American fruit companies."[27] Despite the fact the term "banana republic" originated in Honduras, this particular conflict had nothing to do with that fruit, although President Bonilla did involve himself with foreign banana interests several years later. In 1907 he lost his office. In 1911 the banana company Cuyamel, headed by Sam Zemurray (better known as "Sam the Banana Man"), wanted to break into the Honduran banana market. He found this impossible because the U.S. government had helped the United

Fruit Company create a monopoly there. Bonilla wanted his office back, so Zemurray agreed to help him retake it if Bonilla would allow Cuyamel to do business in Honduras. When the former president agreed, Zemurray supplied him with a gunboat and mercenaries to invade Honduras in 1911. The next year Bonilla took the presidency back. He gave Zemurray his concession. In 1893 Honduras had passed a law that charged a tax of two cents per stem on all bananas exported from the country, so, as an added bonus, Bonilla repealed this as well.[28]

Butler's next duty took him to the Philadelphia Navy Yard on League Island, a post at which he stayed for six months.[29] There an outbreak of meningitis occurred. He successfully stopped it by revamping the yard's sanitation system. Here again he showed his exceptional skill at solving engineering problems.[30] The American military had only embraced the concept that good sanitation reduces disease relatively recently. This idea had originated in 1752 when James Lind, a Scotsman serving in the British army, published the so-called bible on the subject, *Observations on the Diseases of the Army.*[31] The American military failed to heed its advice until the Civil War, when a lack of good hygiene caused mass death. This state of affairs prompted the Federal surgeon general, William A. Hammond, to force the Union Medical Corps to implement such reforms. For this he found himself out of a job and faced with a court-martial. His Confederate counterpart, Samuel Preston Moore, did the same thing, but no one hampered his efforts.[32]

After the Spanish-American War, the military faced massive outbreaks of yellow fever in Cuba, so the Army sent a group chaired by Walter Reed to investigate. When it discovered that mosquitoes spread this particular disease, the Army executed a mass extermination of this pest in Havana, solving the problem.[33] Military and civilian engineers working in Panama applied this same technique to stop yellow fever and malaria there.[34] Without this discovery, the United States could never have succeeded in its next venture into the region.

Like other seafaring international trade nations, America desired to dig a canal somewhere through the middle of Central America to link the Atlantic and Pacific Oceans. The U.S. government initially wanted to build an artificial waterway through Nicaragua, but the French sought to convince their American friends go through Panama instead. They had good reason. Their own effort there had collapsed in failure in 1899 (thanks to the disease-carrying mosquitoes) at a cost of $250 million. If the Americans bought it, the French could recoup some of their money. To achieve this end, they hired William Nelson Cromwell, a New York lawyer and a representative of the Panama Railroad & Steamship Company, to sway American opinion on the matter.[35]

He succeeded. In 1902 the United States bought the rights to the canal.

Secretary of State John Hay negotiated the Hay-Herrán Treaty with Colombia, then in control of Panama, to obtain a one-hundred-year lease for the needed land. In January 1903 the U.S. Senate ratified the treaty, but in August of the same year the Colombian Senate rejected it unanimously, infuriating President Theodore Roosevelt. When he learned of a plot hatched by Cromwell to declare Panamanian independence, he decided to act, or rather not to.[36] In the past, every time the Panamanians had declared independence — and they had fifty-three times already — Colombia invoked its 1846 treaty with America that stipulated the U.S. military would intervene upon request. Roosevelt would refuse to do so this time.[37]

The revolutionaries declared independence on November 3, the day before America held its national elections, so that no one in America would notice a revolution in Central America suspiciously beneficial to U.S. interests.[38] To ensure the revolution's success, Roosevelt sent the USS *Nashville* to offer naval support. In gratitude to their benefactors, the Panamanians signed away a ten-mile-wide strip of land in which the United States would have its own sovereignty. It became known as the Canal Zone. America gave Panama a one-time payment of $10 million plus a guaranteed annual rent of $250,000. The U.S. government pledged to protect the Republic of Panama from its enemies.[39]

Roosevelt ordered Brigadier General George F. Elliott, the Marines' commandant, to Panama to plan for an invasion of Colombia if that country tried to reassert control of its lost territory. On November 4, Major John Lejeune, one of Butler's best friends and a fellow he had fought beside in the past, took a detachment of 400 Marines into Panama in support of this Colombian contingency. He went to work remodeling the existing French buildings in the Canal Zone at a settlement called Empire.[40] Born in Louisiana, Lejeune had attended the U.S. Naval Academy in 1884 and graduated thirteenth in the Class of 1888. He joined the Marines "two years later." Unlike most of his fellow officers, he held deep-seated religious beliefs, subscribed to temperance, and belonged to the Democratic Party. In 1909 he would attend the Army War College, where he distinguished himself as having an exceptional military mind.[41]

Butler followed him and landed in Panama on December 26, 1903,[42] upon an American man-of-war. One day word came that Americans faced imminent danger at the Cana gold mines, located near the border with Colombia. Cana had no lines of communications to the Marine force, so someone had to go there to investigate. Butler and a detachment of 150 Marines boarded a train that took to them to the Pacific side of the Isthmus. From here they climbed into two gunboats and sailed along the coast to the mouth of the Turia River, where they transferred to smaller vessels that cruised to a little settlement called Yaviza.[43]

With the rainy season making travel difficult, Butler deemed taking his men to the mines en masse impracticable. Mounting donkeys, he, a sergeant (who served as his interpreter) and a guide departed. After two days of hard going, they found "the blooming works running along at a merry clip, and the foreigners on the best of terms with the natives. That evening [Butler] had a delightful dinner with the French mine manager in his beautiful mahogany bungalow." Butler trudged back to his men, then headed back to base, the hard journey for nothing.[44]

He stayed in Panama until March 7, 1904.[45] Upon completion of this duty, he returned to Philadelphia. There he became the captain of the Marine guard on board the USS *Lancaster*. In this same year a friend, Richard Peters, invited him over for dinner. There he met Richard's sister, a young beauty named Ethel Conway. Born in Georgia, she had lived most of her life in Philadelphia, where her family had its roots and enjoyed a status of high social prominence. The two fell in love. They married on June 30, 1905, at the All Souls Episcopal Church in Bay Head, New Jersey.[46] Waller, now a colonel, served as the best man.[47] Because Ethel could wiggle her nose like a rabbit, Butler nicknamed her "Bunny," a term of endearment he used until his death. A lifelong Episcopalian, Ethel nonetheless used the Friends' "thee's" and "thou's" at home when conversing with her close family. Molly Swanton, her granddaughter, recalled, "It was well understood among the close family members that Bunny was 'general' at home." Although Mrs. Butler's husband liked to swear profusely, she would not allow him to do so there.[48]

Butler's duty on board the *Lancaster* ended on July 1, 1905. Thereafter he obtained a leave of absence for his honeymoon; he had until October 15 to report to his next station at Cavite in the Philippines. He received authorization to go there via the Mediterranean but his orders did not guarantee the Treasury Department would reimburse his costs.[49] He and his bride took "a month-long cruise through the Mediterranean and Suez Canal,"[50] making stops in Asia that included Ceylon, or modern-day Sri Lanka. Butler liked this destination in particular, quipping in a letter to his mother that it had "modern buildings and hotels where one can sleep without a life insurance policy in one hand and a box of bug powder in the other." He and Ethel also stopped at Penang Island, Malaya, which Butler considered "the prettiest place yet."[51]

After reporting for duty at Cavite, he headed to his new post at Olangapo Naval Base. Located on Subic Bay, forty miles northwest of the mouth of Manila Bay, it served as just one of two American bases in the Philippine Islands. It had originally belonged to the Spanish, who had established it here because ships could not observe this natural deep-water harbor from the open sea. The bay stretched inland for twelve miles and had an average width of five miles. Mountains and hills around its rim provided additional protection from weather and a good defensible position should any foreign power try to attack. The Olangapo Base had a coaling station and a dry dock.[52]

Butler took command of Company E, serving under Major Joe Pendleton, whose loving wife had a bit of a hearing problem. During his two-year stay at this post, Butler and his wife produced their first child, Ethel Peters, born on November 2, 1906. The Butlers called her "Snooks," the nickname of the largest Marine soldier in the Second Regiment. When Butler celebrated her birth, everyone got drunk.[53] Later in the month he requested three months' leave of absence in the United States (no doubt to see Snooks's grandparents and other relatives), and in this same letter he also resigned his commission at the end of that period of time.[54] For reasons unknown, he changed his mind.

His duties mainly kept him at the base. For ten days every month he took his company out for a march across the country. During one such hike, a private went mad and started attacking everyone with an entrenching tool, nearly killing a corporal with it. Once the man was subdued, Butler had him tied him to a tree by his wrists until such time as someone could retrieve him. Back at base, the private faced a court-martial. Some time later, an investigator approached Butler and told him he had done nothing wrong. Butler did not know that anyone had even looked into the matter. To his surprise, the private had claimed Butler tied him to the tree by his thumbs with his toes barely touching the ground, crippling these digits for life. The private's lawyer wrote to a senator in the U.S., launching the investigation.[55]

One other notable thing came out of Butler's trips across the countryside. For heavier arms, Marines routinely brought with them tripod-mounted machine guns such as the M1895 Colt. This gun was heavy and needed at least a two-man crew, so the Marines used pack animals to carry them. Guns transported in this way often came loose and presented an ungainly load to pack animals. Butler designed a special harness (he called it an *aparejo,* the Spanish word for "harness") and saddle frame designed to keep the gun from sliding or falling off an animal's back; it redistributed the gun's weight to ease the burden. Butler applied for and received a patent for his invention,[56] but it failed to make him wealthy; in just a few years' time the armies of the world would start hauling such equipment using trucks.

In 1906 the Navy expected an imminent attack from the Japanese upon the Philippine Islands. The War Department became so concerned about this threat that it discharged all its Japanese employees at Olangapo and Cavite, then placed about "sixty Japanese women of poor character at Olangapo" under surveillance for suspicion of passing valuable information to their countrymen. The War Department put its two Philippine naval bases on a "war basis," and had the Army and Navy practice war games. Army engineers rushed to Olangapo to place six-inch coastal guns there.[57]

Butler received orders to assist in this effort, taking a detachment of fifty men across Subic Bay to do so. He and his men pitched their tents on a mountainside, where they suffered from heavy rains that would not let up. For food they had baked hash, coffee, canned beef, and fried hash. Although a tug passed by them on a regular schedule to supply a Marine detachment located on an island in the bay, this vessel ignored Butler and his men. When they ran out of rations, he decided to do something to remedy the situation. He acquired a small dugout canoe outrigged with a bamboo pole and rigged with flour sacks for sails. With a crew consisting of a private and a corporal, he sailed to the other side of the bay, during which time a storm whipped up the sea, destroying the sails and nearly sinking the canoe. It took five hours to go the four miles across the bay.[58]

At Olangapo Base he and his men filled an old tug with supplies, then sailed her back to their camp. When the tug arrived, she had nowhere to dock because the foul sea had ripped the Marines' makeshift pier apart. The Marines ripped pieces off the tug and used them as rafts to get the supplies to shore. Butler's superiors saw his action as a form of temporary insanity. From their perspective, he had risked his life and that of his men for food, something he could have done when the weather settled. They decided he had suffered from a nervous breakdown and sent him home to Philadelphia.[59]

There he became seriously sick in January 1908, an illness he self-diagnosed as malaria. The military doctors incorrectly identified it as tuberculosis. They told him to find a "high altitude and seek light employment."[60] On February 1 he began an eight-month leave of absence to recover.[61] He found work that fit his needs: he took a position as superintendent of the Fire Creek Coal & Coke Company, located in the mountains of West Virginia. It took its name from the nearby Fire Creek,[62] a waterway about forty miles southeast of the state's capital, Charleston. The mine had started its operations in October 1877. In the year Butler worked there, it produced 24,699 long tons of coal, had payroll costs of $28,280.17, and sold each ton of coal at $1.14 a ton for a total of $28,156.86.[63] It therefore lost $123.31, verifying a quote from Butler that often appeared in newspapers giving an overview of his career: "We made $2.25 the last month.... Then I quit."[64]

He built a small cabin on top of a peak and bought two bulldogs, Clincher and Susan, to protect his family while he worked. He walked to the mine daily. Soon after taking up his new job, he fired his foreman, a fellow named Mike, for drunkenness and refusing to sober up. The next day Mike returned and pushed a pistol into Butler's face. Butler snatched it out of Mike's hand and physically booted him out of his office. He made John Harris his new foreman, and the two became good friends.[65]

He worked alongside his men, although he did not necessarily do well at it. One day he became frustrated when the chute used to fill the coal cars clogged, so he got on top of the coal pile and jumped up and down. This was not the smartest of moves, since the coal let loose, taking him with it. He found himself buried up to his neck in ten tons of coal; bruises covered his entire body. Another time he got into a coal car to prod it forward. It had no brake stick, so when it started moving with him still in it, it flew at a roller-coaster's pace down the side of the mountain. At the bottom it crashed, throwing Butler twenty-five feet forward. He suffered broken ribs and a body full of bruises. His wife, upon seeing him after this accident, told him he "might as well go back to war. More blood seemed to flow here than on the battlefield."[66]

Near the end of September he obtained orders to report to Philadelphia for recruiting duty.[67] On May 13, 1909, he received a promotion to the rank of major. He headed to the Panama Canal Zone to take command of the Third Marine Battalion on March 23, 1910. He would stay at this post until January 1914.[68] Here his battalion settled into Camp Elliott. He became its health administrator,[69] a job he performed so well the U.S. surgeon general, C.J. Stokes, asked him to give a detailed written report on his efforts.[70] His focus on sanitation and disease prevention included daily inspections of "the ground, stables, and wash-houses" to thwart malaria. He made men take quinine for their first three months of service, and required everyone to sleep with mosquito nets. Although the mess hall served government-issued rations, he made it a point to purchase local fresh fruit to ensure a healthy diet for his men. At the camp he introduced his legendary discipline, such as keeping alcohol off the base to maintain good order. Despite this strictness, he did not intend for his men to live in misery. He had a large gymnasium built for their use that included a movie theater, bowling alleys, a shooting gallery, pool tables, a stage for theatrical performances, and a twenty-eight-piece band.[71]

Butler trained his men hard. Among the officers and men under his command, he made a significant impression on a young lieutenant named Alexander A. Vandegrift, a man who would one day become the commandant of the Marine Corps. In his memoir, Vandegrift recalled that Butler taught him, above all else, "the value of leadership" which he demonstrated "not by words but by action." Butler kept the men busy via intense drilling in the morning and learning new skills in the afternoon. One evening, after Vandegrift had finished his duties for the day and taken a shower, he headed to the tennis court, racket in hand. When Butler saw him, "he scratched his head: 'Well, damn it all. If you have enough energy to play tennis in the evening, then something is wrong with my training schedule.'" Butler focused much on his men's education, preparing them for the sort of engineering tasks they might face while in a hostile foreign country. Vandegrift, for example, taught men how to build bridges while others learned how to drive and repair trains.[72]

Butler's duties at Camp Elliott mostly involved mundane administrative problems. Once, for example, he had to set up a court-martial for a Marine who stole money, then tried to cover it up. He also investigated two officers who frequented a whorehouse called the Navajo.[73] In July 1912 a track and field event between the Marines and the Army at Balboa got out of hand. According to Butler's version, no doubt skewed to benefit his men's side, the Army men could not handle losing. While in the city's red-light district, where both sides went afterwards, they got into arguments over their match. A designated man from each side took to the street to settle the matter fist to fist. The Panamanian police stepped in and fired into the crowd, killing two. About 1,000 of the American soldiers rioted, breaking into businesses to acquire firearms to shoot back. The police prevailed and threw many of them into jail. Butler stepped in and insisted on taking custody of these men to discipline them himself. In one jail cell he found a poor soul up to his waist in water and shackled in irons too tight for his wrists. It took a saw to free him.[74]

The Marines had few responsibilities when it came to the administration of the Canal Zone itself. The Canal Zone had a civilian-based police force, a fire department, schools, and its own diversions. One journalist wrote that the Marines "have little to do except during presidential elections in the Republic of Panama. Sometimes the campaign becomes unusually warm and there is rioting. A few United States Marines can quiet the disturbance."[75] True enough, although the Marines had another purpose: they would travel to hot spots in the region when the need arose. Butler, for example, deployed to nearby Nicaragua three times between 1910 and 1912, as chronicled in the next chapter.

In November 1909, Secretary of the Navy George von L. Meyer nominated Butler's close friend Colonel Littleton Waller for the position of commandant of the Marine Corps. Butler's father, who at that time served as the chair of the House Naval Affairs Committee, supported this. Former President Teddy Roosevelt and the current president, William Howard Taft, both wanted Waller as well. Senator Boies Penrose, a Republican from Pennsylvania, opposed his appointment and managed to get William P. Biddle appointed instead.[76] In 1914 Waller was again passed over for this position, this time by George Barnett. For this "slight," Butler, who disliked Barnett anyway, would one day plot that man's downfall.

Some have speculated Waller did not receive the post because of a nasty blemish on his record. This occurred in January 1902 shortly after his return from China to the Philippines on the island of Samar. There the head of the U.S. Army and Marine detachments, Brigadier General Jacob H. "Hell-Roaring Jack" Smith, ordered Waller to kill anyone over the age of ten capable of carrying a gun. Smith felt he had the right to do so under an old army order dating back to the Civil War, General Order 100, which stated that anyone caught fighting against the U.S. military lacking a uniform could suffer immediate execution. Waller had little inclination for indiscriminate slaughter and told his men not to kill women and children.[77]

In January 1902, Waller led an expedition of Marines accompanied by Filipinos to map the route of new telegraph lines. He failed to bring enough rations and, worse, he and his men all fell severely ill. Desperate, Waller took thirteen men with him to find the expected relief party. He left First Lieutenant Alexander S. Williams in charge of the force left behind. When several Filipino bearers tried to kill Williams with his own gun (which failed to fire), several other Marines came to his defense but could not find the strength to raise their rifles and fire at the porters. The next day the relief party came.[78]

As Waller suffered from a crippling fever, word reached him of this incident. In addition to the porters' attack on his lieutenant, Waller learned that several others had stood by and done nothing. He ordered ten of them executed. He further directed the putting to death of an eleventh man, a Filipino scout, who had tried to steal Waller's bolo while he slept. When word of this incident reached Secretary of War Elihu Root, already bombarded with outrage of the American public because of reports of similar atrocities against the native population, he ordered Waller's court-martial.[79]

Waller argued that General Smith's orders about killing anyone over the age of ten capable of bearing a gun, as well as General Order 100, had given him the authority to order the deaths of the Filipinos in question. When cross-examined under oath, Smith denied giving such an order. Three witnesses came forward and testified he had. The court acquitted Waller. With the public still out for blood, the Army reluctantly charged Smith with the sort of vague misconduct of violence that would make his conviction easy. The court found him guilty, so President Roosevelt ordered Smith's immediate retirement.[80]

On December 24, 1912, President Taft came to visit the Panama Canal Zone. During his time there, he inspected the docks at both the Caribbean and Pacific ends, had dinner with Panama's president, looked at fortifications, and met with the head of the Canal Commission, G.W. Goethels.[81] Butler first met the morbidly obese President Taft on board the USS *Tennessee*. Two days later the president stopped by Camp Elliott for an inspection. Butler liked him immensely. Taft spoke to Butler about Pennsylvanian politics and, to Butler's surprise, ate little at the lunch Mrs. Butler had put together. But Taft's brother, Charles, who had come on the trip as well, "took care of the family reputation."[82]

During this visit, Butler, now a master at directing the military drill, paraded his men in front of the president and several top military men accompanying him. Impressed, they requested he send the War Department a copy of "his regulations" with the idea that the U.S. Army should adopt them. Butler *had* used the Army's drill instructions. He tactfully had its manual typed out by an aide, then forwarded the result to those who had requested it.[83]

To make in-country travel easier — to the limited extent possible, considering the state of the Panamanian roads, which suffered from a constant rain that turned them into mud and eroded any sort of crude pavement put down[84] — Butler purchased an automobile, a vehicle made by the American Motor Car Company of Indianapolis, called an American Traveler.[85] Even car buffs might not have heard of this obscure automobile. Its selling points included a chassis that had higher ground clearance than most cars, as well as a much tighter turn radius. The American Motor's slogan said, "A Car for the Discriminating Few," about which historian Beverly Rae Kimes opined, "Unfortunately there weren't enough such people to keep the company in business for long." Established in 1906, American Motor went out of business in 1914, having built a mere 45,000 vehicles.[86] No doubt this particular car appealed to Butler because a used vehicle from a defunct manufacturer cost far less than a new one.

Still, it caused him a number of headaches. The car never ran well, when it ran at all, and Butler's men had a team of mules ready for when it inevitably broke down. It cost him a small fortune to maintain, and when its tires wore out, he found he could not afford the $75 a tire to replace them. So he tied rope around the tire rims and ran it that way for a few months. He had his Marines build a primitive bridge so he could gain access to a wagon road outside the camp.[87]

In 1913 he received orders to leave the country. By now he had spent fifteen years in the Corps. Life experience and a growing family (on July 12, 1909, Ethel bore him his first son, Smedley Darlington Jr., and on October 22, 1913, a second, Thomas Richard)[88] transfigured him from a reckless youth who spent his free time carousing with his friends to a responsible family man who would not brook the sort of behavior he had exhibited as a young officer. His time in the Marines had defined his personality.

4

Uncle Sam's Racketeer

After his retirement, Butler started a one-man crusade against American big business and its use of the Marine Corps as its private army. When he wrote that he had served as "a high-class muscle man for Big Business, for Wall Street and for the bankers," he did not exaggerate. An extensive record of such activities exists. His three ventures into Nicaragua justified his statement that, "in short, I was a racketeer for capitalism."[1]

The American government's interest in Nicaragua resulted from the heavy investments of American capital into its infrastructure beginning with the presidency of José Santos Zelaya in 1893. Armed with progressive policies and instituting a strategy of internal improvements to better his nation, Zelaya nonetheless used tyrannical tactics to achieve his goals. He tortured political enemies, forced wealthy Nicaraguans to give him loans, established trade monopolies, and gave concessions to foreigners and foreign corporations.[2] At this time Nicaragua had two distinct sections: the west, dominated by descendants of the Spanish conquistadores, and the east, better known as the Mosquito Coast. Here lived a mix of native Mosquito people, creoles, some Spaniards, Latinos, and a smattering of British subjects and American citizens. Zelaya aimed to unite these two areas under his firm rule, and did so with military force in 1894.[3]

The outbreak of the Spanish-American War made him nervous about the possibility of American aggression in the future, so he started to implement policies unfavorable to American commercial interests along the Mosquito Coast.[4] Here Americans and other foreigners had established the port of Bluefields, from which they directed their commercial interests in the country's interior, especially mining for minerals such as gold. These foreign businessmen did not appreciate Zelaya's new policies in the least. Several British and Americans allied themselves with the governor of the Mosquito Coast, General Juan Pablo Reyes, and gave him financing to launch a rebellion on February 5, 1899. Reyes immediately reduced the duties on their exports, and cut taxes back to their pre–Zelaya level.[5]

Despite the presence of a U.S. naval vessel, the rebellion ultimately failed and Reyes fled the country. When Zelaya learned American enterprises like Samuel Weil and Company had incited Reyes to rebel, he retaliated by declaring all customs revenue paid to Reyes as invalid. Affected businesses would have to pay it again. They refused, and because of the threat of a U.S. military intervention, Zelaya abandoned this idea. Instead he raised tariffs and scrutinized his country's contracts with foreign firms. Considering that in the first few years of the 1900s each foreign-owned mine annually produced about $50,000 in gold alone, Zelaya could rake in some much-needed revenue if he could get them to pay up.[6]

One of the American corporations operating in Bluefields, the Philadelphia-based La Luz and Los Angeles Mining Company, owned by the Fletcher family of Philadelphia, had connections with the White House. President Taft's secretary of state, a corporate lawyer named Philander Knox, had worked for the Fletchers before taking his government job. The Fletchers desired to see Zelaya ousted, something Knox had no problem arranging if he could find a good pretext for it. When an American lumber baron, George Emery, came to Knox and demanded the State Department aid him in recouping money he claimed Nicaragua owed him, Knox thought he had found an excuse to oust Zelaya. He gave his demands to the Nicaraguan ambassador and, "to Knox's surprise and perhaps disappointment," received everything for which he had asked.[7]

Knox's dislike of Zelaya heightened when the Nicaraguan president borrowed £1.25 million from European instead of American banks to finance a coast-to-coast railroad. Knox tried to stop the loan but failed to do so. Furious, in the summer of 1909 he started a public relations campaign to gain American support for the removal of Zelaya from office. He then persuaded President Taft himself of the necessity of doing this. With the U.S. government backing them, American businessmen conspired to replace Zelaya with the provisional governor of the Mosquito Coast, a conservative named General Juan José Estrada. On October 10, 1909, the general declared himself president, then asked for diplomatic recognition from America. He named the La Luz and Los Angeles Mining Company's treasurer, Adolfo Díaz, as the revolution's treasurer, then went off to make war against Zelaya.[8] For appearance's sake the U.S. had to maintain official neutrality, so it refused to recognize the Estrada government until Zelaya's capitulation.[9]

This did not prevent two American engineers from volunteering to fight for Estrada. When they were caught by Nicaraguan government forces, Zelaya had them executed — a bad move since it gave the United States the leverage it needed to force him to resign, which he did on December 16, 1909. He appointed a lackey, Doctor Don José Madriz, as his successor.[10] Now two sides faced off against one another: the Liberal government headed by Madriz but

still run by Zelaya, and the Conservatives, headed by Estrada, the man unoffi-
cially backed by the United States. As the revolution unfolded, President Taft
sent Marines into the country to reconnoiter in case he had to deploy a full
force there to settle things once and for all. Major Butler took command of
this detachment. It sailed upon a transport, the USS *Buffalo,* to the town of
Corinto, located on Nicaragua's Pacific coast — Zelaya's stronghold.[11]

Butler went ashore to carry out two reconnaissance missions. For the first
he headed to León to assess and report on a fort overlooking this city. He took
with him Captain James C. Breckenridge and Lieutenant Calvin B. Matthews,
the latter serving as his translator. The trek began January 3, 1910.[12] They traveled southeast from El Realejo toward León. Butler kept a record of his observations, noting important details necessary for a possible military expedition,
such as the width, type, and grade of the roads as well as any fords or bridges
a military force might need to cross. León, the first major city they entered
and one located in northwestern Nicaragua, had a population of about 45,000.
A stronghold of Zelaya's Liberal Party, it served as an important railroad hub
and commercial center of León Province.[13]

The fort Butler planned to reconnoiter stood upon a precipice that rose
about three hundred feet above the city and roughly one mile to its southwest.
Surrounded by barbed wire, it had formidable walls and gates. "Good looking
native soldiers with fairly modern firearms" guarded it. In typical Butler fash-
ion, he and Matthews rode to the fort's first gate as if they had business there.
Matthews demanded in his most authoritative tone that the guards let them
pass. They saluted, then let them through. The two used this trick at two more
gates, once when heading up the hill to the fort proper, and once at its entrance,
where they received another crisp salute.[14]

The fort's officers did not fall for the ruse. Butler and Matthews nonetheless managed to avoid capture long enough to get a good overview of the place.
Butler made "mental notes" as he went. When detained, he and Matthews
feigned "extreme innocence" and "apologized profusely" for their intrusion.
They extended their interview as long as they could so as to observe as much
as possible. Finally the guards escorted them out. Butler concluded from his
visit that the fort would prove a formidable place to take if the need arose.[15]

A second reconnaissance mission took Butler and Matthews alongside a
railroad line stretching from Corinto to Diriamba. After passing through León,
the two headed about fifteen miles southeast to Lake Managua, a crater lake
Butler found "beautiful." There stood the city of Managua, which Butler considered a "second class Spanish" town. Although it served as the country's capital, its unpaved streets did not impress him. He and Matthews stayed at the
Grand Hotel, where about thirty German tourists resided.[16]

The two Marines met an American engineer living in the city, who drove them around for some sightseeing. Butler wanted to see Managua's key strategic point, Fort La Lama. One needed special permission from the president himself to visit it. Butler asked his engineer friend, "who [spoke] Spanish like a native," to accompany him there as his interpreter. At first this fellow balked at the idea, but Butler prevailed. At the fort's gates the engineer told the guards he and Butler had come from the German ship *Erma* (probably the one from which all those German tourists had disembarked), and they wanted to see the view at the top of the hill upon which the fort resided. The bluff worked, so up they went, where Butler made his observations. As the sun set, guards hustled the two Americans back down the hill. Butler later drew a good map of the place.[17]

Traveling through coffee plantation country, Butler and Matthews took a train from Managua to a junction called Masaya, and from there to Jinotepe. Butler found this latter place mediocre but loved the beauty of the countryside surrounding it. Here he and Matthews stayed at the Hotel Imperial, really a converted stable with a few "canvas bunks and chairs." In one of those peculiar coincidences that one encounters while traveling far from home, Butler learned the hotel's proprietor had received his college education at Lehigh University, located in Bethlehem, Pennsylvania, just north of Philadelphia. This man spoke perfect English and further astounded Butler by informing him that his brother had received his education at the Norman School in West Chester, Butler's home town.[18]

After a "vile lunch" they took ponies to the end of the railroad's line at Diriamba. There they toured a coffee plantation owned by a Spaniard named Gonzales. They climbed aboard another train that took them into the city of Granada, which Butler considered "the most desirable City of the Republic." It had everything he considered necessary for a modern metropolis: cleanliness, well-built houses and buildings, and the best place he had stayed in yet, the Hotel Alhambra. This city of 15,000 had of late become one of the flashpoints for the country's civil war. About five miles outside its limits a government army of 10,000 faced off with a force of 3,000 rebels. From Granada, Butler and Matthews took a train directly to Corinto, completing their mission.[19]

Butler came away from this trip feeling more cynical than before. Although he considered the Nicaraguan people pleasant enough (at least the well-educated ones), he found the situation at large disgusting. He had heard, for example, that Zelaya had accumulated $22 million while in office despite only earning an annual income of $2,500. Upon stepping down, the former president had managed to keep about $16 million of this.[20] Although it was probably just an exaggeration spread by the opposition, Butler believed it, shaping his overall opinion of the quality of Nicaragua's leaders.

He wrote to his parents: "What makes me mad is that the whole revolution is inspired and financed by Americans who have wild cat investments down here." He felt "shamed" that a Republican administration had its hand in events, adding, "The whole game of these degenerate Americans down here is to force the United States to intervene and by doing so make their investments good.... The poor common people are the only sufferers, as is always the case." He also expressed his distaste for the reporting of the American media,[21] an attitude later reinforced by his time as Philadelphia's director of public safety.

As the war between the Liberal and Conservative factions persisted, Americans and their companies in Bluefields continued to fund their preferred side. General Estrada, by his own admission, received over $1 million in contributions from them. Joseph Beers gave $200,000, Samuel Weil and Company gave another $100,000, and a stockholder of the La Luz and Los Angeles Mining Company, William Adler of New Orleans, provided a ship to carry weapons and ammunition to the rebels.[22]

Bluefields stood on the western shore of the Bluefields Lagoon, itself located on Nicaragua's Pacific coast. Its poorly maintained grid of wide streets covered roughly 250 acres. About 3,000 people lived there, a mix of native Nicaraguans of various ethnicities as well as fifty American citizens, twelve English subjects, and nine Germans. The compiler of a massive American intelligence report on Bluefields, Marine officer Captain R.M. Gilson, offered this assessment of the local population, which demonstrates beyond a doubt the American attitude toward the country overall: "As a whole the natives are lazy and indolent according to our standards but not more so than the inhabitants of most tropical countries.... The native Nicaraguans are not to be trusted under any circumstances.... [They] can be bribed for little or nothing. The negroes are in the main fairly trustworthy."[23] Even the British, at this time at the height of their imperial power and hardly known for their cultural sensitivity, found American treatment of Nicaraguans unsettling. *The Times* of London article, reprinted in the American magazine *Current Literature*, editorialized, "The attitude of the North American towards the inhabitants of South America has never been other than contemptuous. No matter how well educated, how successful in business the latter may be, they are all classed as 'dagoes,' a term which is not and never was meant to be courteous or complimentary."[24]

The Nicaraguan government issued an official decree that no vessel could enter the port of Bluefields without its express permission. If successful, this would prevent rebels from collecting any customs revenues generated. To remedy this, the United States sent the gunboat *Paducah* into Bluefields Bay, then told the Nicaraguan government it would allow any vessel it liked into the port. The *Paducah* would stop the Nicaraguan gunboat in the Bluefields Bay, the *Venus,* from bombarding the town or molesting any shipping into or out of it.[25]

Butler took a detachment of 250 "officers and men" to Bluefields. He had orders telling him that he and his men had come to protect Americans and foreigners in danger from the fighting. Upon his arrival on April 30, 1910, he learned of the real reason for the Marines' presence: they had to defend the customs house. The American consul informed Butler of the dire situation at hand: government forces had pushed the revolutionaries all the way back to their last stronghold, Bluefields itself, and the former occupied Bluefields Bluffs overlooking the city.[26]

Butler decided the Marines would remain neutral. If Estrada's forces did anything to endanger any "white people," he would throw all rebels forces out of the town, or at least disarm them. Butler further declared if Madriz's army tried to take the city, he would give Estrada two choices: surrender the town or go someplace outside of it and fight the Madriz forces far enough away to avoid any unintentional civilian casualties.[27]

The longer Butler stayed in Bluefields, the angrier the situation made him. In a letter to his father, he wrote that if he ever lost his commission, he would do what he could "to stop this butchery of people too weak to help themselves." He figured he and his men could use their machine guns to beat both sides if the need arose. He blamed the situation on the American businessmen in town, whom he hated, for they had come with the expectation of making a financial killing with the help of his Marines.[28]

The Marines' presence changed the dynamics enough that the war's direction shifted. On August 21, Madriz surrendered power to Estrada after the rebels took the city of Granada. Government forces then departed from Bluefields Bluffs. In Managua, a Madriz stronghold, citizens knew full well that the rebel victory had come about because of American interference. They took to the streets chanting "Death to the Yankees!" and threatened American-owned property and businesses, which received a "heavy police guard," leaving any stray American citizens not in sheltered areas to fend for themselves.[29]

Butler and his men stayed in Bluefields until October. As they prepared to leave, a group of shopkeepers approached Butler demanding his men pay their bills. They had racked up $1,600 of unpaid debt. They thought they would get away with not taking care of their tabs by signing their names as "Yankee Doodle," "George Washington," and "Abraham Lincoln." Butler paid up, then identified each man by his handwriting. He deducted the money they owed from their wages for the next six months.[30]

In December 1910, Antonio Rodriguez, a Mexican citizen living in Rock Springs, Texas, allegedly murdered a Mrs. Dem Henderson. A group of Texans retaliated by burning him at the stake. When an American grand jury failed to indict anyone for this lynching, Mexican-American diplomatic relations deteriorated.[31] This incident also sparked a wave of anti–American feeling in Mexico itself that would, in but a few years, cause an outright confrontation between these neighbors and present imminent danger to Americans living in Mexico[32]—a recipe for Marine intervention.

Upon taking complete control of Nicaragua, President Estrada allowed American commercial interests in the country to go wild. Backed by Washington, the American corporation J. & W. Selig & Company, in partnership with Brown Brothers & Company, created a new national bank. As collateral for a loan of $15 million, they gained control over the country's customs, its biggest source of revenue.[33] American businessmen also acquired Nicaragua's railroad. Not all Nicaraguans took kindly to this. A secret anti–American group planned to retaliate, given the chance. This came when Secretary of State Knox himself visited the country. The group had plans to dynamite, poison, or shoot him. While nothing came of this, Knox did suffer indignity when Nicaraguan citizens threw mud at his car's windows as he rode throughout the country. The opposition to him became so vocal it resulted in mass arrests.[34]

America's puppet president of Nicaragua, Estrada, did not stay in office for long. His minister of war, General Luis Mena, turned on him, plotting a rebellion. He had Mena arrested, but the Conservative Party did not support this incarceration, so the rebellious general went free. Realizing his precarious position, Estrada turned the presidency over to his vice-president, Adolfo Díaz, in May 1911. In an interview with the *New York Times,* Estrada accused the United Fruit Company of backing General Mena. He also admitted to accepting large sums of money from American businessmen to help him overthrow his predecessor.[35] Díaz did not get along with Mena any better than Estrada had. At the end of July 1912 a desperate Díaz asked for a meeting with Commander J. Warren Terhune of the American gunboat *Annapolis,* at the time anchored off the coast of Corinto. Díaz begged him to force Mena to resign from office. Terhune refused. Díaz then directed his army to defend Managua, which Mena threatened to attack.[36]

To settle matters, President Taft ordered Admiral William Southerland to occupy Corinto. Between the twentieth of August and the fourth of September, 2,300 Marines and bluejackets occupied the city. The country had two rebel forces lurking about, one contingent in the north and the other in the south. The southern forces belonged to General Mena, the northern to Mena's ally, General Benjamin Zeledón. This latter leader, the son of a carpenter from a provincial town in Honduras, had, like Mena, served as the country's minister of war. Admiral Southerland managed to convince some of the northern rebels to surrender in exchange for a place in the Nicaraguan government, but he refused to offer the same deal to the southern ones.[37]

Butler and his battalion had landed along with Commander Terhune in Corinto almost a week before Southerland on August 14.[38] On that same day Butler received a phone call from George Weitzel, the U.S. minister in Granada. Weitzel asked for Marines to protect Americans and their property, currently under attack by rebels. Butler, Commander Terhune, and a detachment of Marines and bluejackets arrived in Granada the next day.[39]

Butler sent a volunteer, Lieutenant Edward H. Conger (who spoke fluent Spanish), and two privates south to deliver a letter to General Mena.[40] The privates returned without Conger or their guide, reporting that the rebels had blindfolded Conger and taken him to their base, presumably so he could deliver Butler's letter in person. When Conger failed to come back in a reasonable amount of time, Butler started to worry. On the second day after his departure, the missing guide returned with news that General Mena had taken Conger hostage to ensure that Americans left him alone. Minister Weitzel sent a note with a Sergeant George Copland to Mena demanding Conger's release, simultaneously preparing a force to free him.[41] Copland got about halfway to his destination when he met Conger coming the other way. Mena had released him.[42]

Commander Terhune decided to return to Corinto. On August 21 he and fifty seamen boarded a train. As the train entered León, a mob of anti–American Nicaraguans stopped and seized it, an act not inspired by the rebels but one for which they later took credit.[43] When Butler received word that Terhune and his men had started back to Managua without their train, he assumed they lost it after a firefight. He prepared to receive the wounded at the railroad station by bringing in an ambulance.[44]

When Terhune arrived at four in the morning, he informed Butler that he had no casualties. Indeed, he and his men had put up no resistance whatsoever. They abandoned the train and walked about half of the way back to Managua before finding the wood train upon which they completed their journey. For this act, American seamen conferred upon Terhune the nickname "General Walkemback." They further composed and often sang a song derisively entitled "General Walkemback's Retirement."[45] Butler, who thought the whole business made the Americans look like a "laughing stock," had no intention of permitting this to go unchecked.[46] Besides that, the rebels now controlled the American-owned and -run Corinto-León-Managua line, a situation he could not tolerate.[47] After much wrangling, Butler convinced Commander Terhune to allow him to go to León and clear out the rebel forces.[48]

The Marines climbed on board a train loaded up with material and equipment which they used to repair two damaged bridges along the route. Butler's protégé, Lieutenant Vandegrift, came along in command of Company D. When the train reached León's outskirts, a group of about twenty rebels tried to stop it. Through his translator, Butler told them the train would pass. They relented. As it entered León proper, a mob of about 1,000 people armed with everything from rifles to razors tried, unsuccessfully, to encircle it. While still in the city, the train stopped at a station to take on wood and water. Here rebels surrounded it. Butler warned them that he wanted to avoid unnecessary bloodshed and pointed out the stupidity of attacking well-armed and trained Marines. The rebels demanded Butler meet with their general. He refused, telling them their commander would have to come to him. An overweight fellow soon appeared. He demanded Butler drive the train back whence it came.[49]

Lieutenant Vandegrift never forgot how Butler handled the situation. Butler told the rebel general he would have to ask Admiral Southerland, currently in Corinto, what he should do. He had "two husky Marines" crank "up a generator of a spark-gap radio that" could at most "carry ten miles," putting Southerland way out of range. "Standing with feet apart and hands on hips, Butler dictated to an operator who sent out a great shower of sparks and odd noises." After thirty minutes, Butler quietly directed his men to repeat their effort, this time pretending to write out Southerland's orders. "Frowning in concentration Butler read this and then told the general he was sorry but orders were to carry on." The rebel general, disappointed, accepted this and let them pass without resistance![50] Butler also convinced the rebels to reattach a private car Commander Terhune had lost.[51]

As the Marines' train approached a bridge another group of rebels forced them to halt. There yet another general arrived demanding Butler's retreat. According to Butler's own account, the rebel general pushed a pistol into his stomach. Butler snatched the gun from the rebel leader's hand, dumped its cartridges on the ground, then took him hostage until the train crossed the bridge.[52] When word reached the Marines that the rebels had mined the tracks ahead, Butler stuck Vandegrift and another man on top of the train to look for them. At the end of this venture he noticed Vandegrift smiling ever-so-slightly, so he gave him the nickname "Sunny Jim." Later, when Vandegrift made captain, Butler started to call him James instead. Vandegrift found no mines.[53]

At Corinto, Butler attended a council of war directed by Admiral Southerland, who planned to sail to Panama and return with a force of 550 Marines as reinforcements. Butler would head back to Managua the next day. For this trip he took two trains. The lead one carried the materials necessary to do a thorough repair of the entire rail system, and the second carried a force of seamen and Marines totaling over 500 men.[54] These Butler would deploy at strategic places to protect the railroad.[55]

During his return trip through León, Butler and seventy men went ahead of their train to guard a long steel railroad bridge. Soon enough a rebel colonel came and told him they needed to leave the area for their own safety. The rebels and government forces would soon have a battle here. Butler, seeing through the ruse, told the fellow he and his men would lie down flat when that occurred. It never did. Near Managua, rebels attacked, but the train's speed outpaced their efforts. As the train approached its destination, it lost its brakes and blew through the depot where a group of Americans, including the American consul, had gathered to greet it.[56] It took a steep upgrade to stop it.[57]

Now Butler turned his attention back to opening the railroad to Granada. Before his planned mission began, he fell ill with a 104-degree fever. Despite this, he felt duty-bound to go with his men on their forthcoming mission, but he could not get a medical release to do so as long as he suffered from the high fever. He had an orderly get him water and ice, then placed a piece of the ice in his mouth. Although aware of Butler's deception, Chief Pharmacist's Mate Fred G. Leith took Butler's temperature anyway. Finding it "normal," he gave the major permission to return to duty.[58]

Butler rode on the train upon a reclining chair. When it reached the outskirts of Masaya, a city guarded by fortifications built upon two steep hills, rebels fired at the train with a field gun. Butler ordered it to stop. General Zeledón commanded these revolutionaries. Butler got off and traveled several miles to meet with Zeledón, insisting the rebel general let them pass. At first Zeledón agreed, then he heard that a higher-ranking officer, Colonel Pendleton, had arrived on the scene. Ever the egotist, Zeledón demanded to speak to him instead. Pendleton agreed, talking to the rebel general for about two hours, at the end of which Zeledón still refused to allow the Marines to pass. Zeledón now insisted on speaking with Pendleton's superior, Admiral Southerland, and granted the Marines a twenty-four-hour armistice to give them a chance to contact him. Southerland came, but he failed as well. Having had enough of this obstinacy, Colonel Pendleton gathered up a force of about 500 Marines and threatened to attack Masaya's forts if Zeledón did not allow the train to pass the next morning. He gave in.[59]

As the train headed into Masaya proper, a mounted rebel soldier charged straight toward Butler, then, when he got about ten yards away, fired his pistol at him. The shot missed its target, wounding the hand of a corporal. Butler erroneously thought the bullet had hit his subordinate's heart, so he ordered the train stopped. He jumped off the flatcar upon which he rode to shoot the perpetrator, only to find he had forgotten to put his gun belt on. The rebel rider returned, accompanied by some of his companions, and a nasty firefight broke out. As the Marines shot back, Butler directed the train to get moving.[60]

He sent Lieutenant George DeNeale ahead into Granada with a letter to General Mena.[61] Dated September 21, it demanded the rebel general allow the

Managua-Granada rail line to open. The Marines would go through whether Mena liked it or not. Mena ought to just surrender the property in question to avoid bloodshed. The next day Mena replied that he had given instructions to leave Butler's force unmolested. Butler sent him a third letter that included a contract to this effect, and he insisted Mena sign. He did.[62]

Mena had two motivations for doing so. First, before leaving Managua, the Marines had spread rumors they had a force of 1,500 armed men with heavy artillery. To perpetuate the illusion, they stuck "hundreds of extra campaign hats on poles in the bushes about [the] camp," then placed thick logs in their "small, antiquated cannon," covering "the whole length with canvas" to make them look larger and thus more menacing.[63] Second, Mena suffered from Bright's disease, a generic term that encompasses a number of kidney-related afflictions such as stones. The attack had struck him at the beginning August just as the rebellion began. It caused him so much distress he barely had the strength to speak.[64]

Once in Granada, Butler, who had promised Mena that he would practice the strictest neutrality and leave the rebels alone upon his arrival, ordered them rounded up. He did not wish to do this, but a direct order from the secretary of the Navy himself left him with no choice. He and his men went to each of Mena's three barracks, one at a church, another at a cathedral, and the third at a hospital, to detain them.[65] When Admiral Southerland arrived in the city, he held a "council of war" to discuss how to handle Mena himself. Butler suggested they demand Mena's surrender, then offer to take him to Panama or another American-controlled territory for a comfortable exile. He met with Mena's son, Daniel, to negotiate the details. The two then went to Mena's headquarters at San Francisco Cathedral to meet the general in person. Here Butler found the old general lying on a cot "groaning and moaning" from his crippling pain.[66]

Butler did not appear much healthier. Not recovered from his own illness, he sat "like a potentate [on] a wooden camp chair with long stiltlike legs." His fever had caused his eyes to turn deeply bloodshot. Butler recalled in his autobiography that hereafter "the Marines started to call [him] 'Old Gimlet Eye.'"[67] Other explanations as to how he received this appellation exist. The *New York Times* reported it came about because Butler had "a long, large nose and a pair of blazing and protruding eyes, which soon was to gain him the nickname 'Gimlet Eye' and later 'Old Gimlet Eye.'"[68] The *San Antonio Sunday Light* had this version: "'Old Gimlet Eye,' the Marines called him for the vigilance of his inspection, the strictness of discipline, but they knew he would wade through high water and crawl into hell to drag out an enlisted man."[69] Like most nicknames, no one will ever know its precise origin, but Butler liked it so well he used it in the title of his memoir.

Butler and Mena agreed that in exchange for the latter's surrender, the Americans would give Mena and his son safe passage out of the country into exile. Upon hearing this deal, Secretary of the Navy George von Lengerke Meyer vetoed it. He wanted to turn Mena over to the Nicaraguan government. Southerland backed Butler's promise, sending a cable to Washington to that effect. He prevailed.[70] Mena took an American ship for Panama, promising never to return.[71]

On October 3, Admiral Southerland gave General Zeledón an ultimatum: if he did not surrender the Masaya forts within twenty-four hours, American forces would attack. Zeledón declined.[72] The forts in question rested upon two hills, both fortified and defended with heavy artillery and machine guns.[73] Butler described them thus: "The more formidable of these hills is called the Coyatepe, and the lesser the Baranca, the former being about 500 feet high, with extremely steep slopes on all four sides, and the latter (Baranca) about 250 feet high, and with almost perpendicular sides."[74]

When the deadline to surrender passed, Butler received the order from Colonel Pendleton to open up with the artillery. This fired continuously at Coyatepe from eight in the morning until three the next morning. When the ground assault on the hills commenced, the Marines split into two groups: Butler's force attacked from the south while Colonel Pendleton's force of 600 did so from the north.[75] Bluejackets and Nicaraguan government soldiers participated as well, the latter of whom had the mission of taking the city of Masaya itself. In a mere thirty-seven minutes the combined military forces took both hills. Upon seeing this, the Nicaraguan government troops started their assault on Masaya proper, suffering one hundred dead and two hundred wounded. Of the American soldiers, only Marines suffered casualties: four dead and five wounded.[76] This upset Butler, for he believed they had died not in the service of their country but for the benefit of the banking house Brown Brothers, who had a major financial stake in the country.[77]

Although Zeledón and his staff escaped, they only got about twenty miles before the Nicaraguan cavalry "killed or captured" them.[78] Government forces then dragged Zeledón's body through a series of hamlets before burying him in the village of Catarina. One witness of this gruesome procession, a seventeen-year-old named Augusto Sandino, decided on the spot to become politically active. Fifteen years later he led a revolution against the Americans still occupying his country.[79] Through trial and error he perfected his brand of guerrilla warfare against them. When the Americans left in 1933, he kept fighting against the Nicaraguan government until he reached a tentative agreement with it in 1934. Government forces lured him to a meeting at which they arrested and executed him.[80]

In July 1961 a group inspired by him, the Frente Sandinista de Liberación

Nacional (FSLN), formed with the goal of mimicking his guerrilla tactics to overthrow the right-wing dictatorship then in power. The Sandinistas, as they soon became known, wanted to establish a brand of Marxism different from the Soviet style often mimicked in that era. When the Sandinistas' military tactics failed, they turned to organizing the rural and urban poor. Frustrated at a lack of success, they fractured in 1974 into three distinct factions. These reunited in 1979 and overthrew the reigning dictator. Despite their Marxist philosophy, they created a mixed economy and ruled it with a nine-man committee. When the new American president Ronald Regan came into power in 1981, he and his conservative allies could not stand the idea of a successful left-wing government operating anywhere in America, so Reagan started a disinformation and propaganda campaign against them.[81]

A lieutenant colonel in the Marine Corps working out of Reagan's office took this a step further. In cahoots with others in the administration, this officer, Oliver North, illegally sold arms to Iran at inflated prices, then sent the money that he had skimmed off the top to the anti–Sandinista movement in Nicaragua, the Contras. This violated both the Bolan Amendment and Article 1, Section 9, of the Constitution, which made using stolen money for such a purpose an impeachable offense. The incident nearly crippled the Reagan administration and almost caused the president's impeachment. David M. Abshire, who got involved with the damage control aspect of this business, summed up this unexpected blowback in his book *Saving the Reagan Presidency:* "Simply put, the survival of the presidency was threatened."[82] History has shown that Reagan endured, but opinions as to the effect of this incident on his administration vary so greatly even a synopsis of them could fill an entire chapter.

While Butler had helped to spark this chain of events, he had not initiated the policy to deal with Zeledón — that came from President Taft. The deed done, Butler and his battalion left Nicaragua at the end of November. He lived until January 1914 at Camp Elliott in Panama, as chronicled in the previous chapter. After leaving there, his battalion headed to Mexico, where other trouble brewed.[83]

5

Spy and Soldier

Butler took command of the First Marine Provisional Battalion on board the USS *Minnesota* in January 1914.[1] In late February Admiral Frank Friday Fletcher, head of the flotilla of U.S. naval vessels anchored off the coast of Veracruz, asked Butler to do a bit of intelligence gathering. He wanted him to go to Mexico City to gauge the strength of its troops there.[2] America had no dedicated espionage service at this time, so it had to get its intelligence where it could. For Mexico in particular, it often employed the services of the Justice Department's Bureau of Investigation, founded in 1909, and the U.S. Army's War College Division. The former focused on revolutionist activities along the Mexican-American border and the latter on military information and plans.[3]

Turmoil in Mexico and a revolution there caused the U.S. to pay close attention to that country's affairs. Mexico's problems had started in 1910 when Porfirio Díaz, its dictator in the guise of a president, won his ninth term the usual way: fraud. Having occupied this office for thirty-two years, he saw no reason not to continue despite his advanced age of eighty. Supported by the Mexican elite, its military, and the Catholic Church, he ruled with an iron fist, using the national police to impose his will upon the people.[4]

Díaz did have opponents. In 1908 one such individual, Francisco I. Medero, a wealthy landowner who belonged to one of the five richest families in Mexico, published a book titled *La sucesión presidencial en 1910* (The Presidential Succession in 1910). An instant bestseller, it argued that the common people of Mexico should rise up if Díaz ran for another term in 1910. In that year Medero campaigned against Díaz not as a candidate but as one who opposed Díaz's reelection on general principles, and for this he found himself arrested and imprisoned.[5]

With help, he escaped to San Antonio, Texas, where he published a manifesto he had written while in prison: *Plan de San Luis*. It called for the Mexican people to refuse to recognize the Díaz government and launch a revolution. It further offered a populist proposal to redistribute land to the poor. Medero would serve as president of the revolution's provisional government. He called for all this to start on November 20, 1910, and it did. So began the Mexican Revolution, a conflict that would not end until 1940.[6] In 1913 America's ambassador to Mexico, Henry Lane Wilson, convinced two Medero opponents, General Victoriano Huerta and Féliz Díaz, to unite and remove the Mexican president from office. They agreed, then exceeded what Wilson had expected: they had the Mexican president and vice-president assassinated. Horrified, President Woodrow Wilson refused to recognize Huerta as the legitimate ruler of Mexico.[7]

Relations between Mexico and the United States, never stellar since the former lost half a million square miles of its territory to the latter in a mid–nineteenth-century war, had completely deteriorated by the time President Wilson took office. A number of concurrent events contributed to this animosity, such as the burning at the stake of Mexican citizen Antonio Rodríguez by Texans and the lack of justice in that matter. This incident in particular sparked such anti–American feelings in Mexico a number of U.S. citizens felt compelled to leave the country. Other Americans went *into* Mexico to fight against the revolutionaries on behalf of its hated government, further raising the level of hostility. A wave of anti–American propaganda appeared in Mexican newspapers, posters, and billboards. These contained slogans such as "Death to the Yankees!" "Down with Gringos!" and "Kill Díaz and his Yankee friends."[8]

The details of Butler's 1914 spy mission, with nearly a century of time between it and the writing of this work, remain muddled and filled with stories more likely invented than not. The most complete and detailed version appears in Butler's autobiography *Old Gimlet Eye*. In this Butler recalled beginning his mission by taking a train to Mexico City. The superintendent of the train became his conspirator, stopping it from time to time to allow Butler to survey strategic areas. He got off at the city of Puebla de Zaragoza, where he posed as an expert in public utilities to give him access to such facilities. He also wished to visit one of the forts there, so he pretended to chase a butterfly to get onto the premises.[9] About this incident he once commented, "Because I carried a net and studied rocks, they thought I was a nut and let me pass."[10]

In Mexico City Butler went to the American Legation and there became friendly with its acting head, Nelson O'Shaughnessy, who introduced him to a member of the Mexican Secret Service.[11] Butler told this man, a Cuban by birth, he had come to Mexico in search of "a murderer who had fled [to] Mexico from Ohio and who was believed to have joined the Mexican Army. The Cuban gained an audience for Butler at President Huerta's palace." Here Butler met the Mexican president in his bedroom. About this meeting Butler recalled, "I became so intimate with him that I actually sat on the edge of his bed and I prepared an order which he signed giving me free access to every one of the twenty-four military garrisons of the City of Mexico." With this in hand he completed a thorough examination of Mexico City's soldiers, its army's equipment, and its fortresses' defenses.[12]

Butler visited as many of the American residences in the city as he could under the pretext of writing a guidebook. If American forces had to invade Mexico City, they would make it a priority to secure the safety of any American citizens living there. After gathering a sufficient amount of intelligence, Butler placed the maps he had drawn into a false bottom in his travel bag, then hopped onto a train to Veracruz. During the trip two Mexicans kept tabs on him. Convinced they belonged to the Mexican Secret Service, he went into a washroom and, when the train slowed at a fork in the tracks at Veracruz, jumped out the window, heading to the American Consulate. From there he took a boat back to the American fleet.[13]

In 1927 Butler and a Marine first lieutenant, Arthur J. Burks, collaborated in a semi-autobiographical teenage boy's adventure book titled *Walter Garvin in Mexico* that used this mission as its basis. It mixed historical fact and real people with fictitious ones. Its main character, a Marine lieutenant named Walter Garvin, had many of Butler's characteristics, including a Marine emblem tattooed across his chest and Butler's sense of boldness. Like Butler, Garvin posed as a madman, a detective, and the writer of a guidebook. Unlike Butler, he spoke fluent Spanish and faced far more harrowing obstacles than his inspiration. Still, the book's adventure parallels Butler's quite well, and includes all the towns, cities and forts Butler visited during his mission. Although written in a straightforward pulp-fiction style that makes it quite readable, it would nonetheless not suit the young adult market of today. It often refers to Latin American people using derogatory terms, and depicts most Mexicans as brutal and stupid.[14]

On April 21, 1914, the *New York Times* published the U.S. military's entire battle plan for the taking of Veracruz and Mexico City, attributing it to "an officer of large experience" (probably Butler) who had the task to take over and secure the railroad from Veracruz to Mexico City, then enter the latter to rescue any American citizens in danger there.[15] President Wilson wanted any excuse for an American attack on Veracruz because he hoped such an action would lead to Huerta's downfall.[16] A German cargo ship named the *Ypiranga* provided this excuse. This vessel carried a cargo of 15 million rounds of ammunition and "a large supply of small arms." Although America had for a time enacted an embargo against the Huerta government to keep out-of-country weapons from reaching him (during which someone purchased the very weapons upon the *Ypiranga*), by the time the German cargo ship reached Veracruz, the embargo had ended. Thus to prevent the *Ypiranga* from unloading, President Wilson ordered the seizure of Veracruz's customs house, from

which American representatives could then confiscate the weapons if the need
arose.[17]

A flotilla of U.S. naval vessels including six battleships arrived. These
shelled the southern part of the city on the night of April 22, 1914. The flotilla
then unloaded a total of 3,000 Marines into Veracruz.[18] Butler arrived on the
cruiser *Chester*. He reported to Colonel Wendell Cushing Neville — "Buck" to
his close acquaintances — whom Butler considered one of his best friends.[19]
The two had fought together in the Boxer Rebellion. A product of the Norfolk
Academy for naval officers, Neville had seen action in Cuba and served as the
military governor of the province of Basilan on the Philippine island of Zam-
boanga. There he encouraged marriage and performed quite a few ceremonies
himself, making him known as the "marrying governor." Promoted to lieutenant colonel the month before this action, this "even-tempered" fellow
became known as "the loudest of all marines." Like his friend John Lejeune,
he one day would serve as the commandant of the Marine Corps.[20]

Sniper fire plagued the seamen and Marines trying to make it through
the streets of Veracruz. Butler dealt with this threat by ordering his men to
invade a house, clear it of its occupants, then use picks and axes to smash
down a wall that, when removed, offered access into the next dwelling. After
clearing an entire row of residences like this, Marines climbed to the roof to
take out enemy snipers.[21] A rumor spread that a large Mexican force would
soon attack the city from the west, so the Marines spent the night demolishing
houses to create effective barricades. In the morning one of the neighborhood's
residents returned home from work. Butler recalled his reaction: "He would
count the houses from one corner, measure off the land and find a vacant lot.
Then, he would select another corner, pace off — and still find a vacant lot. He
knew his section all right, for the vacant lot was where his home had been."
The Marines compensated everyone whose houses they had demolished,
but it turned out they had destroyed them in futility: the Mexican army
retreated.[22]

With the port secure, Admiral Fletcher ordered a naval lieutenant to board
the *Ypiranga* to tell her captain that he could not unload his cargo, a demand
Fletcher had no legal justification to make. This created a diplomatic incident
for which the U.S. quickly apologized to the German government. To make
amends, Fletcher allowed the *Ypiranga* to unload all its cargo except the munitions. The *Ypiranga* then sailed off to Puerto México and offloaded the weapons
there, making the official reason for invading Veracruz a total failure. Historian
Michael C. Meyer pointed out the "irony" of this situation: "The shipment
was purchased in the United States when the arms embargo was in effect but
was not permitted to be discharged in Veracruz after the embargo had been
repealed."[23] Despite this, the Veracruz attack succeeded with its true aim: it

gave Huerta's enemies the chance they needed to close in, and when they did, he resigned and fled the country in July.[24]

In the aftermath of the Veracruz action, the American military issued Medals of Honor like candy, fifty-six in all.[25] When Butler received one, he returned it, writing a series of letters to the Navy Department explaining why he did not deserve this citation.[26] The secretary of the Navy, Josephus Daniels, told him to keep it. The Department of the Navy explained in detail that if Butler did not take his award, it would diminish its merit for those other military men who also received it for Veracruz. It ordered him to wear it.[27]

The Germans, whose cargo ship had sparked the Veracruz invasion, had more to worry about than a skirmish between Mexico and America. On August 1, 1914, Germany declared war on Russia, and, two days later, on France. This sparked the series of further declarations of war throughout Europe and beyond that developed into World War I, a conflict called the Great or World War until the outbreak of World War II. While other foreign powers busied themselves defending their colonies and fighting one another, the American government used this as an opportunity to further expand its influence into the Caribbean.[28]

It had its eyes on Haiti in particular, and a crisis in that country involving both its national bank and the construction of a railroad would give the U.S. the excuse it needed for intervention. In 1910 an American named James P. McDonald bought the rights to several unfinished Haitian railroad lines, one of which would connect Cap-Haïtien to Port-au-Prince. His company, the Compagnie Nationale des Chemins de Fer d'Haiti, issued bonds to finance the estimated cost of $33,000 per mile of track laid down. The Haitian government agreed to pay six percent interest plus one percent in a sinking fund (money set aside to help to pay the bonds back) in exchange for one-sixth of any profits the railroad made that exceeded twelve percent, and a takeover of all the railroad's land upon the payoff of the bonds. In 1911, National City Bank of New York took control of the railroad. National City made one of its employees, Roger L. Farnham, president of the Compagnie Nationale. When that went bankrupt in 1914, the Haitian government stopped making interest payments; it would not spend another penny until the railroad completed the project in full, and it began foreclosure procedures.[29]

This crisis motivated Haiti's national bank, the Banque Nationale de la République d'Haiti (BNRH), in which Americans had a twenty percent interest, to pursue its own agenda. The BNRH wanted America to take over the country's customs because this would give the U.S. effective control over Haiti's finances and thus, the BNRH projected, create economic stability. To force the Haitian government to agree to such a venture (one which American diplomats proposed six times beginning in 1914), the BNRH, which held a monopoly

on the printing of Haitian paper money, refused to allow the Haitian government to withdraw $2 million of its deposit; without this the government could
not operate. In response to the BNRH's obstinacy, Haitian troops tried to seize
the money by force. The bank responded by asking the U.S. government to
help it transport $500,000 in gold to America for safekeeping. On December
17, 1914, Marines landed in Port-au-Prince and took the gold to the vaults of
National City Bank in New York.[30]

In 1915 Haitian president Jean Vilbrun Guillaume Sam took advantage
of the resulting turmoil by arresting potential political rivals. During his first
four months in office he threw 175 men and boys into Port-au-Prince's prison.
Some of their relatives organized a rebellion with Doctor Ronsalvo Bobo as
their leader. As Sam's power base deteriorated, he ordered General Oscar, the
man "in charge of the huddled prisoners," to do what he needed to if Sam lost
possession of the presidential palace.[31]

When an unsuccessful attack on this edifice came, Sam and his family
fled to the French Legation. General Oscar carried out his orders. He and six
guards slaughtered the prisoners; out of 175, only six escaped, one by faking
his death. The deed done, Oscar hastened to the Dominican Legation for protection. It did him little good. Sixty-year-old General Polynice, whose three
boys Oscar had just murdered, "jumped on his horse" and rode it into the
Dominican Legation. He knocked Oscar over the head with his walking stick,
"dragged him out into the street," then "emptied his revolver into him." A
mob stormed the French Legation and dragged Sam out as well, chopping him
up and dragging the resulting bits and pieces through the street. The American
chargé d'affaires, R.B. Davis Jr., had seen enough. He telegraphed Admiral
William B. Caperton, stationed on the *Washington* at Cap-Haïtien, for help.[32]

This incident gave President Wilson the moral authority he needed to
justify an invasion of Haiti. To strengthen his case, he further claimed the
Germans planned to set up a submarine base in the country.[33] This latter
excuse, true or not, did have a basis in reality: the Germans had a major economic presence in the country, and German loans had probably financed several revolutions.[34]

Haiti, a nation that occupies the western third of the island of Hispaniola,
had suffered through a staggering number of revolutions and civil wars. Part
of this came from its turbulent history and its ethnic makeup. Ten percent of
its population, the French-speaking mulatto elite, controlled the ninety percent
Creole-speaking black population. The mulattoes possessed the country's
wealth and had no intention of giving it up nor sharing it with one another.
The Creole-speaking populace frequently rebelled up in the north. When this
occurred, a member of Haiti's elite inevitably took command. Once in power,
said leader would then head south to Port-au-Prince, the country's seat of

power.[35] Between the day of its independence on January 1, 1804, and the U.S. invasion in 1915, only one Haitian president served a full term (followed by a partial second). Nor had Haiti received official American recognition until the Lincoln administration. With the opening of the Panama Canal, Haiti became strategically important to American interests because a well-used shipping lane passed by it. The U.S. government desired to purchase property for a naval base there but the Haitian constitution forbade the ownership of land by foreigners.[36]

Marines and seamen under the command of Admiral Caperton stormed into Port-au-Prince on July 28, 1915. Upon securing the city, Caperton had all revolutionaries arrested, the city's residents disarmed, and the customs houses seized. He declared martial law on September 3. The Haitian National Assembly — the combined upper and lower houses of its legislature that dealt with constitutional matters— responded by electing Dr. Bobo as the country's new president. Caperton refused to recognize him. He ordered a subordinate, Captain Edward Beach, to find a president agreeable to American interests. Beach located the perfect man for the job: Philippe Sudre Dartiguenave.[37]

A member of the southern elite and the president of the Haitian Senate, Dartiguenave won the endorsement for Haiti's highest elected office from his peers only because of American pressure. Despite this, Dartiguenave resisted becoming a puppet for the Americans, often playing "a double game" to keep as many of his country's own interests intact when he could. As the first southern president to serve since 1876 as well as a civilian backed only by a foreign military, he held no sway with the common people. His base consisted exclusively of the *mulâtre* minority. When he tried to run for reelection in 1922, he found that neither group supported him, so he retired, the first Haitian president to do so in a long time.[38] The day after he took office, the Americans handed him a treaty they had written and told him to sign it. He did so, and the Haitian legislature approved it, with its final ratification occurring on May 16, 1916.[39] It gave the U.S. undisputed control over Haiti's ministries of "Finance ... Agriculture, Health and Sanitation" as well as all "Public Works" and the "Gendarmerie"— a national police force.[40]

Although Caperton had secured Port-au-Prince, he still faced considerable resistance beyond its limits, mainly from rebels who lived in Haiti's "northern and central mountains." The revolutionaries, made up mainly of the poor black population, called themselves *cacos,* a word that in the Creole language meant "birds of prey."[41] Butler arrived in the country on August 10, 1915. Colonel Waller arrived five days later to serve as the senior Marine officer there. He received the task of dealing with the *cacos* in the north. He set up a meeting with their leaders. They refused to recognize the legitimacy of Dartiguenave and insisted they would only support Dr. Bobo. Waller informed them Bobo had voluntarily left the country for exile in Jamaica and would not return. He arranged for a second meeting with the rebels, at which they agreed to disarm by a predetermined deadline in exchange for a say in the new government. Not all of them gave their consent. One group surrounded the northern town of Gonaïves, cutting off its water supply. Waller ordered Major Butler to deal with them.[42]

Butler and a detachment of ninety-five men took a gunboat there, arriving on September 20 at nine in the morning. Although 800 *cacos* encircled the city, Butler wrote to their leader, Pierre Rameau, and told him "where to get off. That evening he replied by burning the railroad track and bridges." Butler took twenty men and pursued them. The Marines faced off with fifty rebels, shooting six and chasing the rest away.[43] At daybreak Butler took fifty men and hunted the *cacos* while at the same time avoiding ambushes. When he caught up with Rameau he told him he did not want to see his *cacos* harassing any Haitians within ten miles of Gonaïves. He yanked Rameau off his horse, humiliating the man so much he lost his leadership role right there and then. The morning after, Butler and his men went on another patrol during which they found six *cacos* robbing some local women. They shot three of them. The *cacos* in the area voluntarily disbanded soon thereafter.[44]

The ensuing peace did not last. Although the Marines had offered the *cacos* money and amnesty in exchange for the rebels' guns, those few who accepted usually went right back to their previous occupation. To counter the problem, Colonel Waller had the border with the Dominican Republic closed up. Next he directed the Marines to systematically force the *cacos* into a mountainous area of about four hundred square miles in size. Here the *cacos* occupied a series of "small French-built stone forts."[45] Butler took a detachment of twenty-seven Marines from Fort Liberté into this area on horseback to locate the *cacos'* strongholds, including one in particular called Fort Capois. They took with them a single machine gun.[46]

The Marines began this action during the rainy season, so they had to fight just as hard against swollen rivers and muddy trails as with any rebels they might encounter. At first they had no luck finding any *cacos*, let alone Fort Capois. When they came across a giant of a black Haitian named Antoine, Butler gave him two options: serve as a guide or face execution. Antoine took the former choice.[47]

On the night of October 24 the Marines and their guide entered a ravine in which they had to ford a deep river. A force of about 400 *cacos* opened fire from three sides behind the cover of bushes. (Butler believed Antoine had given the rebels a signal to attack just then, but the Haitian later refused to leave Butler's side when given the chance.) Luckily the *cacos* did not aim well, and only a horse died during the crossing of the river. The Marines fired back only when necessary, pushing forward to a defensible position.[48] Here Butler ordered his men to set up the machine gun. They discovered that although they still possessed its ammunition, they had lost the gun itself during the river crossing. It had been swept away on the back of the dead horse. Despite the rain and dark, a tough sergeant named Dan Daly volunteered to recover it.[49]

Butler once described Daly as "hard-boiled. You could strike a match on his neck 'whiskers.' Not quite six feet tall, he was heavy-set, strong, with a determined face, keen, piercing eyes, and a square chin.... Children and dogs liked him — a sure sign of a kindly, gentle nature, for you can't fool children and dogs."[50] Born on November 11, 1873, in Glen Cove, New York, Daly had gained a reputation as an amateur pugilist. Butler met him during the Boxer Rebellion in Peking, where Daly had served as an American Legation guard. During the Boxer siege of the Legation Quarter, Daly volunteered to take an exposed position on top of the Tartar Wall. Armed with nothing more than a bayonet-fixed bolt-action rifle, he held off the Chinese all night. In the morning dead Boxers "littered" the area before him. For this he received his first Medal of Honor.[51]

During the Great War, Daly fought in the Battle of Belleau Wood, where he charged the Germans despite overwhelming odds and uttered this famous phrase to his men: "Come on, you sons of bitches! Do you want to live forever?" For this he received medals but not a Medal of Honor. Supposedly he did not get one because he swore too much.[52] Butler and Daly remained friends all their lives. In 1932, a friend of Butler's living in California, F.E. Smith, wrote and described a peculiar incident that had occurred. A man who had suffered from a heart attack appeared at the San Joaquin Hospital claiming Daly's identity. He requested to see Smith, who had served with Daly thirty years earlier. The claimant recited many of the details of Daly's life correctly, but unless he had lost several inches of height and experienced a change in eye color, Smith doubted his identity, adding in his letter that if a fake, this fellow "would be just another imposter." Smith asked Butler for his opinion. Butler telegrammed the following in response: "SERGEANT MAJOR DALY IN NEWYORK [*sic*] IN BEST OF HEALTH."[53]

This colorful sergeant plunged into the darkness to retrieve the lost machine gun at great risk to his life. When he returned from his mile-long trek to the river and back, he had the gun strapped to his back. Despite enemy fire, he had gone swimming to recover it. For this act of bravery, Butler recommended Daly receive his second Medal of Honor, which he did.[54] When morning broke, Butler sent squads to rush the three *caco* positions. This attack drove them away, killing eight and wounding ten. Only one Marine endured an injury.[55]

By the time the Marines returned to Fort Liberté, they had marched a total of "120 miles in 5 days 10½ hours, on 10 meals of coffee, corned beef, and hard tack, fought one continuous fight with 400 devilish Cacos for 21 hours, crossed four mountain ranges, [and] passed through a flood that made [them] sit in trees all night ... [all] without losing a man." Butler headed to Cap-Haïtien for a meeting with his superiors. They gave him a force of 600 men with which he planned to launch a two-week campaign to deal with the rebels in the mountains.[56] He took it to assault Fort Capois. Here the *cacos* abandoned their post and escaped. No one on either side suffered from a wound.[57]

The Marines pushed the *cacos* to a place called Fort Rivière, located along Grande Rivière. It stood upon a quarter-mile-long hogback ridge, a formation with two steep sides and a narrow, nearly pointed top that resembled the back of a pig. The fort had thick walls and a courtyard of about 250 square feet.[58] One could only practically approach from its front. The *cacos* had barricaded its original entrance in favor of using a more defensible drainage culvert through which only one person at a time could pass.[59] The fort presented a formidable obstacle, one Butler's immediate superior, Colonel Eli K. Cole, thought impenetrable. Butler convinced him otherwise.[60] He suggested the American forces make a coordinated attack by splitting into four columns that would converge on the fortress from different directions simultaneously.[61]

On November 16 the Marines left the town of Grande Rivière du Nord at five twenty-five in the morning. They carried with them two machine guns and five days of rations on mules. At La Coupe they met up with a detachment of seamen from the USS *Connecticut.* On November 17 the attack commenced. Butler had the machine guns strategically placed to offer covering fire, then moved his column to the walls.[62] There he and twenty-four men approached the drain tunnel entrance, knowing they had to enter despite fire coming through it from inside the fort. Butler started to crawl first, but an old sergeant, Ross Iams, stopped him, saying, "Sorry, Sir, I was in the Marines before you were and this is my privilege."[63] Butler let him go ahead. In his autobiography, Butler recalled he had trouble gathering up the courage to go through that culvert. When he equivocated, Iams said, "Oh, hell, I'm going through," and did. Next went Private Samuel Gross, then Butler.[64] When Iams reached the end of culvert, "he saw the shadows of the legs of two Cacos armed with machettes [sic] guarding the hole. He took off his hat, put it on the end of his revolver, pushed it through, felt the two machettes [sic] descend on it, and jumped forward into daylight."[65]

The others in Butler's column poured through the culvert. Within, they faced about 300 *cacos* whose weapons included "rifles, clubs, [and] stones." With their superior firepower, the Marines made short work of the rebels. As the enemies fought in close quarters, the other three columns of Americans stormed the walls and made their way in. This ten-minute mêlée resulted in the death, surrender or escape of all the *cacos* within. No seamen or Marines suffered a mortal wound.[66] For this action Butler, Iams and Gross all received Medals of Honor. Franklin Delano Roosevelt, at this time the assistant secretary of the Navy, personally issued Butler and Iams theirs.[67]

About the taking of the fort a newswire story proclaimed, "The fall of Fort Riviere [*sic*] is regarded here as being the end of the opposition to the government of President Sudre Dartiguenave. The country is now practically pacified. There are no rebel bands of any importance in the field."[68] Although this was a bit of wishful thinking on the paper's part, the Marines did ensure the *cacos* could never again use the fort itself as a base. They placed a ton of dynamite within. Its detonation on the eighteenth of November made short work of the old stone and brick fortress.[69]

The Haitians themselves did not collectively celebrate this Marine victory, and some even denied it ever took place. In 1931 the Haitian minister to the United States, Dantes Bellegarde, publicly stated that the fort did not exist and Butler had made up the story of its capture. A furious Butler made a formal complaint to the Department of the Navy. Under pressure, Bellegarde backtracked and said he meant to say he had never heard of the place, not that it did not exist. The secretary of the Haitian Legation, Numa Rigaun, made no such apology, saying, "In Haiti we think General Butler is a very imaginative man. He says he took a fort which so far as is known in Haiti never existed.... He says he blew it up afterwards and that is why we cannot find it today. He says he took it alone by crawling through a hole. It is very amusing."[70]

With the rebellion quashed, America could now get down to the business of administering the country. Its infrastructure had fallen into a dismal condition. When Colonel Cole first arrived at the northern port city of Cap-Haïtien, for example, he found it in a state of decay. Its hospital, run by French nuns, could not offer shelter to those it cared for. The city as whole had little in the way of fresh running water, and those few houses that received it did so at best for a couple of hours every day. No one had cleaned or repaired the streets for years because the city lacked a functioning government. Sanitation did not exist, so the city "stunk to heavens." The prison there had fallen into a state of disrepair so notorious it had become "a national affair." The telegraph and telephone systems no longer functioned. Only schools run by nuns worked well, and not a one — Catholic or secular — existed whatsoever in rural areas. Outside the city nothing but mules could pass on the roads even in the *dry* season. In the wet season they often drowned in mudholes.[71]

It would take quite an investment of time and money to make the needed improvements. To facilitate this, U.S. officials had included in their treaty with Haiti the establishment of a national police force, the Gendarmerie, which the

Americans would run. On October 15, 1915, the secretary of the Navy proclaimed that Marines could serve as its officers. This violated existing U.S. law, so Congress moved to change it, although it would not do so until June 12, 1916. In the meantime the Marines had no legal standing in their positions as Gendarmerie officers.[72] Butler received word on December 3, 1915, that he would head this new organization, and he had to create it from scratch.[73] He became a lieutenant colonel in the Marine Corps on August 29, 1916,[74] but held the rank of major general in his capacity as commandant of the Gendarmerie. All Marines who served as officers in this police force received a rank higher than the one they held in the Corps. Sergeants became first lieutenants; second lieutenants, captains; first lieutenants, majors; captains, colonels; and so forth.[75]

Butler established the Gendarmerie's base of operations at Port-au-Prince, the city in which he would live for a bit over two years. He determined that only white men from the Marines would do as Gendarmerie officers. He later said of black officers at a Senate Hearing: "It is instinctive with them to abuse the inhabitants whenever they are given power." Never mind that every nation on earth has such individuals, and all police forces suffer from this problem to some degree, as Butler would discover in Philadelphia. He added, "The Haitian people are divided into two classes: one class wears shoes and the other does not." He despised the shoe-wearers—a euphemism for the elite creoles—and "took [them] as a joke." He masked his racist attitude with a veneer of goodwill by saying he felt American presence could make Haiti "a first-class black man's country."[76] Despite remarks like these, he proudly proclaimed he had allowed neither corruption nor mistreatment of the Haitian people. He prided himself on eliminating the country's institutionalized system of bribery and proclaimed he had put a stop to it, although he had not.[77]

Butler's racism did not stop here. He once described Antoine, the black man who had helped the Marines locate Fort Capois, as "a hideous, ungainly brute. He must have been the ugliest native in Haiti. His arms hung clumsily to his knees and he looked like an ape." Despite this uncharitable remark, Butler trusted Antoine to be the protector of his children while they lived in Haiti.[78] To excuse Butler's racist attitude as one held by most middle-class white Americans of his generation and leave it at that simply will not do. Butler came from a religion that had dedicated much of its resources toward aiding non–white races, especially Native Americans but also African-Americans. After the founding of the United States, the Friends initiated a strong abolitionist movement, and, following the Civil War, started the Freedmen's Association to help protect, educate, and give practical training to former slaves. (Admittedly some Friends did struggle with the issue of racial equality for blacks and whites for quite some time. As late as 1949 they debated among

themselves whether or not to allow blacks to attend their white schools.[79])
Moreover, some of Butler's white American contemporaries viewed white
supremacy as something utterly despicable. In May and June 1909 journalist
Oscar Garrison Villard and other whites met with black leaders at the National
Negro Committee in New York City to do something about it. Out of this
came the National Association for the Advancement of Colored People
(NAACP), an organization dedicated to establishing racial equality in Amer-
ica.[80]

While Butler saw to it that no Haitians served as Gendarmerie officers,
only President Dartiguenave or the Minister of the Interior had the power to
issue the Gendarmerie orders, and only Dartiguenave could appoint its
officers.[81] Haitian natives from the poor classes filled its enlisted ranks. They
wore surplus Marine uniforms made by prison labor in Port-au-Prince that
had plain buttons instead of those embossed with the Marine emblem. At first
Butler only wanted to admit enlisted men who could read and write. He soon
abandoned this criterion when he discovered he could not find a sufficient
number of qualified applicants. He also required enlistees to stand at a minimum height of five feet four inches and, for reasons never explained, a maximum of six feet.[82]

The Gendarmerie controlled Haiti's utilities and internal improvements,
necessary to get the country's economy to produce the sort of wealth the American companies doing business there needed so they could make profits. First
Haiti needed its roads repaired. Without a decent system of transport, internal
commerce would never improve and therefore the Haitian economy could not
grow. To achieve this, one American official — and no one took credit for this —
found an old, unused Haitian law on the books that stipulated citizens had to
either pay a tax for the upkeep of roads or, if they could not give money, to
do so in labor. Called the *corvée* system, it amounted to nothing more than a
legalized form of slavery. The Gendarmerie began enforcing it in July 1916.
Butler later testified in front of a Senate committee he had ensured no one
abused it. The Senate committee found otherwise. It discovered that Haitian
officials had used the system as a means to collect bribes. Although flawed and
immoral, the *corvée* system resulted in the renovation of the old French-built
system of roads so that by the time Butler left the country in March 1918, 470
miles of rebuilt roads existed. Discontinued on October 18, 1918,[83] use of the
corvée system had unintended consequences that would one day bring Butler
back into the country.

The Gendarmerie rebuilt more than just roads. It directed the repair or
building of irrigation works and cleaned up towns, shaping the country into
something functional once more.[84] Butler asked the minister of the interior
to give the Gendarmerie control of the postal service and permission to build

telegraph and telephone lines; the minister happily agreed.[85] Butler felt it a military necessity to manage these things, but the Haitian minister in Washington refused to sign a treaty that would give the Gendarmerie these powers.[86]

Frustrated, Butler and Waller went to President Dartiguenave and demanded he telegraph his minister in Washington, D.C., and instruct him to sign that treaty. Dartiguenave said he would do so. Butler and Waller had doubts, so Butler returned later to see if the president had dispatched the message or not. He had not. Butler sent Dartiguenave a note telling him to send that telegram by the next morning or else. He sent Sergeant Harold E. Miller to stay with Dartiguenave to encourage the president's resolve.[87]

When Miller saw the president write the telegram in code, he reported this to Butler. Butler obtained a copy of the message, then had a man swipe the Haitian code book to decipher it. As Butler suspected, Dartiguenave had instructed his minister *not* to sign the agreement. Butler confronted the president about this deception, but Dartiguenave insisted he had done no such thing. Butler placed his translated copy on the president's desk. He insisted Dartiguenave write out his order in non–coded French and give it to him to send, which the Haitian president did.[88] Such strong-arm tactics endeared Butler to the Americans with business interests in the country. In December 1916, for example, Roger Farnham, now a vice-president of National City Bank, sent Butler a note praising him for his accomplishments.[89]

Despite all this trouble, in the end, the Gendarmerie failed to take control of the country's postal service or build telegraph and telephone lines as Butler wanted. The latter task fell to American engineers. This embittered Butler so much he felt like quitting but refused to do so because he wanted to set aside "a little nest egg for the future."[90] Butler received, in addition to his Marine pay, $250 a month in his capacity as the head of the Gendarmerie, giving him an additional $3,000 a year. Because of this added pay he had an earned gross income of $7,256.83 in 1917.[91]

Although he did not like his position as chief of the Gendarmerie, he planned to keep it for some time. He rented a house in Port-au-Prince to accommodate his family, who came to live with him.[92] To ferry them about, he ordered a Stutz four-passenger roadster with a "coupled body." He wished to pay $1,000 or $1,100 for it, although he would go as high as $1,200 if the need arose. He wanted to have a model no older than a 1915, plus he needed spare tires and parts. He received his car at the end of January 1918.[93]

6

Général Butler

Butler had to balance his duties as a Marine officer and those as the commandant of the Gendarmerie on a regular basis. Often the line between the two blurred to the point where one could not say with any degree of certainty in which capacity he served. One afternoon in December 1915, Colonel Waller received a note from a distressed President Dartiguenave saying he feared revolutionaries planned to kill him. Could he please come in the evening? Waller did so, bringing Butler with him. The president had heard that rebels planned to revolt against him on January 10. To ease his mind, Waller directed Butler to stay with the president until after Christmas.[1]

Waller already knew about the uprising but made no move to stop it because he wanted it to come off so he could unmask its leaders. He soon found them: Antoine Pierre-Paul and General Codio. After the Marines made short work of this rebellion, Waller locked Codio in prison; Pierre-Paul escaped. Waller later testified before a Senate committee he believed Pierre-Paul had fled to the German Legation for protection. He suspected a cabal of German businessmen had financed the revolt. General Codio and about 150 revolutionaries broke out of the national prison in Port-au-Prince, but before Codio reached the Dominican border, the Marines shot him dead. President Dartiguenave later pardoned Pierre-Paul, who gave him no further trouble.[2]

At the end of August, Butler received an order from Dartiguenave that further distorted the line between Haitian and American interests. The Haitian president told him to take seventy-seven "mounted men" to the Dominican border to root out bandits causing trouble there. Dartiguenave's written order directed Butler to leave on September 5, and in his official report Butler stated he had done so.[3] In a letter to his father, he contradicted this; he wrote that he left on September 1 and had taken with him not mounted gendarmes but Marines. Colonel Waller had ordered him to the Dominican border to look for a revolutionary leader named Celidiano Pantilion and, if he happened upon him, Pierre-Paul (who at this point had not yet received a pardon from Dartiguenave).[4]

69

Whether as gendarmes or Marines, Butler and his men would spark no unintentional international incident by crossing into Dominican territory. Earlier in the year the U.S. had invaded that country and, although it had planned to stay for a short time, remained there until 1924. Thus America controlled the entire island of Hispaniola, making illegal border crossings a moot point. Incidentally, Butler's mission had nothing to do with the guerrilla war against American forces over sugar that broke out in the Dominican Republic in 1917. This occurred in the eastern half of the country, whereas Butler and his men only skirted its western border.[5]

The seventy-six Marines whom Butler commanded for the expedition went well-armed, carrying no less than two machine guns, 10,000 rounds of ammunition, and a pack train of twenty-four mules carrying three weeks' food and supplies. They traveled to Azua in the Dominican Republic, at which point they tracked down rumors they had heard about their target. To investigate them all, Butler split his force into two columns. His detachment traveled "176 miles" and climbed one mountain range that rose to just over 3,000 feet "in 5 days, 8 hours and 45 minutes."[6]

Butler's patrol heard that Pantilion had a "tremendous estate" somewhere in the area. Everyone seemed to know about the bandit leader and his place of residence, but neither was found. Upon discovering "a little, dirty hut," the Marines declared it Pantilion's "estate," thus bringing a successful end to their mission.[7] About going home empty-handed without firing a shot, Butler commented in a letter: "Now when a crowd of roughneck Marines can't find any cause for shooting and burning[,] d — d little exists."[8]

On January 21, 1917, an inspection tour set to visit the islands of Cuba and Hispaniola departed on a ship bound for the Florida Keys. An up-and-coming politician named Franklin Delano Roosevelt, in his capacity as the assistant secretary of the Navy, led it. FDR's entourage included, among others, General George Barnett, the Marines' commandant; John McIlhenny of the U.S. Civil Service; and Livingston Davis, FDR's secretary.[9] The Roosevelt party arrived at Port-au-Prince on January 25. The group took an admiral's barge to shore. There everyone wore dress uniforms despite the heat, Butler and Colonel Cole among them.[10]

FDR had written a speech he planned to give to President Dartiguenave and, with much difficulty, translated it into French himself. He mistook Dartiguenave's representative at the dock for the Haitian president, so he recited the speech to him. Everyone climbed into automobiles and rode to the presidential palace, outside of which they met another delegation. FDR mistook Port-au-Prince's mayor as the president, so he repeated his speech. In the palace itself, the envoys finally met the president and his cabinet, so FDR presented his speech for a third time.[11]

Butler gave a dinner in FDR's honor. He also accompanied the future president to the island of Gonâve for a recreational riding expedition. There FDR sighted the famous wild cattle, said to have arrived on the island with Christopher Columbus's son, Diego. This venture served as a prelude for a longer trip by horseback the Roosevelt party planned to take, during which it would travel from Port-au-Prince to Cap-Haïtien.[12]

This began on January 29 at six in the morning when the Roosevelt party gathered at the American Legation. It took cars north to Croix-des-Bouquets to meet Butler, General Barnett, an escort of 150 mounted gendarmes, and a pack train of sixty animals. On the first day the combined group traveled a staggering forty-three miles, quite a feat in that mountainous terrain when burdened with so many supplies and men.[13] The next day it stopped to skinny-dip in a creek at a place called Hinche.[14] There, much to FDR's amusement, "we found that the entire female population was lining the banks. They had never seen a white man in this condition before and seemed to take it quite calmly." Davis, a fellow not well-adapted to such an adventure, had changed into a bathing suit first.[15]

Now the party split up. Davis joined the group heading west to Citadelle while FDR, Butler, and others departed on a trek that would take them to the ruin of Fort Rivière.[16] FDR wanted to see for himself the place in which he heard Butler and his men had stormed through a drain into the fort. Its imposing location impressed the future president enough for him to award Butler and his sergeant the Medals of Honor mentioned in the previous chapter.[17] The travelers reunited at Cap-Haïtien. From there the Roosevelt party departed for Santo Domingo to do an inspection, which ended abruptly when the Germans declared the waters surrounding the island of Hispaniola a war zone. This forced FDR and his entourage to rush back to Washington so they could deal with the ensuing crisis.[18] General Barnett later wrote Butler a letter thanking him for planning the trip so well, and for making it such a pleasure and success.[19]

In 1916 American officials dissolved the uncooperative Haitian National Assembly. In 1917 new elections brought in replacements, but this version proved just as stubborn as the last. The point of contention came from a wrangle over the ratification of the new constitution, supposedly penned by FDR himself. Although the Haitians had written no fewer than ten constitutions between 1805 and 1916, every one of them denied ownership of Haitian land to foreigners. The U.S. insisted the Haitians remove this restriction, something the Assembly refused to do.[20]

Colonel Cole, now a brigade commander, wrote a memo to his superiors saying he felt the Haitians would not go for this change, and he thus might have to dissolve this newest National Assembly. According to Cole's account, when he approached Dartiguenave about this, the Haitian president said he could only execute such an order with U.S. support. Cole made a formal request to his superiors in Washington to do this. The Navy Department said that yes, he could, but he could *not* use Marines to accomplish it. With this caveat, Cole ordered Butler to dissolve the Assembly in his capacity as head of the Gendarmerie.[21]

Butler's explanation of this incident differs from Cole's in some significant ways. In Butler's version, two of Dartiguenave's cabinet ministers came to him on the morning of June 19. The minister of finance, who spoke perfect English, warned, "The constitutional assembly is making nasty remarks about the President. They are saying he is a bad man, and he is dishonest, and that he is pro-American, and that at 1 o'clock they are going to impeach him." The minister told Butler to dissolve the Assembly. He refused. Only the president could order him to do so. Butler repaired to the presidential palace to confront Dartiguenave himself, but the president feigned illness, refusing to see him. When it became apparent Butler would not leave, Dartiguenave gave in. He told Butler to dissolve the Assembly. Butler refused, saying he needed a written order. Dartiguenave replied that he required cabinet members to witness the signing of such an order, but one of them currently resided in Cap-Haïtien. He again gave Butler a verbal order to dissolve the Assembly, and once more he said no. Dartiguenave rounded up four of his five cabinet ministers, and together they signed the order. By law a cabinet minister had to deliver the message, but all of them declined out of fear for their safety. Butler said he would take it.[22]

He brought a contingent of gendarmes with him to the National Assembly, although he personally went unarmed. The Assembly greeted his arrival with "hisses and jeers." He handed the message to the president of the Senate, Stenio Vincent, who said he would read it out loud. Instead Vincent went into a tirade against Americans in general and Butler in particular. Butler's Haitian gendarmes, used to shooting opposition leaders, loaded their guns and prepared to fire. Butler had his officers order them to unload. Vincent went into another diatribe, and the farce repeated itself. Finally he gave in and read the president's order. The Assembly dissolved. Vincent approached Butler, who expected the senator to bawl him out. Instead Vincent said, "I am hungry." With the standoff over, he wanted Butler to take him out to lunch.[23]

The National Assembly did not reconvene. The next year, on June 12, 1918, America arranged for a direct approval of the new constitution by national referendum, although the Haitian government conveniently failed to explain its purpose to the general population. In a low turnout, it received 98,294 votes of approval versus a mere 769 against. Foreigners could now own Haitian property.[24] Butler had known dissolving the Assembly in the way he had could cause him legal problems at home, so he kept Dartiguenave's original written order. Several years later a Senate committee investigating this incident called him to account. He handed it over to them, protecting himself from any unpleasant consequences.[25]

On April 6, 1917, America declared war on Germany. Butler immediately wrote to his good friend General John Lejeune asking for a transfer to Europe so he could fight for his country.[26] To his horror, he found he had become a victim of his own success as the head of the Gendarmerie. Washington did not want to release him from his post for this reason. Butler found little solace in the explanations he received. One friend assured him Washington would not allow him to leave his post because they could not find a suitable replacement. John McIlhenny, who had accompanied FDR to the island, wrote to Butler and told him that both he and FDR felt that if another man took his post, things in Haiti would quickly decay.[27] (And, as it turned out, they did.)

After all, during his tenure as the Gendarmerie's chief, Butler had overseen the repair and building of roads with a workforce of 6,000 men, the repairing of telegraph and telephone lines, the establishment of a coast guard service that generated its own revenue by hauling freight, and the management of six large plantations. The Gendarmerie took over the finances of all villages, towns and cities.[28] Butler and Cole drew up a plan to create a national school system, and they had four school buildings built in well-traveled areas so the Haitian people would become aware of them. The Marines (possibly in their capacity as gendarmes) built the schools using Haitian-style architecture with materials able to withstand the tropical climate.[29]

Butler launched a furious letter-writing campaign to get out of Haiti. He felt trapped. As his communications fell on deaf ears, his frustration mounted. He wrote to Lejeune: "The service is becoming more and more detestable every day and the knowledge that I am not to be allowed to fight for my country makes it even more unbearable."[30] Having promised his wife he would not use his father's political influence to get what he wanted,[31] he had no choice but to sit tight. After months of pestering anyone he could think of in Washington and elsewhere, he finally received an order to leave Haiti on April 10, 1918. His new post did not improve his chances of seeing combat in Europe. He had to report to a swampy place called Quantico in northern Virginia.[32] Before going there, he took a leave of absence, during which time he had more work done on his teeth, a constant struggle for him.[33] By the time of his retirement he had dentures.[34]

In 1916, with American involvement in the war in Europe a distinct possibility, Congress had authorized an increase in the size of the Marine Corps from about 11,000 officers and men to 15,600, with a contingency to expand to 18,100 if the need arose. Marines usually trained on Navy bases, but with that arm of the military expanding as well, room enough for both did not exist. The Navy needed a new training ground set aside for Marines somewhere on the East Coast. The declaration of war in 1917 finally motivated it to acquire land to build such a facility, one that had to accommodate at least 7,000 men. A board chaired by General Barnett formed to find a suitable location. It recommended an area in Virginia just south of Washington, D.C., called Quantico, land owned by the Quantico Company. The Navy leased 5,300 acres. The first Marines there, commanded by Major Chandler Campbell, arrived on May 14 to set up camp. The recruits started to arrive four days later.[35]

Why anyone would establish a base here defied reason. Nothing more than a muddy swamp, it suffered from mosquito infestations and had no access to potable water, which came in on carts. Disease plagued its occupants, sanitation barely existed, and the Marines took to burning their garbage for lack of a place to send it. To make matters worse, 1917's high temperatures broke all previous records. In 1918 the U.S. government bought this gem for $475,000.[36]

To carry out his work at Quantico, Butler received the temporary rank of full colonel on July 1, 1917, made permanent on March 9, 1919.[37] He figured he had received orders to report here of all places because he had criticized the Navy Department for considering raising the rank of the Marines' commandant to lieutenant general while not offering any sort of rewards for the soldiers fighting in the trenches. Still, his training style served him well. It impressed one raw recruit, Josephus Daniels Jr., so much he wrote to his father, Secretary of the Navy Josephus Daniels Sr., and asked him to have Butler sent to Europe. His father complied. On September 15, 1918, Butler shipped out on the USS *Von Steuben* with Daniels Jr.'s regiment, the Thirteenth, from Hoboken, New Jersey. Two days out to sea, Butler fell ill with the flu.[38]

He had contracted no ordinary influenza. Known as the Spanish flu, it had first struck America on March 4, 1918, at Camp Funston in Kansas, then tapered off during the summer. In the fall it returned, this time at Camp Devens, located thirty-five "miles northwest of Boston," a place meant to accommodate 35,000 men but packed with 45,000. The epidemic swept through at a rapid pace, killing one hundred men per day. Symptoms included fevers that often got to 104°F, and body aches so terrible a light touch caused pain. The flu in and of itself usually did not kill. Death typically resulted from the development of one of the most virulent varieties of pneumonia ever seen, one that often caused death in a matter of hours after contraction. It filled the lungs with fluid, creating a condition called cyanosis—a lack of oxygen in the blood as a result of which the skin took on a blue-blackish hue.[39]

This particular strain of influenza became known as the Spanish flu not because it originated in that country but because Spain had no part in the

Great War and thus its papers did not suffer from censorship. The Spanish press reported the disease caused 8 million deaths there. Although other nations experienced similar losses, they dared not reveal such numbers for fear this information would further demoralize the war effort. In America the Spanish flu killed about 675,000 people. Worldwide it caused an estimated 30 to 40 million deaths.[40]

Doctors thought Butler had developed the pneumonia associated with it, but he had not, so he survived. Still, the flu took its toll on him. When he arrived in Brest, France, on September 24, he could not stand on his own. From this port he and those other American soldiers on board headed to a processing facility called Camp Pontanezen, a place in such terrible shape it made the swamps of Quantico seem pleasant. Upon his recovery, Butler hoped to head straight to the front. On September 25 he received an order attaching him to the Army. To his dismay, he learned he would take command of Camp Pontanezen itself. Despite his misgivings and disappointment, he pledged to do all he could for the men suffering there. Regulations dictated that only a general officer could command this facility, so he received the brevet rank of brigadier general on October 7 at the age of thirty-six.[41] This became permanent on July 4, 1920.[42]

Never did a place need Butler's genius for engineering and organization more than here. Brest itself served as the port of choice for Americans because it had the best deep-water harbor on France's west coast, allowing the largest of transport and cargo ships to dock right at the shore rather than having to anchor far out and thus unload men and supplies using transport boats, a process that slows things down considerably. A staggering 791,000 American soldiers, out of a total of 1,057,000 who came to France, landed at Brest, most of whom went through Camp Pontanezen. This military base, established in April 1918 and built upon an existing Napoleonic-era French encampment, stood on a hill four miles from Brest. Originally consisting of stone barracks surrounded by a stone wall, it soon expanded to one mile wide and one and a half miles long. It had no roads or sidewalks. Making things worse, cold temperatures and constant rains that started in October had turned it into a muddy "quagmire." Heavy rains continued to fall through November and worsened in December. When the war ended in the former month, the camp had to abruptly reverse itself to process hundreds of thousands of men for their return home.[43]

The expanded portion of the camp contained steel barracks and enough tents to accommodate up to 5,000 men, but none of these shelters had floors, meaning those living within had to contend with mud. Few stoves were available to provide warmth, exacerbating the misery. The camp's water supply had suffered contamination from fertilizer runoff from nearby fields, so potable water came from springs located two kilometers away.[44] The camp could barely keep up with the number of sick. Two hours after taking command, Butler received word that the USS *Leviathan* had arrived and, of the 10,000 on board, he would have to retrieve 4,000 of them because the flu made them too weak to move on their own. The camp possessed a mere nine trucks and two horse-drawn ambulances to get the job done, and only 250 beds in the camp hospital. Butler released his regiment, the Thirteenth, from quarantine, then used it to complete the task.[45]

Mud presented the greatest problem. Although General James G. Har-bord, commander of services and supplies in Tours, and his chief quarter-master, Colonel Henry Smithers, did their best to give Butler the provisions he asked for, even they found it nearly impossible to procure certain items from the supply warehouses. Butler's immediate superior, General Eli A. Helmick, also accommodated Butler's needs when possible. When Helmick temporarily left his post to deal with matters elsewhere in France, he left Butler in charge. Butler used this newfound authority to march 7,000 men down to the supply warehouses to raid its inventory of spare duckboards—wooden boards used to line the bottom of trenches. While there, Butler decided to lib-erate a number of "shovels, axes, picks and kettles" as well.[46]

Carrying a duckboard on his shoulder, Butler led his column of men in a march back to camp. At a crossroads an MP stopped him, insisting he yield to an oncoming Cadillac. It had a general's star on it. Butler, dressed as an enlisted man, replied, "Just a minute … that's my car." The MP replied, "If yer don't back off and give that car gangway, I'll show you who you are." Butler put his duckboard down and showed the MP the star on his shoulder, then complimented the fellow for doing his job well. For this Butler earned "the sobriquet of 'General Duckboard.'"[47]

Butler constantly worried not so much about his own career (although he did this, too) as for the men under his care. He expressed this in a letter to his wife: "Last night I went to sleep finally[,] nearly worried to death, this trying to keep 65000 [*sic*] men fed, with never enough stuff on hand to do it more than one meal in advance." He feared he would find himself held accountable for the wretched conditions despite his Herculean efforts to rem-edy them. His worst fears became a reality when George P. Brown of the *Wash-ington Post* visited the camp during a time when Butler had business in Tours. Although Brown published a scathing article, it nonetheless praised Butler for his efforts to improve things.[48]

Although Butler did not know it at the time, General Harbord, fearful for his subordinate's reputation and career, decided to do something proactive. He heard that Mary Roberts Rinehart, a popular American writer known for her mysteries and other work that appeared in *The Saturday Evening Post*,

Rooms from Camp Pontanezen after Butler came to the camp and made it livable. From the Smedley D. Butler Collection, courtesy of the Marine Corps Archives and Special Collections Department at the Gray Research Center, Quantico.

resided in Paris just then.[49] At this time Rinehart happened to serve as Secretary of War Newton Baker's eyes and ears in Europe, so a good word from her would exonerate Butler's reputation.[50]

Rinehart figured she would write "a blistering report," especially upon her first sight of the place. Because of the pervasive mud she had to don "high rubber boots" and a slicker. To her surprise, she found the camp's morale exceptional. She soon learned why. General Butler, whom she described as "that dynamo of energy" and "no red tape man," had defied regulations by issuing "double rations of food," serving "hot soup all day long to those who needed it," and handing out a blanket to every man in the camp. The lunch she had there tasted better than anything she had so far eaten at the nearby hotel in which she stayed. Her hotel had no water in the bathrooms, no working plumbing — it had trench latrines in its basement — and no heat in its rooms, forcing her to cover herself up with a blanket as she wrote her report. In contrast, Camp Pontanezen had all these things. She asked Butler what he required. He told her, stressing a particular need for wood to burn. When she radioed her report to the secretary of war, he saw to it Butler received all he had requested.[51]

Things improved thereafter. Butler had electricity introduced and proper sidewalks installed. To ensure the camp's water quality, he ordered its stores chlorinated and inspected regularly. He had the beds at Camp Hospital No. 33, one of several, expanded to 2,800 and, even when "taxed to their utmost capacity," the hospitals never failed to meet the needs of their patients. All 450 barracks and 5,500 tents had floors installed.[52] Ten large kitchens provided the food needed to feed the mass of men passing through. Butler once held a contest among them to see who could "produce the best all round results" with the winners gaining a week's leave of absence.[53]

Visitors inspecting the place came with unsettling frequency and included FDR, General Pershing (whose eyes Butler did not like and whose voice he deemed "weak" and "insincere"), General Harbord (along with a man from the Associated Press who later wrote he had never before seen such an efficient feeding operation, one that the Army planned to copy all over France), President Wilson's close friend Colonel Edward M. House, French generals and admirals, and Secretary of the Navy Daniels and his wife. Of these visitors, Pershing would have the most impact on Butler's time in France. He gave Butler command of the Fifth Marine Brigade, made up of two regiments, on April 9, 1919.[54]

In early June, Pershing appeared at the camp and asked Butler if he and his fellow Marines would like to get back into Marine uniforms instead of wearing the standard one of the American Expeditionary Force. Butler said yes, realizing he and his men had received a rare privilege, as most Marines could not do this. Pershing thought much of Butler's efforts to make the camp into what it had become, and he let him know it, much to Butler's embarrassment. Pershing personally awarded Butler and General Harbord medals for their work behind the lines.[55] Butler received the Distinguished Service Medal for the Army and Navy. The French awarded him their *Ordre de l'étoile noire*— the Order of the Black Star.[56]

As Butler had struggled to keep pace with the soldiers passing through his camp, the United States gave criminals the greatest gift they had ever received from the government: the Eighteenth Amendment. This made the manufacture and sale of alcohol illegal in America. It would go into effect at the end of January 1920.[57]

On June 30, Butler received orders to go home. He took six weeks' leave and spent it in West Chester. Thereafter he reported to Quantico as its chief of staff under General Lejeune.[58] Lejeune became the Marines' commandant shortly thereafter, replacing George Barnett, a man Butler never liked, particularly since Barnett had managed to gain his post over Butler's good friend Waller. Butler's father had much to do with Barnett's removal.[59] The day Lejeune took his new post, he arrived at Barnett's office a bit too early. Barnett informed Lejeune that he still had to obey his orders and he would stand at attention while Barnett told him something. He dressed Lejeune down. At noon Barnett dutifully stood up and told Lejeune he now had the position of commandant. Two of Barnett's aides-de-camp each pulled a star from their commander's shoulders before he left the office. Butler sat in a parked car across the street and watched the whole thing.[60] Upon taking the post on July 1, 1920, Major General Lejeune made Butler the commandant of Quantico.[61] Butler had little time to take up his new duties before he received orders to travel to Haiti and the Dominican Republic for temporary duty to investigate accusations of Marine atrocities.[62]

In the Dominican Republic the Marines had taken to treating the predominately black population as second-class citizens in much the same way as white supremacists treated the African-American population in the United States at the time. Problems ranged from "Marine rudeness" to outright brutality. Once, for example, a group of armed Marines invaded a Dominican party uninvited, then proceeded to drink all the alcohol there. A more serious incident occurred in December 1920. Four armed Marines broke into the house of a teenage girl named Altagracia de la Rosa, raped her, and then took her mother hostage for ten days. Although it was a well-documented incident, no one brought charges against these men.[63]

In Haiti, meanwhile, the commandant of the Gendarmerie, Colonel Alexander Williams, about whom we shall hear more later, asked for reinforcements. Another *caco* rebellion had broken out, one directed at the Americans. It had its origins with the bitterness created by Butler's use of the *corvée* system as well as a rumor circulating among the Haitian population claiming the Americans planned to reintroduce slavery. Charlemagne Masséna Péralte, a member of Haiti's elite class with a French education, led the rebellion. He had turned against the Americans after receiving a sentence of five years at hard labor for attempting to steal the Gendarmerie's payroll. He escaped from prison, then started this revolution.[64]

The *cacos* attacked Port-au-Prince on October 7, 1919, although Marine intelligence had anticipated it, so it failed. A Marine sergeant who served as a captain in the Gendarmerie, Herman H. Hanneken, took charge of apprehending Péralte. Failing to draw him out for a conventional fight, Hanneken, sixteen gendarmes, and a guide — all dressed in camouflage — headed out on the night of October 31 with the sole purpose of finding Péralte. They sneaked past six *caco* checkpoints to reach the rebel leader's camp. There the guide pointed Péralte out to Hanneken, who proceeded to fire two rounds of his Colt .45 pistol into the *caco* leader, killing him. A moment later a *caco* threw a blanket over the campfire, so Corporal William R. Button opened up on the rebels with his Browning Automatic Rifle, a weapon developed for the trenches of Europe and designed to kill en masse with certainty.[65] When stories like this reached the ears of General Barnett in 1919, he wrote a report to Secretary of the Navy Daniels. Daniels in turn ordered the investigation that Lejeune and Butler now spearheaded.[66]

They arrived in Port-au-Prince on September 4, staying there until September 13, at which time they headed into the Dominican Republic. While in Haiti, Butler met President Dartiguenave for the first time in several years. The president "almost kissed" him. He awarded Butler the *Médaillon militaire du Haïti* for his service as chief of the Gendarmerie.[67] Butler found the state of the country appalling. He complained bitterly in a letter to his mother about the poor condition of the roads and other infrastructural improvements he had worked so hard to have built up.[68]

In his final report, Lejeune wrote that he had found no problems with the Marines in Haiti, effectively giving those who had committed the atrocities or had just abused Haitians an exoneration. Secretary of the Navy Daniels "convened a court of inquiry" to investigate some specific incidents. Rear Admiral Henry T. Mayo served as its president, so it became known as the Mayo Court of Inquiry. In a travesty of justice, the Mayo Court deemed two unjustified homicides and sixteen other serious incidents "isolated." It saw no overall problem with the way the Marines had behaved on the island, especially since the men involved in any illegal activities had faced justice. It concluded that no "indiscriminate killing of natives" by Marines had occurred on the island of Hispaniola.[69] The Senate, too, held inquiries at which Butler testified in October 1921.[70] Neither the Mayo Court nor the Senate admitted the truth that Marines had indeed committed outrages against the native populations of both Haiti and the Dominican Republic.[71]

Despite Butler's hope that America's interference in Haiti would benefit its people, American policies ultimately failed to do so. In 1929 the left-wing journal of opinion, *The Nation,* summed up: "Fourteen years of Yankee rule in Haiti have been an ignoble failure." The system of government installed by the United States had turned into a "military despotism" that propped up "a native dictatorship." The Marine in charge of the island, General John H. Russell, had permitted "the puppet government which the marines installed in office to accumulate such a high tide of resentment" that no one respected it. Moreover, thirteen years after Butler dissolved the National Assembly, no elections had yet taken place. If America left the Haitian people alone, things would work out far better than the economic and political disaster caused by U.S. interference.[72]

Upon his return to Quantico, Butler decided to make the base the pride of the Marine Corps. He had a tough job ahead of him. Swamps and swamp-like conditions still prevailed, and were so bad in the spring the Marines had to use tractors with caterpillar treads to move artillery.[73] Beyond remedying this situation, Butler wished to "beautify" the base and make it a "show place" for the Corps. He decided to build a sports stadium, one that would one day bear his name, and not just any arena would do. He wanted "'the world's largest stadium.'"[74]

Given a budget of a mere $5,000 to accomplish it, he spent the entire sum on cement. To continue construction, then, he had to get creative. He obtained "sand and gravel" for "free from local contractors," then found the iron he needed by gathering up surplus salvaged from Marine bases that had closed after the Great War ended. For steel he convinced the Richmond, Fredericksburg and Potomac Railroad to donate their old rails. The Marines, including officers and Butler himself, provided the labor. All Marines had to participate in its construction one way or another. When three musicians told Butler they did not want to do manual labor on the project for fear of hurting their hands, he agreed, then declared that so long as the men worked, musicians such as these would provide them with music. Although it was not completed until after World War II, the Marines nonetheless utilized the stadium early on.[75]

Butler formed a Marine football team. In 1923, as part of the Marine Corps' anniversary, it traveled to Ann Arbor to play the University of Michigan's team. Many Marines volunteered to have part of their salaries docked to finance the cost of attending.[76] Butler took much pride in the team. At a game in Philadelphia, for example, he personally roared a cheer and clanged

Although no record of this photograph's exact place and time exist, its wilderness setting and the number of VIPs around General Smedley Butler (center) suggests someone took this shot during one of the Marines' summer exercises in which they reenacted Civil War battles. From the Smedley D. Butler Collection, courtesy of the Marine Corps Archives and Special Collections Department at the Gray Research Center, Quantico.

a pair of cymbals to drum up support for the Marines. At a football game in 1928 an incident occurred in which a Navy band leader kicked the team's mascot, a bulldog named Jiggs, when he did not get out of his way.[77] Butler "ordered a charge of the opposing stands" in response.[78] Although considered "possibly apocryphal" by the writers of Quantico: Crossroads of the Marine Corps, the story may have a basis in reality. Butler received a letter from D.C. Gurnee, the general secretary of the Maryland Society for the Prevention of Cruelty to Animals, in which this fellow complained that during a clash between the Army and Marines at a game, Jiggs had gotten hurt. He asked Butler to refrain from bringing his dog onto the field in the future out of fear for Jiggs's safety.[79]

Beyond athletics, Butler attracted positive publicity for the Corps by having his Marines reenact famous Civil War battles around Quantico for public entertainment every summer. In June and July 1921, a Marine Brigade "fought" the Battle of the Wilderness using "155mm guns pulled by 10 ton tractors" as well as its air force. President Harding himself watched the spectacle from a canvas White House constructed for him.[80] One day the Marines would use modern equipment, and another they would fight a battle using historic tactics.[81] In 1922 the Marines refought Pickett's Charge at Gettysburg and in 1923 New Market in Shenandoah Valley.[82]

In this latter year Butler suffered a major financial setback. He lost $5,000 — a small fortune in those days— when a bank in the nearby town of Quantico failed.[83] Banks had no kind of insurance then, so when they shut their doors for good, anyone with money in them would lose it all. Perhaps it ought to come as no surprise that when Butler received an unexpected employment opportunity, he took it despite not really wanting it.

7

The War on Drinking

One morning in 1924, Butler purchased an extra edition of a Philadelphia newspaper with a headline reporting his death at the hands of gunmen. Although unknown persons had taken shots at him the night before as he left a police station, they had missed. He had jumped into his car and given chase but had lost the perpetrators.[1] These men wanted him dead not as a Marine officer but as Philadelphia's director of public safety, a job he started on January 7, 1924. He had received the offer for it two months earlier after W. Freeland Kendrick won the mayor's office by pledging to rid the city of crime and corruption. To achieve this, Kendrick and his advisors came up with the idea that they needed to hire someone outside of Philadelphia's convoluted (and corrupt) politics to take the cabinet post of director of public safety, the person in charge of the police and fire departments. They wanted to fill the position with a professional military man, figuring such an individual would bring discipline to the police department's ranks. Someone suggested Butler. Not only did he have Pennsylvanian residency, a requirement, but he also possessed law enforcement experience.[2]

A friend of Kendrick's called Butler in November 1923 and arranged for a secret meeting with the mayor-elect at the Bellevue-Stratford Hotel in Philadelphia. Kendrick, at least in Butler's account, begged him to take the job.[3] Butler agreed on two conditions: first, Kendrick would not interfere with the way he ran the police, and second, he could quit at any time should he decide he did not have this freedom. Kendrick consented. Butler did not wish to resign from the Marines, so Kendrick asked President Coolidge to grant him a year's leave of absence, which he did.[4] When Kendrick publicly announced Butler as his choice, the mayor said, "We are personal friends. I met him after the World War." When asked about this comment, Butler retorted, "I never met Kendrick till two weeks ago."[5] In fact he had. During his time as Quantico's commander, one of Butler's fellow Shriners had asked him to invite Kendrick, the Potentate of the Philadelphia Temple to which Butler belonged, for a visit to the base. Butler invited Kendrick and the entire Temple for lunch.[6]

Butler had little enthusiasm for his new job. He wrote to friends that he would treat it as nothing more than another detail. He figured he would fail miserably at it.[7] Still, after losing a small fortune to a bank failure, he needed this job for the extra money it would bring him. It paid an impressive $15,000 a year.[8] Despite his money problems, in September of his first year in office, he, at the suggestion of his wife, gave $2,000 of his own money (which came from his unspent Marine pay) to the widow of a policeman whose baseball game benefit had suffered cancellation due to rain.[9]

Butler wore his Marine uniform when Kendrick swore him in. Half an hour later he reappeared in a uniform "he himself had designed" that made him look more like a superhero than a police chief. It was "blue with gold trim, its cape, taken from his Marine mess jacket, revealing a flaring red lining." He called the city's inspectors to his office and told them their lieutenants had forty-eight hours to clean up the city or they would suffer demotions. Any police officer offered a bribe should report the incident to him. He had beds placed in City Hall for himself and the police chief so they could oversee this drive,[10] which targeted speak-easies in particular. Of the estimated 1,200 saloons operating in the city, the police shut down 973 during this two-day assault. Butler planned more of these drives in the future.[11]

Pennsylvania in general and Philadelphia in particular had ignored the enforcement of Prohibition until a progressive governor named Gifford Pinchot took office in 1923. An environmentalist and forester by profession, he had founded the U.S. Forestry Service under President Theodore Roosevelt. When he first started running for public offices, he did so as a Progressive. Unable to win any elections that way, he switched to the Republican Party. He won the governorship by attacking utility companies and alcohol. When he found he could not get any money to enforce the Volstead Act[12] from the state legislator, he funded it using a donation of $150,000 from the Women's Christian Temperance Union.[13] He supported Butler and would serve as one of his high-placed allies in state politics for years to come.

Butler had plans to militarize the city itself. He wanted to set up twenty-one booths containing two armed guards positioned at points of entry and exit to the city, wire all police stations to one another directly to improve communications, and create a "bandit chasing squad" composed of fast cars and motorcycles. Not content with merely going after vice, he decided to pursue reckless driving as well by setting up a series of "colored lights and arrows to act as guides for motorists."[14]

In his first month in office he launched a total of three forty-eight-hour drives. Although temperance supporters loved him, most politicians and judges did not. Magistrates refused to issue search warrants for private homes even if police suspected their owners sold liquor out of them. Cafés shut down one

Butler (right) shakes hands with an unidentified police officer in this photograph taken either in 1925 or 1926. Here he wears the uniform of the office he then held, that of Philadelphia's Director of Public Safety. He designed it himself. From the Smedley D. Butler Collection, courtesy of the Marine Corps Archives and Special Collections Department at the Gray Research Center, Quantico.

day and reopened the next. When trials occurred, judges often suspended sentences or meted out minor fines. Only one jurist, Harry S. McDevitt, ever supported Butler's efforts. As the months passed, councilmen and other city elite publicly and privately implored Kendrick to leave certain places—the ones they frequented—alone. Several real estate agents tried to get Butler to raid only the "little places." Butler refused. His sense of treating everyone equally no matter what their social or economic standing dictated he would grant no such favors.[15] Years later he recalled this sentiment: "My foolish notion that the laws of our country applied to rich and poor alike accounted for the growing feeling of antipathy toward me."[16]

Butler issued .45 caliber army revolvers to the city's 1,600 firemen, giving them the authority and mandate to assist the police in fighting crime. He abolished "all district detectives" and gave lieutenants the ability to decide if their men would serve in uniform or plain clothes. He wanted to establish a "secret service" akin to Scotland Yard. Station houses from now on would display pennants. Blue represented a clean district, red that the district did well, and white that "it is lying down on the job." The firemen enthusiastically supported their new director. Butler announced, "Unless we make it safe by February for a child to go anywhere in Philadelphia, we've failed in our duty."[17]

This made for good publicity but did little to address the city's underlying problems. Its Republican political machine ran things with a level of corruption that made Al Capone's operation look honest. Often referred to as "the organization," it was controlled by Congressman "Boss" William S. Vare. His family had made its fortune through municipal contracts for things such as garbage collection and road repairs. No one got elected in Philadelphia without the machine's backing.[18] For reasons of his own, Vare wanted Butler in office. Vare recommended one of his own men for the chief of police, a post Butler appointed. Not only did Butler decline, he later demoted this Vare man for corruption.[19] The machine maintained its power by disenfranchising voters and controlling every aspect of the election "from registration to balloting." Police did nothing to arrest repeat voters. The machine, after winning time and again, looted the city's coffers with "graft, payoffs, and kickbacks."[20]

The machine's power so disgusted journalist Imogen B. Oakley that he wrote an article in which he compared it with the dictatorship of Benito Mussolini. He called it the "invisible dictatorship." Butler, when nearing the end of his tenure in 1925, said seventy-five percent of cases brought before the city's magistrates with concrete evidence suffered dismissal because of this invisible dictatorship's manipulation.[21] The machine supported saloon keepers, madams of brothels, and owners of gambling establishments because these people could "deliver votes." They in turn owed fealty to the city's ward bosses. The city's elite stood at the top of this scheme. They frequently met at night in "the lobby" of a different "fashionable" and "respectable" hotel. There they whispered to one another in a corner and at midnight departed for a secret location. Because of this ritual, this group became known as the "Midnight Club." A writer for *New Republic* magazine managed to attend one of these secret gatherings, held in this case at the house of a prominent (but unnamed) citizen of Philadelphia. There the group discussed gossip and politics — stuff that never got into the papers. Here Superintendent William Mills admitted to taking bribes. This statement turned the discussion to the subject of Butler, whom the group deemed "crazy" because he had suspended a number of older police officers considered close friends with Boss Vare. They complained that Butler did not play the game fairly — what "a poor sport."[22]

Since the turn of the century, Philadelphia's police force had seen reforms, but not long-lasting ones. In 1912, for example, things in the department started to change when reform mayor Rudolph Blankenburg took office with the intent of cleaning up the police department. His superintendent, a former military man named James Robinson, militarized the force. He began "regular physical exercise drills" and trained the men in "boxing, wrestling, and running." He had new uniforms introduced as well as a sixty-five-piece band for "ceremonial occasions." He revised the patrolmans' manual for the first time since 1897 and founded a police academy called the School of Instruction. To graduate, potential officers had to pass "written and oral" exams with a score of seventy or better. To keep men on the beat from tiring out, he changed the shift rotation from two a day to three. When Blankenburg left office in 1915, many of his reforms either stopped or became tools for the politicians.[23]

Butler faced many obstacles to success. Federal interference kept his men from inspecting breweries until April 1924. Since Prohibition did not stop the distillation of alcohol for industrial purposes (thus allowing factories to make products such as perfumes and medicine), Butler had to contend with the fact that much of this product got into the hands of the bootleggers every month. More tragically, industrial distilleries produced mainly isopropyl, or wood, alcohol, a substance quite poisonous to humans, and it often got into alcoholic beverages. One coroner reported he saw ten to twelve deaths a day as a result of people drinking such poisonous concoctions.[24]

In April 1924 reporter Maxwell Hyde, a journalist with sources in Philadelphia's underworld, did a story on what the professional criminals thought of Butler and his efforts. Hyde interviewed an underworld boss who boasted he could do more to clean up Philadelphia's crime in one day than "a million Butlers could do in a million years." Despite Butler's efforts, the underworld boss asserted that not one prostitute had left the streets, nor had booze or gambling reduced in volume whatsoever, something Hyde verified in part by finding a glass of beer at the low price of ten cents. Butler had merely forced these activities into secret places but accomplished little else. Yet, the crime figured noted, Butler had done the city one useful service: he had gotten poisonous alcohol off the streets.[25]

The anonymous underworld figure told Hyde he could hire a hit man for $1,000, and many such men made the city their base of operations, often going to other places across the country to fulfill their contracts. Big-league bandits used the city as their headquarters. Illegal lotteries amounted to $100,000 worth of tickets sold each week. One local Sunday paper attacked Butler not because it hated him on ideological grounds but because its owner had ties to the criminal underworld. Hyde, who did not write this article to criticize Butler but rather Philadelphia's population, summed his sentiment up thus:

"Philadelphia will not rid itself of the criminal element unless the entire citizenship gets behind Butler, and thus far many feel that he has done little but make speeches. One man will never clean-up Philadelphia. It will take a 'movement.' And that 'movement' must include every decent man, woman and child in the city."[26]

Butler's time as the director of public safety transformed him into a lifelong Prohibitionist who never touched alcohol again.[27] Yet the harder he tried, the less success he had. In 1923, for example, the police arrested 1,413 people for allegedly running speak-easies and sent seventy-eight percent of the cases to grand juries. In 1924 the police under Butler arrested "four times as many on the same charge ... and almost twice again as many in 1925." Of these, juries convicted sixty-six percent of those tried in 1923, sixty-two percent in 1924, and a meager twenty percent in 1925. Of those convicted in 1925, only four percent received anything more than a "light fine," something that speak-easy operators considered part of the cost of doing business.[28]

Butler did not improve his sometimes tenuous relationship with his police force when he made public attacks on his own men. In an April 1924 newspaper interview, for example, he launched into a tirade against lieutenants who had "'double-crossed' him." A full half of his forty-two lieutenants had allowed gambling houses to reopen. He would do something about it, too: "That means that they have got to suffer for it. Some will be fired, others will be shifted to different districts, some will be demoted and still others will be allowed to resign and obtain their pensions."[29]

As a commanding officer in the Marines, Butler had never criticized his own men publicly — only praised them — and for this they loved him. That he did something so contrary to his usual command style suggests the sort of frustration and strain from which he suffered. Perhaps he experienced exhaustion — not the euphemistic sort celebrities come down with when they have mental breakdowns or drug problems, but a true lack of rest. He worked eighteen hours daily, and in the first three months in office gave one or two speeches a day.[30] His wife and children never saw him despite his residency in the city.[31]

While the political machine hated Butler, his popularity with the citizens made it difficult to move against him in the open. Some machine lackeys close to Kendrick worked to sour Butler's relationship with him. It worked.[32] In July 1924 tensions came to a head when Butler drew up plans for the reapportionment of police districts to keep them out of the control of ward bosses. Kendrick planned to ask for Butler's resignation if he did this, but Butler would not back down. Rumor said Governor Pinchot would interfere and not only ensure that Butler kept his job, but would retain it for Kendrick's full four-year term.[33] Anticipating dismissal, Butler made a speech to the police imploring them to continue with his programs should Kendrick fire him. Before suffering from this fate, he wanted to raise $150,000 for the widows of fallen officers as well as prosecute anyone distributing poisonous alcohol. He also suggested the creation of a police air force.[34]

The Federation of Churches and the Pennsylvania Law Enforcement Association intervened, resulting in Butler and Kendrick's reconciliation.[35] Now Kendrick publicly supported Butler's redistricting plan, pointing out it would free up about $3 million worth of real estate the city could use for other purposes, and it would save the police department about $1 million a year.[36] Kendrick further asked President Coolidge to grant Butler another year of leave from the Marines. The president agreed, but he told the mayor in a letter he would give Butler no more time. He did not think the emergency that had called for Butler's presence in the first place could possibly extend beyond this.[37]

Butler's second year resulted in less success and more aggravation. Hotel operators complained that his strict enforcement of Prohibition had hurt their business.[38] In September 1925 he showed no signs he wanted to leave at the year's end. In a speech he said, "I have tried every method conceivable to put an end to crime and the flow of rum. From now on until the time I leave Philadelphia it is going to be a war to the finish." The same article that recorded those words proclaimed Butler's "war on banditry was successful. The city was so well patrolled by swift motor cars carrying police and detectives that hold-ups were more dangerous to the thieves than to their selected victims. Crimes of violence of all kinds decreased. There were thirty-five fewer murders in the city than in 1923 and thirty-six fewer manslaughters."[39]

Governor Pinchot went to Washington, D.C., to meet with President Coolidge and request a third year's leave of absence for Butler. Coolidge made no promises.[40] Kendrick and Senator George Wharton Pepper of Pennsylvania also asked this of the president, but in early November, Coolidge declined. Butler would have to return to duty at the beginning of 1926. He could only stay if he resigned his commission from the Corps.[41] As Butler pondered whether he wished to stay or go, a city magistrate and two clerks raided the ballroom of Philadelphia's Ritz-Carlton, a posh hotel. There they found liquor violations. Upon learning of this, Butler proposed padlocking the premises until the prosecution of the case concluded. In effect, he wanted to shut the hotel down just at a time of the year when it would have its best business with Christmas and New Year's. He also wanted to revoke the dancing license of the Bellevue-Stratford Hotel for similar violations. With the city's sesquicentennial coming up in 1926, hotels across the city feared such tactics would ruin their potential boom in business.[42]

Oblivious to their protests and influence, Butler resigned his Marine commission. On the same day he sent it off to Washington, Kendrick fired him. His excuse: "I don't want you in my cabinet as a resigned officer." Kendrick named Butler's assistant, George W. Elliott, as the new director of public safety.[43] Fortunately for Butler, he had the option of retracting his resignation from the Corps, which he did.[44] His career as director of public safety ended as unexpectedly as it had begun.

Debate over Butler's success continues to this day. While most literature on the subject has a favorable assessment of him, writer Samuel Walker, in his book *A Critical History of Police Reform: The Emergence of Professionalism*, had nothing but contempt for Butler in general and his policies in particular. He criticized Butler for shutting down the School of Instruction in favor of on-the-beat training, and Walker thought Butler's bandit squad did more for good publicity than it did reducing or fighting crime. Nor did he like Butler's habit of promoting and demoting officers on a whim rather than going through formal channels.[45] Butler had also abolished the police and firemen's unions,[46] a move that gave him more control over them but did much to harm their overall collective bargaining position after his departure.

Boss Vare successfully ran his own man for mayor after Kendrick's term ended. This fellow, Harry A. Markey, named Harry C. Davis as his director of public safety. Davis undid Butler's police redistricting plan, nullifying his most important contribution of removing politics from the police force.[47] Within two years of Butler's departure, a grand jury indicted high-ranking members of Philadelphia's police for corruption. These men had belonged to Unit No. 1, a special task force that Butler himself had organized. The jury found evidence that some of its members had set up a protection racket, one which extorted money from bootleggers in exchange for leaving them alone.[48] Another investigation, this one in 1927, revealed that the heads of a bootleg whiskey ring had "banked more than $10 million. This organization gave the police "millions of dollars in bribes, as shown by several truckloads of account books and ledgers seized at one alcohol-denaturing plant." It also had links to eleven murders the from the previous year.[49] Based on incidents such as these, one can safely conclude Butler's reforms did not last.

Governor Pinchot, Butler's staunchest and most reliable political ally, tried for the Republican nomination for U.S. Senator in 1926. He faced the incumbent, Senator Pepper, as well as Boss Vare, and lost to both. When Vare won the general election in the fall, Pinchot, in his capacity as governor, refused to seat him on the grounds Vare had run a corrupt campaign. The Senate agreed, so Vare never served in Washington. Pinchot would run and win the governorship again in 1930,[50] something that would have an effect on Butler's own dabbling in politics.

Philadelphia's citizens had a different attitude towards Butler's abrupt departure. Letters of support poured in. One fellow, an African-American man named William M. Betts, wrote Butler praising him for treating his people fairly and for standing up to the politicians and corruption. The Universal Publication Syndicate wrote that it would not support Kendrick's political ally, Governor Pinchot, for so much as "a street-cleaning job." Others outside the city, impressed by Butler's tenure as director, offered him a variety of jobs. W.B. Shafer Jr., the president of the Pennsytown Corporation in Norfolk, Virginia, asked if Butler would manage a multi-million-dollar development. The city of Syracuse, New York, asked him to serve as its commissioner of public safety. Butler declined them all. His experience pushed him into a depression, one that still lingered as late as April the next year.[51]

Still, he had made some lifelong friends during his tenure, including that of journalists Paul Comly French of the *Philadelphia Record* and E.Z. Dimitman of the *Philadelphia Public Ledger*. French would later play a part in "unmasking" an alleged conspiracy to remove President Franklin D. Roosevelt from office and replace him with a fascist dictator. Dimitman — "Dimmy" to his friends — often worked with Butler as either a co-author or ghostwriter of newspaper and magazine articles. Their first collaboration occurred right after Butler lost his job. They wrote a thirty-part series titled "Smashing Crime and Vice" that ran in newspapers across the country. For this venture, Dimitman and Butler divided the proceeds in half, with Butler donating his portion to a fund for prosecuting politicians interfering with Philadelphia's police.[52]

As Butler prepared to leave for his next duty station, a civil war raged throughout China. Fighting threatened the International Settlement in Shanghai, the section in which a variety of Western powers, including the United States, had interests and citizens. On October 17, 1926, the Chinese general defending the city, Sun Chuan-Fang, suffered a major setback when one of his munitions ships blew up, killing 1,200 crewmen and troops on board. More disturbingly, the Chinese had fired upon a British gunboat, inviting the possibility of another foreign intervention similar to the Boxer Rebellion.[53]

On January 2, 1926, Butler and his family climbed on board the S.S. *Columbia*, a ship sailing from Brooklyn on a twenty-six-day trip to San Diego via the Panama Canal. Butler would report for duty at the naval base there, taking command of its Marine barracks.[54] Shortly after arriving in the city, Colonel Alexander Williams, who had served as Butler's second-in-command in the Haitian Gendarmerie and whom Butler had recommended as his replacement when he left, invited Butler and his wife to a party.[55] There Butler saw about twenty people drinking cocktails, and, of those present, Williams consumed the most. Embarrassed, Butler stepped outside to the porch because he had no desire to report the incident. About nine at night some of the guests suggested the Butlers join them at the dance held at the Hotel del Coronado. Having already planned to do so they drove there, leaving Williams behind.[56]

SMEDLEY BUTLER is gone. But he, is not forgotten, by any means, although some would have it so.

THE EVENING BULLETIN—PHILADELPHIA, FRIDAY, JANUARY

GENERAL BUTLER AND HIS FAMILY SAIL FOR SAN DIEGO

On Board the S. S. Colombia Just Before Sailing From Brooklyn Yesterday Afternoon—From reader's left: Smedley D., Jr., Brigadier General Smedley Darlington Butler, Miss Ethel, Mrs. Butler and Thomas Richard Butler. The former Director of Public Safety is sailing by way of the Panama Canal and the trip will take twenty-six days. Upon arrival at San Diego General Butler will assume command of the marine post.

This photograph from *The Evening Bulletin*, January 2, 1926, shows Butler and his family as they ready themselves to sail to San Diego for his new posting there. Clipping courtesy of Molly (Butler) Swanton.

Things went well for the first half hour until Butler heard "a commotion." Investigating, he saw a drunk Williams "making a great show of himself." Two Marine officers present grabbed the colonel by the arms, dragged him out, and drove him home. Now Butler faced a quandary. He did not desire to report Williams, but he thought he could not allow this show of public drunkenness to go unanswered. He ultimately had Williams arrested on this charge, deciding to do so in part because he felt he should treat a colonel just the same as a private in matters such as these.[57]

In Washington, D.C., his decision roused the anger of Congress. Debate occurred over the incident on the House floor, much of it critical of Butler. One Democratic representative from New York, for example, thought it unseemly that Butler, Williams's guest, should repay Williams's hospitality like this. Perhaps, he suggested, "Butler should be drummed out of the service."[58] Despite such ire, Williams did not suffer unduly other than an infringement on his reputation. Butler had made a technical arrest, which only removed Williams from his command of the Fourth Regiment but did not confine him either to a jail or at home. While Williams awaited a court-martial, his friends found witnesses who swore he had gone to the dance sober.[59]

Shortly before this debacle began, Butler had ten infected teeth pulled. Complications from this caused him a serious illness— probably the infection had spread beyond his mouth. Doctors confined him to home for two months' rest. To make matters worse, the bad publicity from the Williams affair soured the people of San Diego against him and his family. He quickly learned this firsthand when he made plans to attend a luncheon held by the city's Chamber of Commerce. When its members learned he would appear, quite a few of them called Butler's commanding officer, Admiral Ashley H. Robertson, and told him that because of Butler's presence, they would not attend. In a letter to his friend E.Z. Dimitman, Butler complained, "We [he and his family] have been ostracized as if we had small pox."[60] Sometimes cinema owners, upon learning that a member of Butler's family sat in the theater, would project his image on the screen to get the crowd to boo and hiss.[61]

In a letter to another friend, Butler complained about San Diego in general: "I do not like the duty nor the location. This is a terrible town and has more bums than the whole of Philadelphia." In retaliation for the unfair treatment he felt he had received, he threatened to take all his Marines to a base in another city. Making good on this threat would cause the city much economic harm. Butler estimated the city made about $10,000 a day off of Marines in any given month,[62] a likely figure, considering the Navy as whole spent about $500,000 a month for supplies and $2 million a month on payroll. Indeed, the San Diego base, the biggest on the West Coast, served as a port for "government ships … destroyers, cruisers, tenders, submarines, aircraft detachments" and "tugs." Its Naval Training Station alone had twenty-eight buildings and educated around 2,000 officers at a time. The Marine Barracks, which Butler commanded, could accommodate 5,500 officers and men.[63]

Butler said nothing to the press about the Williams incident because the Navy Department had a policy forbidding its officers from making public statements about ongoing investigations. Because of his silence, the press and therefore the public did not know his side of the story, such as the detail that he had discussed bringing charges against Williams with Admiral Robertson first, and only did so upon the admiral's recommendation. Moreover, Butler only charged Williams for public drunkenness and conduct unbecoming an officer for the incident at the Hotel del Coronado, not at his home, one of the "facts" that had soured public and Congressional opinion against him.[64]

Williams's court-martial occurred in April. His defense team introduced two Marine captains who accused Butler of "browbeating" them into saying they had seen Colonel Williams drunk. A third officer, Captain Clifton B. Cates, told the court Butler had rejected his first written statement on the matter, telling him: "You go back now and tell the truth or you'll get into trouble." Cates testified that Butler forced him to add to his report he had seen Williams "sick, drunk or doped." The court looked into this charge by interviewing a variety of men under Butler's command.[65] Williams's defense further insisted their client had not suffered from intoxication at all, but rather from the effects of a prescription drug he had taken for a urinary infection. The defense found two doctors to testify to this. They also besmirched Butler's reputation by declaring that on the night Butler had seen Williams drunk, the general could barely see out of one eye — so how could a man so blinded recognize someone drunk? The doctors further asserted that Butler had at the time also suffered "from a near nervous breakdown" because of his time in Philadelphia as well as his bad reaction to having ten teeth pulled at once. Thus he had imagined the whole thing.[66]

The court did not agree. On April 19 it convicted Williams for public drunkenness. The verdict pleased Butler. Despite the bad press he had received over the matter, he boldly declared, "Now I am going to dry up this marine base. There will be a housecleaning and there will be no more cocktail parties in which marine officers under my command are the guests."[67] On May 21, Williams received his punishment: he would stay a colonel but lose four numbers on the promotion list, meaning that instead of having seventeen other colonels under him, he now only had thirteen.[68] He died a few months later in a car accident at his new post in San Francisco.[69]

Despite this crisis, Butler continued to perform his duties as commander of the Marines in San Diego. Upon his arrival in January, Admiral Robertson had complained to him that the naval base served as a den for bootleggers, affecting morale. He asked Butler to do something about it.[70] Butler set about his task first by eliminating liquor, then improving overall morale by generating positive publicity about the Marines. Here he employed the same ploy he had used at Quantico: he directed his men to reenact the Battle of San Pasqual, one that had occurred during the Mexican War, and he invited the public to watch. The base received another boost of improved public relations when MGM came to film parts of its movie *Tell It to the Marines*. This motion picture, starring Lon Chaney Sr., featured Marines from the base doing drills, living in barracks, and working on board ships.[71] Butler worked closely with the movie makers and their cast, including its star. MGM's chief executive, Louis B. Mayer, wrote a kind letter of thanks to General Lejeune in which he praised Butler.[72]

On October 16, 1926, Lejeune agreed to a request by U.S. Postmaster General Harry S. New for the use of Marines to guard mail trucks, cars and railroad terminals, which of late had suffered from a series of robberies by armed bandits.[73] Butler took command of the Marines in the Western District, an area encompassing roughly the western half of the country. He gave orders for guards to challenge suspicious persons. If such individuals refused to move along, the Marines could open fire with their guns. Butler had them equipped with tear gas to avoid casualties and to deal with large numbers at once.[74]

Many towns hosting Marine mail guards asked Butler to make a speech

Butler and his dog, Jiggs, in a photograph taken between scenes during the filming of the 1926 MGM movie *Tell It to the Marines*. From the Smedley D. Butler Collection, courtesy of the Marine Corps Archives and Special Collections Department at the Gray Research Center, Quantico.

there. He would agree, but only if the town gave his men "free Theater and Movie privileges" and offered to "entertain them" with a minimum of "two big dinners—Privates and all."[75] At the end of January 1927, Marines started to return to their bases. General Lejeune publicly stated they had gotten the job done and therefore did not need to stay on this emergency detachment.

In reality he had recalled them so he could ship them off to Nicaragua, once again a hot spot. Of the 2,400 Marine mail guards, only 1,000 would remain.[76]

Butler found himself still suffering from the Williams affair. One day, for example, he and his daughter went to a football game between the Marines and the Army. Few Marines sat in the bleachers as most had left the base for mail guard duty. The 2,500 naval men and officers in attendance rooted for the Army. When not doing that, they spent the remainder of their time "hissing and jeering" Butler. To his satisfaction, the Marines beat the Army in a score of "13 to 0."[77]

In February 1927, Butler received an order to head to China. He would arrive in Shanghai on March 25.[78] *The News,* a paper out Fredericksburg, Maryland, reported the reason for his mission: "General Smedley Butler, Uncle Sam's cleanup man, whose record includes distinguished service in China, Nicaragua, Philadelphia and at a California cocktail party, is back in China again at the head of his marines." There they would protect American citizens in danger from the ongoing civil war. When asked about his son's mission by the press, Butler's father commented, "What I want to know is why in the name of heaven those nationals [U.S. citizens] aren't dragged out by force!"[79] A good question to which Butler would soon find the answer.

8

Standard Oil's Man

On March 24, 1927, a contingent of Cantonese soldiers who had rebelled and broken off from their main army invaded and looted the city of Nanking. They spared no foreigner or native. They attacked the British and Japanese Consulates, where the British consul suffered a wound and his Japanese counterpart death. Cantonese forces shelled the Standard Oil compound, killing and wounding Americans there.[1] They also moved into the city proper and began extensive looting. C. Stanley Smith, an American missionary who worked for the University of Nanking, suffered this fate. Cantonese soldiers broke into his house with him still in it, and stole what they could grab, including a typewriter and Peking rug. They ransacked his library. After leaving, local Chinese civilians rushed in to take what they could as well, including his bed! They wrecked the place, ripping up pipes and smashing the bathtubs. Then more soldiers came, hitting Smith and threatening him with death. They literally took the clothes off his back by absconding with his coat, overcoat, and shoes. Smith's Chinese servants disguised their employer and helped him make his escape. A Buddhist family and, later, an elderly Buddhist woman risked their lives to hide him in their homes and to feed him. In retaliation for Chinese looting, two U.S. destroyers and one British cruiser fired shells into the city. American, British, and a smattering of Japanese soldiers moved in to extract their nationals and bring them back to the safety of their ships, Smith included.[2]

Incidents like this set Butler on edge. He arrived in Shanghai just a day after this event began. Since he was the commander of the Third Brigade, a force that included all Marines stationed in China,[3] the Nanking looting profoundly influenced the way he planned to deal with the Chinese people. He well knew that if the Chinese in Shanghai, about one million of them in all, rose up against the 35,000 Westerners living there, things would get ugly.[4]

Shanghai itself stood on the banks of the Whangpoo River. A series of treaties imposed upon the Chinese by Western powers had split it into five distinct sections, or municipalities. Europeans, Americans and Japanese con-

trolled the International Settlement, the largest of these. The
French ruled independently in
their French Concession to the
south of that. The Chinese administered the remaining three municipalities in the city's south and
southeast.[5] The International Settlement contained 800,000 people.
Its governing body, the Municipal
Council, controlled the harbor and
its customs houses in partnership
with the Chinese government.[6]

Butler had come to the city on
board a civilian liner run by Dollar
Line called the *President Pierce.*
Upon disembarking, he reported to
the man in charge of all naval and
Marine forces in the country,
Admiral Clarence S. Williams,
under whom he had never served.
Butler found Williams "chilly."
The admiral's frigid attitude
toward his new subordinate
stemmed in part because no one

Butler's 1928 official Marine portrait. From
the Smedley D. Butler Collection, courtesy
of the Marine Corps Archives and Special
Collections Department at the Gray
Research Center, Quantico.

had consulted him about bringing a general officer of the Corps to Shanghai
nor told him what day this officer would arrive.[7]

Williams asked Butler's assessment of the situation. Butler answered that
he thought he did not have enough Marines on hand to do the job. Williams
replied, "So you're one of these fellow[s] who wants to build a big job for himself and get promotion." Butler would have none of this: "I am not of the
'Gimme Family' and never yelled for help unless I believed it necessary. I would
very much rather do this job with what I have, 'Admiral.'... You asked me for
my opinion and I gave it to you. Now, if you don't care to take my advise [*sic*]
and some Americans are murdered in this town, and you sit quietly here with
half of the Marines available in the United States doing nothing but guarding
coal piles, you will be held responsible." The meeting ended with that.[8]

Butler repaired to the headquarters of the Fourth Marine Regiment, commanded by Colonel Charles "Charlie" Hill, the man who had replaced Colonel
Williams upon his arrest in San Diego. Butler deemed the regiment's headquarters unacceptable. It occupied a condemned house with no heat or sani-

Butler (center, walking) inspecting the barracks in Shanghai, 1927. From the Smedley D. Butler Collection, courtesy of the Marine Corps Archives and Special Collections Department at the Gray Research Center, Quantico.

tation, a situation exacerbated by Shanghai's winter weather, consisting mainly of a cold rain that sapped warmth from the body. Butler rented a different Chinese-built house as a replacement. Its first floor contained the office, the second billeted the officers—two to a room, including Butler—and the third the clerks. Heated by "little open fires," it provided a "dry and comfortable" setting. Outside, orderlies and two squads of troops set up tents heated by small stoves.[9]

Despite the fact that the 20,000 British troops stationed in the International Settlement had set up fifteen miles of barbed wire, "bomb screens" and "impromptu forts of sandbags and bamboo" to guard the streets,[10] Butler observed that the two-man Marines patrols making their policing rounds on foot throughout their section of the city suffered from both physical and mental strain, the former because of the amount of distance they had to traverse and the latter for fear of attacks by Chinese mobs. Such inefficient patrols spread the Marines so thin that if trouble occurred in one place, they could not gather en masse fast enough to deal with it. Butler replaced these with patrols that used trucks in which an officer and eight enlisted men carried a Thompson machine gun and a Browning Automatic Rifle.[11]

Butler desired to replace the trucks his Marines used with armored vehicles. He requested six Christie tanks,[12] which he had seen in action in 1922 while in command of Quantico. Invented by J. Walter Christie, these could run on either wheels or tracks. They also had an amphibious capability, crossing water with the aid of two propellers. When Butler and Lejeune saw a second-generation version in action, they thought it might work well for the Marine Expeditionary Force. Butler convinced Lejeune to buy one. He wanted to use it as a surprise weapon during a practice amphibious landing at Culebra planned to take place between December 1923 and February 1924. When brought into action, it lacked the power to reach the shore, although it did well in Culebra's lagoon. Despite this limitation, Butler thought these vehicles would do for Shanghai, but he never received any because Christie no longer made them.[13]

Butler's frequent discussions with Admiral Williams warmed their relationship considerably. Butler wrote to Lejeune: "I have never served with one better. He is a fine, clear-headed thinker, with plenty of nerve, and incidentally you might assure the Secretary of the Navy that, from our [the Marines'] standpoint his selection is a dandy." The admiral had Butler help him compose two telegrams. One asked the American minister in Peking to please keep the Marines in Shanghai and the U.S. Army out, and the other, written to General Lejeune, requested Marine reinforcements. In reply to the latter, Lejeune sent Butler the Sixth Marine Regiment. Upon its arrival, Butler had it set up camp at the Standard Oil compound on the outskirts of the city. He wanted it there rather than in the city proper because he did not desire to further upset Shanghai's indigenous population, one which already felt as if foreigners had taken over their city.[14]

He had no inclination to abuse the Chinese people under American control. He noted in a letter to his mother: "The British are brutal with the Chinamen but I won't permit our people to even touch them — we must be gentle but firm — and the funny thing is that we control our police district much more easily than do the other and rougher foreigners."[15] The British elite living in the city did not like Butler's approach. These businessmen desired the outright conquest of China. They had little or no contact with the average Chinese citizens, and held nothing but disdain for them.[16]

For the most part Westerners living in the city who interacted with the Chinese people daily wanted them to rule themselves, but the aforementioned firebrand British elite, sometimes called the Shanghai Club, had more power and influence. When they learned the Americans had no intention of outright intervention in the country and the Marine Sixth Regiment would not enter the city, they accused American officers of losing their nerve. This goaded the Marines into making a parade through the city, complete with their band, but did nothing to convince Butler and Admiral Williams to do any more than this. The Shanghai Club held its belligerent stance because its members feared if China reasserted control of the city, they might lose their special economic shelters, causing their profits to plunge.[17]

In May, Butler planned an inspection tour taking him first to Tientsin, then to Peking. Admiral Williams asked him if he would mind taking Mrs. Williams so she could see the country before his impending retirement. Butler agreed. His journey began using a route similar to the one he had traveled during his first time in China back in 1900. He started this venture in Tangu, and from there went to Tientsin, then Peking.[18]

Much had changed in the country since Butler's last visit, not all of it physical in nature. After the allies put down the Boxer Rebellion, they had imposed the harsh Boxer Protocol, which called for the execution of ten Chinese officials and the exile or suicide of many others. The Chinese government had to pay a large indemnity and make a humiliating apology to the German and Japanese governments. In order to raise the money for the payment of the reparations, the allies imposed a tariff on external trade. (The United States waived most of this fee and used the rest of the money to establish Qinghua University in Peking. No others on the winning side did anything like this.) All this sparked a fierce Chinese feeling of nationalism. In 1911 the strain foisted upon China by foreign intervention proved too much. A mutiny of officers in the Chinese New Army forced the emperor to abdicate. They established the Chinese Republic.[19]

A national leader named Sun Yatsen emerged to create a parliamentary democracy based on European models. Alas, the former imperial war minister, Yuan Shih-kai, wanted power for himself, so he made himself China's dictator. His death in 1916 resulted a power vacuum. Military governors scrambled to take control, fighting among themselves for dominance. The foreign press called them "warlords." In response to this chaos, Sun formed the Kuomintang, or Chinese National People's Party, which received Soviet funding in exchange for allying itself with the Chinese Communist Party. The two formed the National Revolutionary Army with the mission of attacking and subduing the northern warlords. When Sun died in 1925, a conservative military man named Chiang Kai-shek took over the party.[20] In 1927 he turned on the Communists, violently expelling them from the Kuomintang. Many of those not shot went into hiding.[21] Chiang made Nanking the new capital. The Communists established bases of their own in the south.[22] A civil war between the two erupted.

In Peking, two of Butler's aides, Major Vandegrift and Captain Ray A. Robinson (whom Butler called "Torchy"), detached themselves so they could work on coordinating with the American forces stationed in the city to develop an evacuation plan. If Chinese forces attacked the city, Americans would go to the relative safety of Tientsin rather than risking entrapment as had happened during the Boxer Rebellion. After Butler met with the American minister, John V.A. MacMurray, he wrote to Lejeune in a "secret" letter that "the American Minister is tired out. He is a nervous wreck." MacMurray wanted America to invade China and felt slighted because the American government had "not adopted his plan." Butler figured the poor fellow would soon have a breakdown. He suggested that the American government replace him with Williams upon the admiral's retirement.[23]

MacMurray often took a hard-line position, but two American officials kept him in check. These men, Secretary of State Frank B. Kellogg and his chief of the Division for Affairs in East Asia, Nelson Johnson, had no interest in treating the Chinese as anything less than equals. They wanted the Chinese to rule themselves without foreign intervention. In contrast, MacMurray "believed that leniency would breed more antiforeignism." On January 27, 1927, Kellogg issued a policy statement in which he proclaimed America wanted to renegotiate international treaties with China, which he felt contained unfair conditions. If Britain, America's closest ally in this matter, did not agree, the United States might do so on its own. Kellogg declared America would not require that the Chinese officials doing the negotiating must also ensure peace, only that they represent the Chinese people or its authorities.[24]

Not long after his return to Shanghai, Butler concluded that the large number of policemen working alongside British soldiers in the International Settlement could deal with any problems that cropped up better than the Marines.[25] The settlement's police force, arranged by the British, had in its ranks 1,200 Chinese citizens and 2,000 intimidating Sikhs imported from India.[26] With that in mind, Butler convinced Admiral Williams to allow him to move most of his Marines to Tientsin because of the Chinese threat to Peking. MacMurray did not want to evacuate this city despite orders from the State Department to do so, and he made himself a "nervous wreck" trying to decide if he would obey such an order if it came. The entire Sixth Regiment arrived in Tientsin on June 4, billeting at the Standard Oil compound there. Butler continued on to Peking for another meeting with MacMurray. He felt "sick" when MacMurray started to complain that an American evacuation from Peking would result in America's losing "face." Although Butler admitted to Lejeune that as a Marine he would enjoy nothing more than a good scrap, as the man in charge, he had a responsibility to do just the opposite.[27]

To keep the Pei-Ho River open — the main supply route from the coast to Tientsin — Butler introduced two aviation fields, one at Tientsin and the other at a place called Hsin Ho, about ten miles up from the river's mouth. Not only did this give the Marines control of both ends of the river, the fifteen-minute flight sped up communication between them. Air travel also reduced the transportation time of mail and people. Butler himself took flights from time to time. By agreement with the Chinese, these could not stray from a narrow path between Hsin Ho and Tientsin, although Butler hoped to expand them to Peking.[28] The Marines flew Coleman Curtiss JN-4 biplanes, known better as Jennies. They also used them for reconnaissance missions to keep an eye on Chiang Kai-shek's army. When the Japanese started to fly observation planes over the Americans during their maneuvers, Vandegrift asked them to stop. They did not, so he had Marine fliers sneak up on the Japanese planes to give them a good scare. They accomplished such stealth by flying with the sun behind them. The ploy worked; the Japanese ceased their spying.[29]

During the summer of 1927 things at Tientsin fell into a predictable routine. After July 4 the heat got so bad that Butler ordered the Marines to stop all regular work after eight in the morning because two men had died from the heat. He requisitioned fans to ease conditions. He also allowed the Marines to strip to a minimum of regulation clothing. Even he, never troubled by high temperatures before, found the intense heat bothersome.[30]

In a letter to Lejeune, he noted he had seen a report from the Chamber of Commerce stating that since the Marines arrived in China and settled in, American business had increased by twenty-five percent in the last five months. Butler attributed this in part to the difference in how his Marines treated the Chinese people compared to other foreign powers. He had made it a point to keep friendly relations with them and even hired a prominent Chinese businessman as a translator, a fellow with many contacts who could make arrangements for the Marines an American could not. Butler asked Lejeune for money to use for entertaining Chinese officials. Since "none of the other foreigners pay attention to them," he thought doing so could benefit American business interests considerably. Even hardliner MacMurray agreed with this idea.[31]

In another public relations move, Butler turned his Marines at Tientsin into "a spit and polish outfit." To that end, he directed a number of parades and reviews, something that Vandegrift recalled as "not a simple matter in a crowded city." The Marines nickel-plated their bayonets, removed camouflage from their helmets and painted them with a green over which they applied a lacquer to make them shine.[32] Some of the Marines so equipped returned to the United States. When General Lejeune saw the modified bayonets, he wrote to Butler: "I feel sure, of course, that some irresponsible young officer had thought to put it over on the other companies by nickel-plating his bayonets, and I hope you will go after him, as it is a flagrant breach of orders to make changes of this kind in the arms and accoutrements issued to the service."[33] Lejeune had the nickel removed from bayonets at considerable expense to the Marines. He insisted that only blued bayonets would do.[34]

Butler's constant traveling and work took its toll. He became so ill he had to stay in the Rockefeller-financed Peking Union Medical Hospital for three weeks. While there he did little but rest. He had severe digestive trouble, which he complained always flared up during times of stress. Although his doctors wanted him to stay longer, duty called, so he left. He wrote to Lejeune that he needed the presence of his wife, still in San Diego, to help him get better.[35] Lejeune wrote back and admonished his friend, telling him he needed to stop pushing himself so hard and thus make himself sick. Not only did Lejeune's personal affection merit this attitude, Lejeune felt Butler's value to the Corps dictated the brigadier general keep himself in good health. Still, Lejeune could at least do one thing for his friend. Although the Corps designated Butler's station as temporary and therefore would not pay for permanent housing nor cover the cost of bringing Mrs. Butler to the country, Lejeune made an exception. He decided the commanding general in China deserved this privilege, so he attempted to place her on the government transport ship USS *Chaumont*, which, as it turned out, had no room for her. Mrs. Butler sent a note to Lejeune telling him she had arranged to head to China on a civilian steamer departing on October 6.[36]

On September 9, 1927, Rear Admiral Mark Bristol arrived in Shanghai to replace the now retired Admiral Williams.[37] Bristol wanted to move most of the Marines out of Tientsin back to Shanghai. Butler observed that the admiral "had never seen a brigade of Marines, much less had never had one under his command. He looked upon such a large force of Marines as a menace to his supremacy and particularly did he look upon me, personally, with great suspicion.... He regarded five thousand Marines as just [the same as] sixty guards of ships, and intended to handle them as such." Still, when Butler made a compelling argument that the Marines should stay in Tientsin, Bristol relented.[38]

Mrs. Butler, minus the children, arrived on November 5, so Butler rented two rooms at a Tientsin hotel for them to stay for the winter. He could afford nothing better; he had to pay the rent on his house in San Diego, put Smedley Jr. through college, and provide for the entertainment of American officials out of his own pocket.[39] As a brigadier general, he made $530 a month.[40] Mrs. Butler left China on February 22, 1928. The trip home cost less than anticipated because she managed to find passage on an Army mail transport. Butler vowed that she would never again take a military ship anywhere. The Army had placed her in the worst stateroom it could find and gave her a "disagreeable" nurse as a roommate, making her trip miserable. Butler wrote to Lejeune, "The majority of the officers of the United States Service, Army and Navy, dislike me personally and are only too glad to get an opportunity to take it out on my wife."[41] This state of affairs had resulted from Butler's willingness to shirk red tape and to protect his men from tyrannical officers. Despite such an unpleasant end to her stay in China, Mrs. Butler had fallen in love with the country.

She displayed the "Chinese treasures" she brought home with her alongside her collection of American antiquities.[42] She made one more trip back and, when she was not there, Butler's daughter Ethel (whom Butler still lovingly referred to as "Snooks") came to stay with him.[43]

On December 23 things got interesting in Tientsin. That night a fire broke out in the candle-making factory at the Standard Oil of New York compound at which the Marines stood guard. The compound contained $25 million worth of inventory. "Thousands of tons of paraffin wax in wood cases" had ignited, and, thanks to their inherent nature, they burned really well. The blaze posed a serious threat both to those fighting it and to Tientsin itself. It threatened six tanks containing three million gallons of oil each, and one can imagine the sort of destruction that would have resulted if those had ignited.[44]

Of all the American corporate interests in China, Standard Oil by far had the greatest value there. When it entered the Chinese market at the beginning of the twentieth century, the country had no viable source of petroleum. It imported 100 percent of such products. Standard Oil used its initial investment in the Chinese Republic to set up a distribution network designed for efficiency. It employed "specially trained men" who went "into the heart of China" to do business and network with local merchants. The bulk of Standard Oil's revenues came from the sale of kerosene as well as its "improved and cheaper kerosene" lamps.[45] Its Chinese name, Mei Foo, "became a household word." Kerosene replaced vegetable oil as the fuel of choice for lamps and stoves.[46] While no evidence exists to say that the State Department deployed Marines to China to protect or fight for Standard Oil in particular, that company certainly benefited from the stability brought by the American military's presence. After his retirement, Butler asserted the Marines had gone to China for the advantage of Standard Oil.[47]

Certainly their presence during the fire made a difference. When it broke out at ten-fifty on a Saturday morning, Butler dispatched 400 Marines to aid in the fight against it. Arriving a little later to assess the situation for himself, he realized he had not brought in enough men. He had hands-on experience fighting fires because as Philadelphia's director of public safety he had worked side by side with the firefighters under his command. (Indeed, he marveled that he finally found something beneficial from that otherwise horrid experience.)[48]

Two warehouses blazed, one with candle grease, the other with 80,000 cases of kerosene. Next to the kerosene store stood a warehouse containing 500,000 five-gallon tins of gasoline, the entire source of the Marines' fuel supply. Butler called in 1,000 more of his men to save the warehouse containing this fuel, which stood a mere fifteen feet from the blaze. They dug a dirt barrier around it, creating a firewall out of anything they could pile upon it, including

The aftermath of the Standard Oil fire in Tientsin that occurred on Christmas Day, 1927. From the Smedley D. Butler Collection, courtesy of the Marine Corps Archives and Special Collections Department at the Gray Research Center, Quantico.

"empty drums, iron doors, pieces of tin and corrugated iron[,] and dirt." To douse the fire, they had to use buckets of water equipped with hand pumps because whoever had started the blaze had also knocked the fire hose pump system out of commission. The side of the gasoline warehouse turned red-hot but did not burst into flame.[49]

By seven that night they thought they had things under control. Then, at three in the morning, a drain or sewer blew up, threatening to spew boiling oil into the river. The Marines built a barrier around it, making a sort of cauldron that boiled and burned the oil away before it escaped. The Marines fought the blaze side by side with local Chinese and other Europeans who came on the scene, working directly with the Chinese themselves and even eating with them, something the other foreigners would not do. The fire burned well into Tuesday. Butler reported to Lejeune that an American intelligence service in the area had blamed the fire on "a big Red organization."[50]

On December 21 a former grandmaster of the Masons named William Rhodes Hervey gave a well-received speech at a dinner held at a Masonic Temple in California. In it he outlined the recent revival of the Masons in postwar Europe as well as in Mexico. He praised Italy's dictator, Benito Mussolini, who he thought had done wonders for Italy. He claimed Mussolini had "abolished beggary." All men worked "in some capacity" for eight hours a day or faced jail time for refusing.[51] Butler would one day make a speech about Mussolini too, although his opinion would differ considerably from Hervey's.

In early 1928 Admiral Bristol decided he wanted to reduce the Marine presence in northern China as a goodwill gesture toward the Chinese. Butler thought this would lead to disaster. He argued that no Chinese people or officials "objected to our presence here," and if the Marines departed, the local warlord, Chang-tso-lin, might attempt to take Tientsin so he could help himself to the $75 million worth of silver bars there.[52] Butler wrote to Lejeune and warned him of Bristol's intent. He implored Lejeune to use his influence to stop this if possible. Although Lejeune could not halt the reduction altogether, he managed to limit it to 630 enlisted men and 38 officers.[53]

On May 26 Butler's greatest ally in Washington, his father, Thomas S. Butler, died of a heart attack at his apartment in the Burlington Hotel in Washington, D.C.[54] Thomas had already suffered from one massive but non–fatal heart attack on April 30 in his Capitol office, and still another had followed at his apartment. Hope existed he might recover. He had a fifty percent chance of improvement, and would probably make it if he lasted sixty days. He did not. Samuel and Maud Butler stood by Thomas's side when he died.[55] General Lejeune, a good friend of Thomas's, attended the funeral in Philadelphia. Smedley could not make it home in time to do so.[56]

He "wept" upon hearing the news. In despair, he "wrote his mother" six weeks later, expressing his sorrow. His father, he believed, had killed himself over all matters naval, so perhaps he would have to do the same when it came to the Marine Corps. Smedley's despair blinded his memory; he could not remember the last time he had seen his father. He pleaded to his mother: "Be sure to write me fully any message that Father may have left for me, and if in his suffering he didn't leave any — make up one. It will be all the same — I must have something to go on."[57] His father's death made him feel "very far from home."[58]

In early September, a storm washed out a bridge on the Tientsin-Peking Highway. The Chinese "fiddled around for a week" but did nothing, so Butler directed some of his men to build a bridge there. They did so, improving about a mile of road as well. The grateful Chinese of a nearby town placed a brass tablet on one of its stone piers and inscribed upon it Butler's name. They considered Butler a fellow Chinese citizen. At the ceremonial opening, where Chinese citizens and officials came, Butler had the Marines demonstrate the benefit of scraping to create a better road surface. The Marines, with the aid of 1,500 men loaned to him from a Chinese general, worked to improve more of the road.[59]

In September Butler became the recipient of an honor that no Westerner, so far as anyone at the American Legation knew, had ever before received: an

Butler and Chinese road authorities at "Butler's Bridge." Marine engineer Captain F. M. Howard designed the bridge and Butler directed the construction. From the Smedley D. Butler Collection, courtesy of the Marine Corps Archives and Special Collections Department at the Gray Research Center, Quantico.

Umbrella of Ten Thousand Blessings, something not awarded to anyone in the Tientsin-Peking area for seventeen years. The people of Ta Chih Ku, a Tientsin suburb of 40,000 that Butler had known as Boxer Village, had given it to him. Ta Chih Ku had seen "some of the most severe fighting between the Chinese and the Allies" during the Boxer Rebellion. About this Butler commented, "Just laugh at the people who tell you that the Chinese will not fight, or that they make poor soldiers. In 1900 at the Boxer village more than 5,000 of them were killed by the Allies in one day of terrific battle." Butler described the presentation ceremony as "quite spectacular" and noted that fifty "old notables" had presented it to him.[60]

According to Chinese legend, the Umbrella of Ten Thousand Blessings had its inspiration during a battle between barbarians and a Chinese "tribal leader" named Huangli in 2697 B.C. Overhead floated clouds of many colors, so the Blessing Umbrella became a memorial of this battle. At first making them out of colorful flowers, umbrella makers soon switched to silk, which in turn became a symbol for the emperor. When the common people started to use paper umbrellas during in the Han Dynasty, high-ranking officials took to carrying (with Imperial permission) colorful silk ones during processions. Buddhist monasteries adopted it as well, using it alongside Buddha representations.[61]

The large red satin umbrella Butler received had "200 tags, each about an inch wide and six inches long" containing the names of the city's elders. Two banners accompanied it. One read, "The Chinese love General Butler as they love China," and the other, "General Butler loves China as he loves America." Butler received this gift because he had saved Ta Chih Ku from looting by an enemy Chinese army.[62] He elaborated on this event in his autobiography, telling this improbable tale: while he was driving through the city in a car that lacked a muffler, the machine-gun-like sound it emitted had alarmed the invaders. When they saw his vehicle blocking a "narrow street," they assumed he had his Marines behind him, and thus retreated.[63] Butler later received an unprecedented *second* umbrella from another town, this one grateful because he had ordered his engineers to replace the washed-out bridge.[64]

The Chinese people on the whole had more problems than just looters and floods. A terrible famine had swept through Shantung Province caused by "three years of bad crops, merciless taxation, civil war, exploitation by bandits and uncontrolled armies, a locust pest and no rain." An estimated four million people wandered homeless throughout the region, eating "boiled chaff, grass roots and the bark of trees." Some of its counties had no people left at all. Chinese families became so desperate they sold their daughters as concubines for anywhere between $4 and $25 a girl. Despite "bumper crops" in the Yangtse Valley and Manchuria, Chinese mismanagement of resources had left the people of Shantung Province with nothing.[65]

Butler offered the services of his brigade to assist in distributing aid to these poor souls. He considered staying in China longer than planned to deal with this humanitarian disaster. The Chinese people had in fact petitioned the American government to let him do so. He could not in good conscience "forsake them." He wrote to his mother: "For some reason they trust me and it is some great satisfaction to find some people who do, for thee knows full well that Americans do not regard me in any light except that of a fool — so it might be that we will settle here in China where the people will at least tolerate us."[66]

Butler received one more gift before leaving his post. The commander of Japanese forces in North China, a fellow named Aria, presented him with a samurai sword. Butler had no idea what he had done to deserve this rare gift. U.S. Minister MacMurray never heard of any American receiving such a present. He held the opinion that the Japanese offered it because the previous year Butler had resisted their plans to attack the Chinese, and they "like[d] somebody to oppose them."[67] The Japanese plan involved a coalition of foreign powers in the country to launch an offensive against Chiang Kai-shek's army, but when Butler refused to commit his Marines, the plan collapsed.[68]

On January 8, Butler received an order that upon the disbandment of the Third Brigade, he would head home to the West Coast "on or about" January 15.[69] For his time in Shanghai itself he received the Yangtze Service Medal No.

119.[70] On March 5, 1929, another of Butler's best friends, Wendell Cushing Neville, became the new commandant of the Marine Corps.[71] Back in the U.S., Butler took command of Quantico for a second time. On July 13, just weeks before his forty-ninth birthday, he received a promotion to the rank of major general, the youngest Marine ever to obtain it.[72] His second tenure as the commandant of Quantico would bring him far more trouble than the first.

9

The Mussolini Affair

With his retirement nearing and his savings not great, Butler turned to two sources of new income during his second tenure as Quantico's commander: writing articles and giving lectures for a fee. For his articles he frequently collaborated with E.Z. Dimitman, the Philadelphian journalist with whom he had become friends while serving as Philadelphia's director of public safety.[1] Butler often wrote a rough sketch of what he had in mind, dictating it to an aide, then he would send it to Dimitman to "write it up in the correct form." Dimitman returned the material to Butler and asked him to fill in certain details. The two split their profits fifty-fifty; sometimes Dimitman's name appeared as a co-writer, sometimes not.[2]

On the night of December 5, 1929, Butler flew out of Quantico on a government airplane to make a speech at the Pittsburgh Builders' Exchange. In it he said the Marines had rigged elections in Nicaragua. He further spoke about the Marines' manipulation of the government in Haiti, such as when they had appointed an illiterate man to the post of secretary of public instruction and cults, recommended to them by the fellow's barber. No less a person than Sinclair Lewis seized upon the these revelations. He sent a letter to the Senate demanding an investigation into Butler's allegation that America had rigged Nicaraguan elections.[3]

Secretary of the Navy Charles F. Adams demanded a written explanation from Butler. He did not like Butler's references to Nicaragua in general and his accusation that "the opposition candidates in Nicaragua were declared bandits when it became necessary to elect our man to office" in particular.[4] After receiving Butler's account, Adams stated publicly he would take no action against Butler because he felt that the general's report on the matter had sufficiently explained what he had really meant.[5] Privately he summoned Butler and administered "a stiff reprimand." Butler retorted, "This is the first time in my service of thirty-two years that I've ever been hauled on the carpet and treated like an unruly schoolboy…. If I'm not behaving well it is because I'm not accustomed to reprimands, and you can't expect me to turn my cheek meekly for official slaps." Adams coldly dismissed Butler from his office, saying he never wanted to see the general there again.[6] Butler never grasped the idea that as an active officer in the Marine Corps, his words reflected on both the Corps and the U.S. government itself, and some might take them as official policy. While no one in the government tried to restrain his right to free speech, he did have to face consequences if he did not sound diplomatic.

In September 1929, members of the American Legion of West Chester, Pennsylvania, formed a "Butler-for-Governor Club" in a bid to get him to run in 1930. When asked about it, Butler said he did not seek the position, but if the people of Pennsylvania wanted him to run, he would.[7] Privately he thought little of the idea per se, feeling it did no harm because "it serves as good publicity for my speech making engagements, for all of which I am getting paid and the more publicity the better the pay."[8]

Other than his run-in with Secretary Adams, the year of 1929 went well for him; 1930 did not. On February 28 of that year, General Wendell Cushing Neville, the commandant of the Marine Corps, suffered a severe stroke from which he did not recover sufficiently to take up his duties again. He died on July 8, 1930.[9] Butler, who had written to his mother and father in 1927 saying he would never do well for this post,[10] nonetheless decided to use what pull he had to obtain it. A contingent of supporters from Pittsburgh traveled to Washington on his behalf to disabuse those opposing him of the notion that he had said anything disloyal about the American government during the speech he gave about Nicaragua. This group also solicited Secretary of the Navy Adams himself, who gave them a "cool, and even rude reception." Although Adams did not support Butler's nomination, others in President Hoover's cabinet did, including James J. Davis, the secretary of labor. Butler received backing — both real and in spirit — from others as well. Senator David Aiken Reed of Pennsylvania told Butler he thought he would get the appointment. A naval officer friend informed him the Navy Department had received 2,500 telegrams in support of his appointment. Pennsylvania's Governor Pinchot, in office once more, sent a telegram to President Hoover and Secretary Adams backing Butler's nomination. From Philadelphia came similar messages from its mayor, its Chamber of Commerce, and a variety of other organizations and associations. Even President Wilson's widow endorsed Butler.[11]

He did not receive the coveted post. It went to an "underdog" named Ben Hebard Fuller. Butler's good friend Vandegrift later commented that this "nearly broke Butler's heart."[12] Fuller, much to Butler's dismay, had graduated from the Naval Academy, an institution Butler felt lacked the ability to teach officers how to command. Fuller had a well-rounded education despite his having graduated in 1889 with such a low standing in the Academy he did not qualify for a naval officer's commission. Two years later he joined the Corps as an officer, and by 1899 found himself a captain stationed at Cavite in the Philippines. Military historian Merrill L. Bartlett assessed Fuller's ability as an administrator for the next twenty years by noting he "served in such traditional assignments satisfactorily if not superbly."[13]

Throughout his career, Fuller furthered his military education. He attended the Army Field Officer's Course at Fort Leavenworth as well as the Naval War College, although during the Great War neither helped him get to the front. He received the temporary rank of brigadier general during this conflict, but upon its conclusion the Corps downsized and those who had not served in a combat or support role lost any provisional ranks they had received. Butler therefore held a higher rank than Fuller until the latter's appointment as the assistant commandant of the Marine Corps under Generals Lejeune and Neville. Despite Butler's low opinion of the man, Fuller did well as head of the Marines, fighting hard to keep the Hoover Administration from dismantling the Corps.[14]

After Fuller's appointment, life in the Marines got downright miserable for Butler. He decided he would stay for another fifteen years to "block every Naval Academy man who comes around." Only a general court-martial could remove him. He wrote to his brother that he would do nothing "to make any false steps and give them any loopholes" they could use against him. He failed to keep this promise, as we shall see. President Hoover and Secretary Adams, meanwhile, seemed intent, at least from Butler's perspective, to force him out. When, for example, Secretary Adams appointed Butler to "an Interdepartmental Board to recommend to Congress a uniform system of promotion and pay for the four military services affected," the type of committee upon which Quantico's commander always served, President Hoover removed him from it.[15]

Fuller slighted Butler by telling him he needed to focus more on running Quantico and less on giving speeches. Secretary Adams came to the base to inspect it in July 1930. Despite Butler's showing off its efficiency and parading his men in good order, Adams had nothing positive to say to him in private. Adams complained that the base trained men at a greater expense than any other military operation in the United States. He called the football stadium "one of [Butler's] damned follies," and considered the clubhouse then under construction another one. Butler pointed out that neither effort had cost the government a penny[16]; for the clubhouse, the Marines had provided the labor and used materials found on base. Adams did not care. He further berated Butler for draining a swamp to expand the landing area for airplanes.[17]

Adams publicly praised the Marines with a speech given to the officers and men gathered at a gymnasium on the base. When he concluded, Butler stood up and informed "the men that he would allow all who could be spared to leave camp until Tuesday morning to aid in the conserving of the water supply." Suffering from a severe drought, Quantico had to have water brought in tanks on barges. On the base the laundering of clothes stopped, men bathed in the Potomac, and the construction of a concrete tank designed to hold two million gallons of water began.[18]

Despite this, Butler maintained discipline. When he realized that Marines kept indulging to excess in the bootleg liquor they obtained in the nearby town of Quantico, for example, he forbade them from going there. This immediately crippled the town's economy because it received ninety percent of its revenue from the Marines. Butler would relent only when the town cleaned itself up. When Quantico's mayor committed to doing so, Butler allowed his men to return.[19]

On Monday, January 19, 1931, Butler made a speech that would affect his career as no other before had. He spoke at the Contemporary Club of Philadelphia. His speech, "How to Prevent War," contained comments such as: "An eel which has just taken a bath in olive oil is a non–skid device compared to a treaty," and "I'm afraid that nations are just collections of human beings and in some there are certain to be some bad eggs who don't understand law and treaties."[20] He rounded this line of thought with this: "Right now there are several embryo fellows coming up in Europe getting themselves all girded up and ready to jump on somebody. One of these is Benito Mussolini. He is polishing all the brass hats in Italy. He is getting very Roman." If that did not insult the Italian dictator enough, Butler then related a story about Mussolini a friend had told him. In 1926 this friend, whom Butler did not name, had taken a car ride with Mussolini in which the dictator drove too fast. He hit a small child, killing it. Upon realizing this, Butler's friend screamed, but Mussolini shrugged this off, saying, "It was only one life.... What is one life in the affairs of a State?"[21]

Although audience members later insisted Butler had delivered these comments in a "jocular vein," his words stung nonetheless. Butler still had not learned his lesson that as a high-ranking and well-known military officer, he could spark an international incident by saying things such as this, which he did. He had naïvely not expected anything he related to get into the papers, believing all his remarks would stay confidential. The next morning they appeared in the *Philadelphia Record,* supposedly given to that paper by a bootlegger whom Butler had once arrested.[22] About the speech, *Literary Digest* opined, "There is a nearly unanimous editorial agreement that Smedley D. Butler talks too much. We could fill up this page with the names of newspapers which talk about the General's 'loquacity,' 'loose tongue,' 'soap-box oratory,' 'wagging jaw,' 'yellow oratory,' 'habit of loose speech,' [and] 'blatant way.'"[23]

Mussolini personally sent a telegram of complaint to the Italian ambassador in Washington, who in turn forwarded it to the secretary of state. Mussolini stated he had "never driven around Italy with an American and I challenge General Butler to prove the contrary. I have never run over any child, or man, or woman." Had he done so, he would have stopped to help. On January 29 the dictator demanded an apology. He received one, but not from Butler. It came from the secretary of state. The next day the Italian ambassador accepted it, and said he considered the matter closed.[24]

Secretary Adams wrote Butler a terse letter with an attached copy of the article from the *Philadelphia Record*. Adams ordered Butler to affirm or refute its accuracy.[25] (Butler not only kept Adams's letter demanding this explanation, but when several Haitian officials accused him of lying about his fight at Fort Rivière, he paraphrased it in his letter to the Department of the Navy demanding an inquiry into the Haitians' accusations.[26]) In his reply to Adams, Butler clarified a few points. He had not called Mussolini a "mad dog" as reported in some papers. He apologized and swore he had nothing but respect for the Italian dictator. He had told the story about Mussolini's killing of a child to emphasize his point about how different states viewed "Welfare and Life."[27]

Much to Butler's horror, Adams and others in the Hoover administration did not let the matter drop. On January 29, Butler received an official notice from General Fuller that as of ten-thirty that morning he should consider himself under arrest pending a general court-martial! He had to confine himself to the post and turn command over the Brigadier General Randolph C. Berkeley. Despite this trouble, Butler refused to publicly divulge the name of the friend who told him the offending story.[28] A fellow named Clarence H. White knew this person's identity, and he told the papers. The tale had come from no less a person than journalist Cornelius Vanderbilt Jr., one of the heirs to the Vanderbilt fortune.[29] With Vanderbilt's name now public, Butler wrote to his booking agent, Louis J. Alger, and asked him if he could get a signed affidavit from Vanderbilt that the journalist had indeed told the tale. Butler thought it might help his case.[30]

Although Mussolini denied ever meeting Vanderbilt, the Italian government later checked its records as to whom had met with Mussolini in 1926, and it found that yes, the two men had met, but, no, Mussolini had not taken Vanderbilt for a drive.[31] When asked, Vanderbilt responded that Butler had gotten his story all wrong, but in fact the version he related matched Butler's with few variations.[32] In 1959 Vanderbilt expanded upon it, writing an account of the incident in his book *Man of the World: My Life on Five Continents.* It went like this. While in Italy, Vanderbilt made it known he wanted to meet Mussolini. The dictator invited him to his offices at Chigi Palace. Neither man spoke the other's native language, so they communicated in poor French. Mussolini asked his new journalist friend if he wanted to see Rome with him. Vanderbilt "jumped at the opportunity." The two got into Mussolini's Fiat. The dictator had a lead foot, zipping about at an unsafe speed. Followed by two limousines, he unexpectedly headed out of Rome to Naples, his driving so reckless Vanderbilt feared for his life.[33]

The next day they traveled to the Riviera, staying for the night. On the third day together they went from Turin to Milan, then to Venice. Heading back to Rome via the Apennines, they passed through a village where a small boy (variations of this story sometimes identified the child as a girl) tried to cross the road before the Fiat reached him. The boy did not make it. Vanderbilt felt a bump and saw the boy lying on the road behind him. Mussolini put "a hand" on Vanderbilt's "right knee" and said, "Never look back, Mr. Vanderbilt, never look back in life." They drove on to Rome without stopping.[34]

A fiery Democratic senator from Alabama, the outgoing James Thomas Heflin, defended Butler on the Senate floor. He read into the record an article found in the newspaper *Il Nuovo Mondo*. This paper claimed it had evidence confirming that Mussolini had indeed run over a child with his car. Heflin challenged, "Let the American people sit in on the trial.... Let us know if this mad monarch is to have the world kowtowing to him."[35] One must treat *Il Nuovo Mondo's* report with some skepticism. Established in New York City by Frank Bellanca, the paper opposed fascism, promoted unionism, and supported the American-based Anti-Fascist Alliance of North America. It featured "the writings of Italian exiles" and made the Italian government so "nervous" that its minister in Washington as well as other agents made daily reports on the paper's content to Italy's foreign ministry. The Italian government tried to pressure the State Department to shut it down. Although nothing came of this, it nonetheless ceased publication in 1930 on its own.[36]

Butler refused to apologize. He received hundreds of letters and telegrams on this subject. Most of them praised him. Some did not. E.L. Stevenson of Yonkers, New York, for example, called Butler's words "shameful." The Sons of the Order of Italy demanded Butler reveal the name of the man who had told him this scurrilous story (this before Vanderbilt's identity became public).[37] Butler telegrammed his friend Josephus Daniels and asked him if he could solicit John W. Davis, the former 1924 Democratic presidential candidate and one of the nation's top lawyers, to take his case. Daniels replied via telegram that he would do just that. The governor of New York, Franklin D. Roosevelt, telegraphed Butler and told him that he would do the same.[38] Davis did not take the case.

For his defense Butler retained his old friend and comrade-in-arms Henry Leonard, now a prominent lawyer, and Robert S. Morris, a former ambassador to Japan. Since General Fuller had confined Butler to Quantico, he found it difficult to prepare for his defense. To allow him to create a proper one, he needed to go beyond Quantico's confines. Feeling humiliated at having to do so, he wrote General Fuller and requested permission to travel to Maryland, Pennsylvania, New York, and Washington, D.C. Fuller acquiesced. Butler headed to the District of Columbia to meet with Leonard at his house. Leonard pointed out that public opinion had turned on the Hoover administration on this matter, and the longer it dragged on, the better the chance the government would drop it.[39]

Butler faced two charges: the all-encompassing "conduct to the prejudice of good order and discipline" and "conduct unbecoming an officer and a gentleman."[40] As Leonard had predicted, the State Department realized prosecuting Butler might cause the U.S. government embarrassment, a sentiment with which the Italian ambassador in Washington agreed. Without consulting the Navy Department, the State Department approached Leonard with a deal on February 6. In exchange for dropping the court-martial, Butler would accept a reprimand, lose his command at Quantico, and receive the ambiguous status of one who has "waiting orders." Leonard rejected the proposal. The State Department countered with another one: if Butler took the reprimand, he could stay on active duty but would lose his command of Quantico. This, too, Leonard declined.[41]

The State Department asked Leonard what he would accept. He wanted "a minor reprimand" which he himself would write. Butler would continue as commandant of Quantico. The State Department said this sounded good so long as Butler wrote a public letter as to what had occurred, and he never published the original explanation he had sent to Secretary Adams. Leonard agreed, although he stipulated the public letter would *not* contain an apology to Mussolini. The State Department consented. In his public letter Butler expressed his regret for embarrassing the American government.[42] Soon after its publication, the fifty-year-old Butler announced his intention to retire from the Corps in the fall. At this time he would begin a lecturing tour with Louis Alger as his booking agent. He had a contract spanning from October 1931 to May 1932. He insisted his decision to retire had nothing to do with the recent Mussolini incident.[43]

He gave a more detailed explanation about his choice to retire early in a piece he wrote for the magazine *Liberty: A Weekly for Everybody*. The article's title said it all: "To Hell with the Admirals!" He wanted to retire because he had found himself passed over for the position of commandant of the Marines. In his view, the Navy did not give him this command because he had not attended the Naval Academy at Annapolis. The admirals did not value men who learned their trade in the field rather than the classroom. With the position of commandant unavailable, he had nothing to look forward to—no rank or combat role would ever again come his way. Better to leave now while he had his health and many years to go rather than stick things out until the age of 65. The article, a bitter piece interspersed with excerpts from his official military record, continued in this vein until its end. Either Butler or the editor thought fit to add this final line: "The opinions or assertions contained herein are the private ones of the writer and are not to be construed as official or reflecting the views of the Navy Department or the Naval Service at large."[44]

On the day Butler departed from Quantico, he lowered his flag, one that had "a red field and two white stars."[45] He left his post on September 30, 1931. With a salute of thirteen guns, he drove off in an automobile.[46] He headed to Newtown Square, Pennsylvania, a rural town outside of Philadelphia at which he moved to a ten-acre farm he had recently purchased. Upon it had stood a burned-out farmhouse. An early estimate for the cost of remodeling this as well as adding a garage amounted to $21,879. Located at 1819 Goshen Road, the finished house had a great hall with a high ceiling designed to accommodate his blessing umbrellas and other memorabilia. To pay for it, Butler took out a mortgage from the Philadelphia Loan Agency, which then sold it to the Reconstruction Finance Corporation.[47]

He began his new career as a fulltime professional speaker during one of the worst years of the Great Depression. Despite this, he kept busy. From January 19 to September 28, 1931, he made seventy-five speeches. Venues included a diverse range of places such as the New England Iron and Hardware Association, the Bristol Fathers Association, the Brown Prep School, the Women's Club in East Orange, New Jersey, and a number of American Legion posts.[48] His fees varied, ranging anywhere from $100 to $500, with an average of about $250 per speech.[49]

Sometimes radio stations broadcast his lectures. Radio station WELK, for example, pledged to air his speech to the 312th Field Artillery at the Elks Lodge one evening in Philadelphia. Here Butler told the story of the attack on Fort Rivière in Haiti. When he uttered the word "Hell," WELK's owner and announcer, Howard Miller, cut Butler off the air, truncating the general's speech by about five minutes. The station quickly announced to its listeners: "We are sorry if you have been offended by General Butler's use of profane and obscene language."[50]

Those in attendance at the Elks as well as the public listening to the program did not take kindly to such censorship. Listeners flooded newspapers with complaints. Butler himself stormed into the WELK studio and confronted Miller, demanding to know what obscenity he had uttered. Miller explained that the FCC forbade him to broadcast the word "Hell." Butler's close friend, Judge Harry McDevitt, calmed the storm. He went on the air, said Butler had only used the word while quoting a sergeant, and pointed out everyone knew how sergeants spoke. Butler had meant no offense. McDevitt offered an apology to the listeners upset that the station had cut Butler off.[51] When Butler spoke in Baltimore a month later, the radio station broadcasting his speech there allowed him three "damns" and two "hells" every ten minutes. He did not violate the condition, so his stayed on the air the whole time.[52]

During the last months of his tenure as commandant of Quantico, Butler had taken a leave of absence to make a two-month speaking tour. Despite his own financial difficulties, he did something that demonstrated what his men had always known: he put the needs of others above his own. He announced he would donate half the money he made on his latest lecture tour to the Philadelphia Committee for Unemployment Relief. He told the press: "My wife and I followed the unemployment situation each day in the newspapers.... We were convinced that we should make some sacrifice for the relief of the poor fellows with no jobs.... I want to do everything I can to help." He figured that he could donate $1,000 a week to the relief fund.[53]

The unemployment crisis facing the nation worried Butler. He feared the eruption of "mob violence" and "revolution" unless someone did something radical. He offered a solution: the "taxation of wealth." Congress would use this money for direct relief of the unemployed as well as public works projects such as building schools and roads. Butler told the press he had conversed with fourteen wealthy men with a combined $5 million in assets who said they would agree to a fifty percent tax on the their fortunes.[54]

Under his plan, the common people would make sacrifices, too. Those aged nineteen and under could not work at all. Instead they would attend trade schools to learn a useful skill. To facilitate the numbers involved, America would have to construct 50,000 to 60,000 schools. This would create thousands of jobs because of the need to hire construction workers and teachers. Also, slumlords would have to tear down their tenements and erect decent buildings filled with all the modern appliances currently available. This, too, would generate jobs because the increased demand for appliances would create a call for new factories and the workers to fill them.[55]

Butler decided to make an attempt to implement his suggestions. He announced his interest in running for public office. He thought he may try for the U.S. Senate, possibly challenging one of Pennsylvania's sitting senators, James J. Davis, in the 1932 Republican primary. Backed by Governor Pinchot, Butler made a formal announcement on March 2, 1932. He planned to run on a dry platform. He announced, "I enter this fight as a dry and you can spell it out in capital letters. D-R-Y."[56]

Although Prohibition had prompted him to swear off drinking for the rest of his life, when it became legal again he did keep alcohol under lock and key at his home to serve to guests, and he sometimes bought Mrs. Butler a drink or two when they went out to a restaurant.[57] He also accepted it as a gift. During the waning years of Prohibition, a friend of his, Marshall Keck, wrote him a letter in which he said he had received two quart bottles of Scotch whiskey for Christmas. He planned to mail Butler one. The whiskey had come from another friend's stash that preceded Prohibition (making it legal). Keck assured Butler he would like this gift. In fact, Keck made drinking alcohol a running theme throughout his letter. As it progressed, his typing deteriorated, simulating the slurring of a drunk.[58]

Butler's campaign platform also included a pledge to "clean up" the Senate. About this he said, "They're afraid of me because I am always fighting.... I won't quit, and if you elect me to the Senate I am going to tell those boys there to get out of my way. I represent 10,000,000 people, and I am going to have some say in this government."[59] Few listened. Davis beat him in the primary "by more than 2 to 1." The day after the election, when a few votes still needed counting, Davis had 528,116 votes versus Butler's 267,843.[60] Butler ran for no more public offices. Hereafter his lifelong allegiance to the Republican Party waned. He backed and campaigned for Democratic presidential candidate Franklin D. Roosevelt in the same year.[61]

Still another campaign grabbed the headlines at this time. At the end of the Great War, the government had found itself embarrassed by the fact its civilian work force had received better pay than the soldiers in the trenches. To make amends, Congress decided to give veterans $1 for every day served domestically and $1.50 for every day served overseas. Paid out after twenty years, the initial sum set aside for this purpose earned six percent interest "compounded annually." A total of 3.6 million veterans held certificates for this bonus. Because of the hard times, veterans of the Great War wanted their promised bonus now rather than when it came due in 1945. Congressman Wright Patman, a Texas Democrat, wrote in *Congressional Digest* that he wanted to do just that. He reckoned the bonus came due on October 1, 1931, rather than the projected date of 1945. Ogden L. Mills, the secretary of the treasury, penned a rebuttal in which he argued paying it now would cost the government too much. It would devalue currency and create bank runs.[62]

To lobby for the bonus, veterans gathered into what they called the Bonus Expeditionary Force, which became better known as the Bonus Army. In the summer a number of its members, many accompanied by their wives and children, decided to head to Washington, D.C., to make their case directly to the president and Congress. They elected a cool-headed former sergeant named Walter W. Walters as their leader. He wanted no violence and, upon his army's arrival in Washington, D.C., found a sympathetic ally in the city's chief of police, Pelham D. Glassford. This noble fellow, once in the military himself, arranged for the veterans arriving in the city to receive a hot meal. He found them a place to quarter near the Capitol at Anacostia Flats, then spent his own money to create a commissary. For that the men elected him their secretary-treasurer.[63]

Butler supported the movement in general and those in Washington, D.C., in particular. During his ill-fated senatorial bid, he campaigned for the immediate payment of the bonus, although he had balked at the idea of just printing money to cover the cost. On July 19 he came to Anacostia Flats to speak to the 16,000 Bonus men there. Walters introduced him and asked if he would take command of the Army. Butler declined. As the sun set behind him, he "took off his coat, rolled up his sleeves, and opened his collar," then roared into speech-making action. He praised Walters and told the men they would do well to follow him. He complimented the men themselves for their discipline and service to their country. He urged them to stay put until they got what they wanted, telling them: "You have as much right to lobby here as the United States Steel Corporation." He told them they needed to exercise their right to vote so they could change things in November (in other words: vote for FDR for president). After the speech, Butler inspected the camp, then stayed the night.[64]

Other Bonus Armies settled outside of Washington, D.C. One did so in Johnstown, Pennsylvania. This city's mayor, Eddie McCloskey, asked both Butler and Governor Pinchot to come to help boost morale. The camp faced food shortages and serious sanitation issues. For his part, Butler sent a telegram to the mayor saying he could not come at this time. He suggested the men go home for a while. No one at the camp liked this plan, nor did the mayor. Moreover, some of the men in the camp of 6,188 thought Butler would soon come and lead them. One of its leaders went so far as to claim he had seen a telegram from Butler in which the general promised to gather an army of 750,000 "Khaki Shirts" to march on Washington, an allusion to Mussolini's Blackshirts.[65]

In Washington, D.C., itself, President Hoover publicly ignored the Bonus Army. On the sly he made sure that the camp had supplies and access to cheap army rations. He had far more sympathy for them than they perceived, wanting no harm to come to anyone in the camp. When money from supporters poured into the camp to help sustain it for a prolonged period, Hoover decided he wanted the bonus men moved out of Washington's business district to avoid any potential riots. The Army's chief of staff, General Douglas MacArthur, received orders to direct them to move. MacArthur considered the Bonus Army a communist threat and believed it planned a bloody coup.[66]

MacArthur brought into the city general infantry, six tanks, and a machine gun squadron. As he led his men down Pennsylvania Avenue, he directed them to fire tear gas into "old buildings" to clear squatters out. He had these derelicts burned down after the occupants fled. Next he turned his attention to the Anacostia Flats camp. Here he planned to move its residents out using tear gas, although Hoover had issued an order that MacArthur first clear it of women and children. MacArthur nonetheless gave the command to fire tear gas into the crowded camp before anyone had time to evacuate. The gas killed a baby, blinded a child, and caused acute harm to thousands of others. Two veterans died from gunshot wounds. MacArthur's men burned the camp to the ground.[67] One of MacArthur's biographers, Geoffrey Perret, asserted that MacArthur had in fact *not* disobeyed Hoover. Perret argued, rather convincingly, that MacArthur failed to receive Hoover's order because his chief of staff, George Van Horn Mosley, had purposely not delivered it.[68] Even if true, this does not exonerate MacArthur in the least. He had authorized a tear-gas attack on the camp knowing full well that it contained women and children, and he could have decided to wait until they left.

On January 4, 1932, Butler and his wife formally announced the engagement of their only daughter, Ethel Peters, to Lieutenant John Wehle of the Marine Corps, whom she had met at Quantico. The couple married in West Chester on May 5 at Holy Trinity Church.[69] Near the end of the year Butler wrote a frank letter to his new son-in-law in which he expressed his thoughts as to how he liked his retirement. He complained about money, or the lack thereof, and predicted if things did not improve, he would have to live in just one room of his house so he and his wife could take on boarders. Mrs. Butler contemplated opening a hot dog stand. Butler found the cost of coal bothersome. He mentioned that his wife and a Filipino houseboy named Pedro (a former orderly from Quantico) constantly fought with one another. Despite this, "she would not part with him for the world." Butler himself employed a secretary.[70]

After Pedro departed, the Butlers hired an African-American man named William Williams. Butler's granddaughter Molly Swanton recalled, "William was a jack of all trades, who cooked, cleaned, grew the vegetable garden, etc. He is remembered very fondly by everyone — even me. William lived during the week in an apartment over the separate garage there. His wife, a lovely lady named Julia, used to care for the grandchildren from time to time, and is also remembered with love."[71] Thus Butler's "impoverishment" hardly qualified as such. People who can afford servants cannot consider themselves poor.

10

An Unsettling Proposal

On or about July 1, 1933, Butler received a call from Jack Quinn of Washington, D.C., a man to whom he had never before spoken.[1] Quinn said he belonged to the American Legion. He knew two disabled veterans who would like to come out and visit. Could they do so? Butler said yes. Five hours later a private Packard limousine stopped at his house. Out of it two men emerged. Butler invited them in. They gave their names as Bill Doyle and Jerry MacGuire. Doyle came from Massachusetts and MacGuire from Connecticut, and each said he had once served as the Legion's state commander.[2]

It took them awhile before they got to the reason for their visit. They wanted to unseat "the royal family in control of the American Legion." They asked Butler to attend the upcoming national convention in Chicago as a distinguished guest to help them do so. Butler pointed out he had not received an invitation. They told him they had planned for that; they would arrange for the Honolulu Legion to invite him. But he did not live in Hawaii. They did not seem concerned about this technicality. Butler refused.[3]

His visitors seemed a bit taken aback: did Butler not want to remove the "royal family"? Well, he did, feeling those in charge of the Legion often cheated the average soldiers who belonged. Nonetheless, he still declined. Although he could see that his visitors wanted to embarrass the Legion, he suspected they had a more insidious agenda, one he did not trust. "Two or three days later" Doyle and MacGuire returned in the same car. They said forget the "delegate idea." Now they wanted Butler to assemble several hundred veterans and put them on a special train. They would go to the American Legion's Chicago convention as plants in the audience. At some point they would shout for General Butler to talk, and he would make a speech.[4]

"Make a speech about what?" Butler asked. They handed him one. Butler pointed out the men he knew who might want to go to the convention could never afford to pay for the train tickets or stay in Chicago for five days. MacGuire and Doyle told him they would cover this cost. To which Butler retorted, "How can you pay it? You are disabled soldiers. How do you get the money to do that?" They had friends. Butler began "to smell a rat." He accused them of having no money. They showed him a bank book for an account of $42,000. About this Butler observed, "Wounded soldiers do not have limousines or that kind of money."[5]

At the beginning of August, MacGuire returned to Butler's house once more. This time he did not have Doyle with him nor did this fellow ever see Butler again. At this meeting Butler insisted MacGuire tell him where he had acquired all the money he showed him earlier. MacGuire informed him nine men had donated it, the largest contributor having given $9,000. Butler wanted to know their purpose of doing so. MacGuire answered that they wanted the World War veterans to receive their bonus pay as soon as possible. Butler did not buy this, later commenting, "Well, I knew that people who had $9,000 to give away were not in favor of the bonus. That looked fishy right away." To reiterate the seriousness of his position, MacGuire showed Butler a different bank book, this one listing the sum of $64,000. Butler demanded MacGuire give him the names of the donors. MacGuire identified one as Grayson Mallet-Prevost Murphy, the man for whom he worked.[6]

Readers unfamiliar with this person need not rack their brains trying to remember him from their history lessons in school. He had little fame outside of New York City in his own day, and no historically significant role to play in any other events save the one related now. In his youth he joined the U.S. Army to fight in the Spanish-American War, during which he saw combat, rising from private to captain. He attended West Point, graduating in 1903. He left the Army in 1907 to work in business. During the Great War he served as the first European commissioner of the American Red Cross, then as an Army staff officer. He received the rank of colonel and several decorations before leaving this service. Thereafter he directed a variety of companies that included Goodyear Tire & Rubber Company, Anaconda Copper Mining Company, and the Bethlehem Steel Corporation. In 1921 he founded G.M.-P. Murphy & Company with the purpose of selling stocks and bonds, joining the New York Stock Exchange in 1925. MacGuire worked for it as a bond salesman.[7]

Butler asked MacGuire what Murphy had to do with the soldier's bonus. Why should a man with his sort of money care about the issue of the bonus payment? MacGuire replied that Murphy had underwritten "the formation of the American Legion for $125,000 ... and had not gotten all of it back yet."[8] Murphy wanted Legionnaires to receive their bonus pay with the hope they would use this money to fill the Legion's coffers, and thus it could repay him. MacGuire's story had a flaw: Murphy's name does not appear on the list of the Legion's founders, and records showed he never held "any major position" in the Legion at the national level.[9]

At the beginning of September, Butler attended a reunion of the National

Guard's Twenty-Ninth Division in Newark, New Jersey. Here MacGuire made an unexpected appearance. Butler took him to his hotel room to have a private discussion. MacGuire asked if the general planned to go to Legion's Chicago convention. Butler snapped that he would not. MacGuire wanted to know why. Butler replied, "You people are bluffing. You have not got any money." MacGuire responded by taking from his hip pocket a wad of thousand-dollar bills; he threw them on the hotel bed.[10]

Butler asked, "What's all this?" MacGuire answered, "This is for you, for expenses. You will need some money to pay them." Here MacGuire referred to the soldiers he wanted Butler to take with him to the Legion's Chicago convention. Butler demanded to know where MacGuire had gotten all this money. MacGuire replied that the night before he had received it for his mysterious cause, but had not yet deposited it. Butler warned, "Don't you try to give me any thousand-dollar bill. Remember, I was a cop once. Every one of the numbers on these bills has been taken.... If I try to cash one of those thousand-dollar bills, you would have me by the neck." He told MacGuire to put the money away, not wanting anyone to see it on the bed.[11]

Butler again asked MacGuire for the names of the men giving him all this money, warning he would not speak with him again unless he did so. MacGuire agreed. He said he would send one of these benefactors over to see Butler. Butler asked, "Who is he?" MacGuire told him: Robert Sterling Clark, a banker. Butler knew of him. During the Boxer Rebellion he had served as a second lieutenant and received the nickname "Millionaire Lieutenant" because an aunt and uncle had left him $10 million. Butler remembered Clark as "sort of batty, sort of queer, did all sorts of extravagant things. He used to go exploring around China and wrote a book on it, on explorations. He was never taken seriously by anybody."[12]

Like Murphy, Robert Sterling Clark neither had national fame nor did he make the history books. He graduated from Yale's Sheffield Scientific School with a degree in civil engineering, then went to China where, according to his obituary (and contrary to Butler's recollection), he gathered "information that the War Department later used on a map of that country." He had inherited a large piece of the Singer Sewing Machine Company fortune, and used it to, among other things, collect art and racehorses.[13]

At the week's end, Butler, who had forgotten about MacGuire's promise, received a phone call from Clark. Clark asked if he could come down from New York and have lunch on Sunday. Butler agreed. He would meet Clark at the railroad station. Butler recognized him immediately despite not having seen him for thirty-four years. He took him to his house, where they had lunch. Afterwards they went to the porch and Clark got down to business. He asked Butler if he had the speech that MacGuire and Doyle had given him.[14]

Butler did, adding, "They wrote a hell of a good speech, too." When Butler mentioned that MacGuire and Doyle claimed to have penned it, Clark laughed, saying, "That speech cost a lot of money." He had found this humorous because he knew Doyle and MacGuire had lied; Clark's lawyer, Albert Christmas, in fact wrote it. The speech called for the payment of the veterans' bonus in gold, not paper money, which would only be possible if the United States returned to the gold standard, from which it had recently departed.[15]

FDR had ordered this change in April 1933 to try to stem the tide of gold leaving the country to foreign nations. The Federal Reserve opposed FDR's machinations because it did not think they would work. It unwillingly transferred its powers to the president on a temporary basis. FDR thought returning consumer prices to pre–Depression levels would help to ease the economic suffering of the masses. Under his rule, no one could exchange U.S. currency for an equal amount of gold, nor would America issue gold coinage. Although deemed "necessary" at the time, America's gold reserves still amounted to $2.7 billion. A gold buy-back began as well.[16] Economic conservatives like Murphy and Clark found the concept of abandoning the gold standard horrifying. They thought it madness and predicted it would result in the destruction of the dollar's power. While history has shown this did not happen, none of FDR's gold manipulation measures worked. By September 1934 wholesale prices, for example, had risen a mere twenty-six percent, and retail prices "less than that."[17]

In response to FDR's policies, a group of Wall Street financiers used their personal wealth to create a public relations firm called the Committee for a Sound Dollar and Sound Currency, officially incorporated in December 1933. The Committee desired to force the government to return to the gold standard. It capitalized with $31,000 "for salaries, traveling expenses, printing of propaganda, legal fees, and incidentals." By late 1934 its account had dwindled to $24. MacGuire handled its money.[18]

Clark reasoned if the Legion passed a resolution calling for a return to the gold standard, former soldiers would rally to this cause and march en masse in favor of it. Getting Butler to speak on the gold standard's behalf would bolster its popularity among them. Clark feared if America did not return to the gold standard, all Americans would lose their fortunes. He had $30 million and said he would spend half to "save the other half." Butler refused, "I am not going to get these soldiers marching around and stirred up over the gold standard. What the hell does a solider know about the gold standard?"[19]

To which Clark responded, "Why do you want to be so stubborn? Why do you want to be different from other people? We can take care of you. You have got a mortgage on this house…. That can all be taken care of. It is perfectly legal, perfectly proper." This aroused Butler's anger. He spat back: "Do you know what you are trying to do? You are trying to bribe me in my own house.... You come out into the hall, I want to show you something." There he showed Clark his Marine memorabilia, including ribbons and medals. Butler said, "You are trying to buy me away from my own kind." He meant the veterans. He told Clark to take a look at his citations and think about that.[20]

Clark asked to use Butler's phone. He called MacGuire at the Palmer House, a hotel in Chicago, and told MacGuire to send telegrams and do what he needed to do, but to forget about Butler. The general had excellent reasons why he would not attend the convention and Clark accepted these. He would not go the convention himself, either; he planned to stay in Canada for a while. Clark and Butler had a pleasant conversation about unimportant matters thereafter. Around six in the evening Clark returned to the train station.[21] He and his compatriots at the Committee for a Sound Dollar never again contacted or bothered Butler. Only MacGuire would continue to do so, an important point to remember later.

MacGuire stopped at Butler's house "on his way back from the convention. This time he came in a hired limousine" to report the convention had passed the gold standard resolution. He returned to Butler's house one more time after this to ask Butler to make a speech about the gold standard in Boston at a dinner for soldiers. It would pay $1,000 and include a hired car to take him there and back. Butler had never received such a fee for a speech, although he would always agree to speak to soldiers, but not for money. Undaunted, MacGuire said, "Well, then, we will think of something else." Here MacGuire insinuated he had come on behalf of the Committee for a Sound Dollar, but he did not outright say he had.[22]

In early November, Butler headed to Brooklyn to campaign on behalf of a former Marine running for a municipal office. As he waited for a train to take him home, MacGuire unexpectedly appeared. He asked about Butler's plans to go on a speaking campaign on behalf of the Veterans of Foreign Wars.[23] (The head of the V.F.W., Butler's good friend James E. Van Zandt, had asked him to do so.[24]) Butler said he aimed to rally these former soldiers to oppose war. He believed the country's democracy faced serious threats and knew veterans would stand on the side of it, adding, "I believe that sooner or later we are going to have a showdown, because I have had so many invitations to head societies and to join societies, all of them with a camouflaged patriotic intent. They are rackets, all of them."[25]

Over the years Butler received many peculiar offers and proposals. In 1926, for example, the former U.S. vice-counsel general to France asked Butler if he would like to start an international detective agency. A group called the Technocrats wished him to join their organization. A man named John H.

Skaley wanted him to finance his invention, "a device to locate gold, silver, copper (or other metals if I desired), oil or water."[26] J.E. Shields, a wounded veteran, wrote Butler on behalf of the Order of American Ex-Service Men of the State of Washington. Shields' rambling letter involved phrases such as "*Christ's Chosen Children*" and made a reference to the "Cattle Buying Methods" of American politicians—whatever that meant. His group sought Butler's support.[27] Butler had good reason to worry about the country's state of mind.

MacGuire asked if he could go with Butler on his tour. He wished to rally the soldiers to create a "super organization to maintain the democracy." Butler told him he wanted nothing to do with this scheme. He did not like the large sums of money involved. MacGuire just replied with a vagueness he did not wish to change the current form of government, but he made no definite statements as to what he wanted beyond preserving democracy. He did not board the train.[28]

At the end of November, Butler began his four-month speaking tour for the V.F.W. He neither saw nor heard from MacGuire during that time. Then, in February, MacGuire sent him a post card from Nice, France, on which he wrote that he had enjoyed his time there. Butler received another post card from Berlin in April or May.[29] A third, postmarked May 30, 1934, came from Paris.[30] Aside from these missives, Butler did not hear from MacGuire until August 1934, when he called Butler at home and asked if he would meet in Philadelphia. Butler replied his wife needed to go into the city anyway, so they could get together at the railroad station. MacGuire wanted to meet at the Bellevue-Stratford Hotel, the same place where Butler had received a job offer from Mayor Kendrick. In a disused café, MacGuire told Butler he had gone to Europe to examine its various veterans groups' reactions to the current economic crisis. He did not think the Italian Fascists or German Nazis had a good setup. He admired the French right-wing paramilitary group called the Croix de Feu (Cross of Fire), which, by MacGuire's estimate, had a half million men.[31] This organization, which had begun as an apolitical veterans' group, took a political stance in 1931 when a fellow named Colonel François de la Rocque took it over. Under his leadership it made "veiled allusions to an impending H hour" and often held "massive, disciplined, and menacing parades." In 1936 the newly elected French government outlawed all such groups, so the Croix de Feu transformed itself into a political party called Parti Social Français,[32] which, as history has shown, did not affect French politics in any significant way.

MacGuire wanted to create an organization like this in America, one with half a million men. Butler asked, "What do you want to do with it when you get it up?" MacGuire wanted to "support the President." Butler pointed out the president did not need the backing of such a group. MacGuire explained that the president had nearly run out of money and would need more. To get it, he would have to change the way the government collected its revenue. MacGuire wanted his proposed group to ensure this did not happen. He did not say so outright, but he opposed FDR's raising taxes on the rich.[33]

MacGuire reckoned the "overworked" president also needed help to do his job. He required "a secretary of general affairs—a sort of supersecretary." MacGuire's fantasy did not stop there: "You know, the American people will swallow that. We have got the newspapers. We will start a campaign that the President's health is failing. Everybody can tell that by looking at him, and the dumb American people will fall for it in a second." Then came the bombshell: he asked if Butler would like to head his proposed army with the insinuation that Butler would then become the new secretary of general affairs. Alarmed, Butler replied, "I am interested in it, but I do not know about heading it." He told MacGuire he had a "hobby" of protecting democracy, warning, "If you get these 500,000 soldiers advocating anything smelling of Fascism, I am going to get 500,000 more and lick the hell out of you, and we will have a real war right at home."[34]

This nameless group of conspirators MacGuire claimed to represent planned to change the order of presidential succession so the secretary of general affairs would take office should the president resign and the vice-president could not or would not replace him. MacGuire figured FDR would probably have to resign. Butler pointed out that executing this whole scheme would cost a great deal of money. MacGuire assured the general the organization he represented had $3 million to start with and could raise another $300 million. Clark, for example, planned to donate $15 million for the cause. The organization would pay enlisted men $15 a month and captains $35 a month.[35]

MacGuire said he believed only a "man on a white horse" such as Butler could save capitalism. He proposed Butler march this army into Washington, D.C., itself. If Butler did not accept, MacGuire informed him that those he represented might then ask either Hanford MacNider, a former head of the American Legion, or General Douglas MacArthur.[36] MacGuire said that while the "Morgan interests" (the J.P. Morgan banking empire) did not trust Butler, he had pushed for Butler's involvement anyway.[37]

Butler had heard enough. He asked his journalist friend Paul Comly French to look into the matter.[38] One might find it odd that the always-skeptical Butler took any of this seriously, but he had a good reason for doing so. Despite his quirks, MacGuire had an insider's knowledge of the business world and American politics that gave his proposal a sheen of credibility. MacGuire had, for example, told Butler about the formation of the American Liberty League—an organization about which we shall learn more later—approximately two weeks before it went public. He predicted that Al Smith, the ex-governor of New York and one of FDR's closest political allies, would break with the president and attack him in his magazine *New Outlook*. A month later he did. Another time MacGuire foretold Hanford MacNider would come out in favor of payment of the veterans' bonus, which at that time he publicly opposed. Three weeks later he did.[39]

Butler's journalist friend French, a member of the Society of Friends, had worked briefly as Butler's personal secretary, this experience reinforcing French's staunch pacifism. As a reporter for the *Philadelphia Record,* French had covered the Lindbergh kidnapping and had an active role in the Writer's Union and the WPA Writer's Guild. A man rarely seen without a pipe in his mouth and known as a name-dropper, he championed the cause of giving conscientious objectors to war the right to choose non–military service such as working for the Civilian Public Service.[40]

French managed to get an interview out of MacGuire because Butler called him and said he would make no final decision about his proposal unless MacGuire agreed to see the journalist. For the interview, French went to MacGuire's New York City office on the twelfth floor of 52 Broadway.[41] Although reluctant to speak at first, MacGuire soon opened up. He said, "We need a Fascist Government in this country ... to save the nation from the Communists who would tear down all that has been built up in America. The only men who have the patriotism to do it are the soldiers, and Smedley Butler is the ideal leader. He could organize a million men overnight." MacGuire further asserted he would have no problem raising $100,000 to pay for the equipping and maintaining of such an army. He could obtain weapons from the Remington Arms Company using credit provided by the DuPont family. If FDR played along, he could stay in power as a figurehead, just as Mussolini had done for the king of Italy. Raising an army could solve the nation's unemployment problem by drafting all out-of-work men of the right age into military labor camps.[42]

On November 21, 1934, French published his story in the *Philadelphia Record* and, simultaneously, the *New York Evening Post*. The *Record* ran with the headline "GEN. BUTLER CHARGES FASCIST PLOT."[43] Mainstream press reaction, save for a few exceptions like the *San Francisco Chronicle*, treated the story as a fantasy.[44] The *New York Times* ran with the headline "Gen. Butler Bares 'Fascist Plot' to Seize Government by Force." It placed "Fascist Plot" in quotations as a qualifier because it clearly did not take Butler's accusations seriously.[45] *Time* magazine thought even less about them. It ran an article titled "Plot Without Plotters" in which it began with a tongue-in-cheek account of Butler's leading a half-million man army into Washington, D.C., for a successful takeover of the government.[46]

Many of those allegedly involved with the plot denied any knowledge of such a scheme. Thomas W. Lamont, a J.P. Morgan and Company partner, said, "Perfect moonshine! Too unuterably [*sic*] ridiculous to comment upon!" Murphy called it "a fantasy! I can't imagine how any one could produce it or any sane person believe it." MacGuire said, "It's a joke — a publicity stunt. I know nothing about it. The matter is made out of whole cloth. I deny the story completely."[47] Robert Sterling Clark "freely admitted trying to get General Butler to use his influence with the Legion against dollar devaluation, but stoutly declared: 'I am neither a Fascist nor a Communist, but an American.' He threatened a libel suit 'unless the whole affair is relegated to the funny sheets by Sunday.'"[48]

Butler received a variety of letters from people around the country supporting him for revealing the plot. The American Legion's Post 37 in Philadelphia endorsed his charges and thanked him for exposing it to the "proper authorities."[49] Richard St. Clair of San Francisco wrote that he had always known the American Legion worked for Wall Street, and considered "Randolf [*sic*] Hearst," the newspaper tycoon, one those behind the Fascist plot. St. Clair's letter exhibited all the characteristics of the conspiracy theorist: it contained much speculation and not one piece of evidence to back it.[50]

MacGuire's proposition caught the attention of the Special Committee on Un-American Activities Authorized to Investigate Nazi Propaganda and Certain Other Propaganda Activities, one chaired by Representative John W. McCormack and vice-chaired by Representative Samuel Dickstein.[51] Established on March 20, 1934, it had formed as a reaction to the alarming rate at which foreign governments had fallen to fascists and communists. It preceded the more the famous House Un-American Activities Committee, or HUAC. After its various investigations, of which MacGuire's proposals only made up a part, its final report contained "more than 4,300 pages."[52] Better known as the McCormack-Dickstein Committee, it contacted Butler, who cooperated fully and who made it clear to the press the Committee had subpoenaed *him*, he had not approached it.[53]

A friend of Butler's from Washington, D.C., Chas M. Kelley, related the story of how Dickstein had become aware of the plot. Using what he termed "unimpeachable sources," Kelley reported that in August 1933 one of the "London Rothschilds came to New York" to meet "with certain financiers" to stir up interest in establishing a fascist movement in America. The Rothschilds feared a communist takeover. Somehow Dickstein managed to attend one of these meetings, and when he heard the allegations of a communist usurpation he became "all hot and bothered." Although he learned of MacGuire's proposals to Butler here, he cared little for fascists or Nazis and did not seem inclined to pursue this matter; he only wanted to uncover communist plots. Kelley further accused Randolph Hearst of involvement with the plot because the newspaper mogul he had gone to Europe and "hobnobbed with both Mussolini and Hitler."[54]

On November 20 the McCormack-Dickstein Committee began its hearings on this matter at the Association of the Bar of the City of New York. The Committee started its inquiry by interviewing Captain Samuel Glazier, camp commandant of the Civilian Conservation Corps base in Elkridge, Maryland. Someone had alleged that the army proposed by MacGuire would use the camp as its rallying point. McCormack and Dickstein then questioned Butler, French, MacGuire, two bankers, one accountant, and Albert Christmas, Robert Sterling Clark's lawyer.[55]

McCormack and Dickstein interviewed MacGuire for much of the five days they spent looking into the matter. MacGuire began his testimony by stating his name, Gerald C. MacGuire, and his occu-

A 1934 press photograph in which Butler tells of his role in uncovering a plot by American businessmen to establish a fascist dictatorship in the United States. From the Smedley D. Butler Collection, courtesy of the Marine Corps Archives and Special Collections Department at the Gray Research Center, Quantico.

pation, bond salesman. Born in 1898 in New Haven, Connecticut, he had graduated from New Haven High School and later Hopkins School in New York City. He had a wife, five children, two brothers and three sisters.[56] As a bond salesman, he made $75 a week.[57] One newspaper account described him as "short, quite heavy, with a small, bullet-shaped head, close-cropped, and bright blue eyes." He spoke "in a plaintive voice with a faint East Side accent."[58] MacGuire claimed he had worked as an aide to FDR during his time as the assistant secretary of the Navy. When French researched this, he found that MacGuire had served as an ensign in the Navy, but no record existed about his being an aide to Roosevelt.[59] MacGuire told another reporter he had sailed on board the naval transport *Aulus* during the Great War, "but he would not say what his rank was."[60]

Butler had also done a background check on MacGuire. He learned MacGuire had served in the Navy during the Great War, during which he suffered a head wound, resulting in the placement of "a silver plate" in his head. Butler assessed him as follows: "Now, he is a very cagey individual. He always approaches everything from afar. He is really a very nice, plausible fellow. But I gather … that due to this wound in his head, he is a little inconsistent, a little flighty."[61]

When asked to recount his side of the story by the McCormack-Dickstein Committee, MacGuire often contradicted Butler and French's statements. MacGuire testified he had never served as the state commander in Connecticut's American Legion nor made that claim. He said he had personally called Butler from Philadelphia to ask if he and Doyle could meet with him, and no mysterious fellow named Jack had gotten involved in any way. He had known Butler for several years before this, and further intimated he had a close relationship with Butler by claiming Butler once spoke to him about Colonel Williams's court martial.[62]

MacGuire and Doyle went to Butler's house solely for purpose of asking him to run as the Legion's national commander. For that the general would need to go to the upcoming convention in Chicago. MacGuire admitted to telling Butler he could come as a delegate from Hawaii.[63] Interestingly, William Doyle, whom the Committee did not call to testify, reported that he had never asked Butler to become the Legion's national commander. He said, "In fact, he couldn't be a candidate if he wanted to, because he wasn't a delegate."[64] MacGuire, on the other hand, said, "I had always been a great admirer of General Butler and I thought that he would be a fine man to be commander of the Legion." MacGuire confirmed that he asked Butler to speak on behalf of the Committee for a Sound Dollar, but denied ever giving Butler a speech. He had never asked Butler to gather up several hundred veterans and bring them to the Legion's Chicago convention to demand he address it. Nor had he shown Butler a bank book.[65]

Representative McCormack asked MacGuire about the incident at Newark at which Butler asserted MacGuire had thrown thousand-dollar bills on a hotel bed. MacGuire admitted going to Newark to see the general, but said he never tossed any money on a bed. McCormack asked, "How did you happen to be at this convention of the Twenty-ninth?" Butler had invited him, although MacGuire could not recall if he had done so verbally or in writing. MacGuire met Butler there for lunch.[66]

McCormack wanted to know MacGuire's connection with Richard Sterling Clark, and whether or not he had mentioned Clark's name to Butler. MacGuire had, but he did not know if Butler and Clark met or not. McCormack followed this up: "Did he ever call you up in Chicago from General Butler's home?" MacGuire answered, "No, sir; to my recollection he did not." MacGuire remembered meeting Butler at the Bellevue-Stratford Hotel in

Philadelphia and speaking about his trip to Europe. He had made no mention about examining fascist governments during the conversation, although he did say he thought Hitler would not last another year in power, and he acknowledged his admiration for the Croix de Feu. MacGuire went on to say that he had frequently warned the general to *avoid* organizations such as the one Butler accused the bond salesman of proposing. Indeed, MacGuire claimed to have once said to Butler: "General, you are crazy to get mixed up in these kinds of things." He further warned that the group wanting to replace the current government with a fascist one "was just another racket, that those boys wanted his [Butler's] name, because he is a membership getter."[67]

McCormack and Dickstein spent most of their interview with MacGuire focused on where he had acquired all the money he showed Butler. Presumably the congressmen hoped to trace it back to the plot's financiers, if any. This avenue of questioning uncovered nothing more than a confusing cacophony of numbers, bank statements, and contradictory information. McCormack and Dickstein determined MacGuire had received money from Clark, Christmas, Murphy, and a fellow named Mr. Frew, and that some of it had gone to the Committee for a Sound Dollar, some for the purchasing of bonds, and the rest for MacGuire's European trip.[68] McCormack and Dickstein traced none of it back to a mysterious organization bent on replacing FDR with a fascist dictator.

11

The Plot Unravels

MacGuire's second day of testimony started a pattern of contradictions amounting to perjury. He often changed his story. When, for example, Representative McCormack asked again if he or Doyle had called Butler from a hotel in Philadelphia to set up their first meeting, MacGuire answered that he could not remember, although in his previous testimony he said he had made the call from that location. McCormack persisted, inquiring if perhaps a fellow named "Jack" had phoned Butler to arrange the meeting? MacGuire suddenly remembered he had, saying, "I had plainly forgotten the incident." He met Jack for the first time in his life in Washington, D.C., at the Mayflower Hotel, but he could not remember the man's last name nor did he know much about him. Yet in his previous testimony he had named this fellow, Jack Quinn, as a founding member of the Committee for a Sound Dollar.[1]

Inconsistencies such as these abounded throughout the rest of his testimony. At the end of the second day's interview, McCormack asked MacGuire about his trip to Europe. MacGuire said he had left on December 1, 1933. About five weeks into the trip, his wife joined him. He went there on behalf of Clark. McCormack wanted to know if MacGuire had written any reports or memorandums about his trip. Yes, he penned letters from time to time as well as a final report when he got home, and he possessed copies. Would he produce those? He would. When MacGuire returned for a third day of testimony, he reported that he never made a final written report after all, just a verbal one. He did have copies of the letters he sent home to Clark, which he handed over. He had only gone to Europe to evaluate the economic conditions there in an effort to aid Clark in deciding in what countries he might want to do business.[2]

On another day, McCormack wanted to know if perhaps MacGuire had traveled to Europe to evaluate the various paramilitary groups and totalitarian governments as suggested by his letters. McCormack considered parts of MacGuire's letters ample evidence of his interest in paramilitary groups. One of MacGuire's letters, for example, reported, "There is no question but that another severe [political] crisis is imminent [here in France]. There have been various pieces of information given me to the effect that the Communists have been arming and are scattered in the outlying districts of Paris." MacGuire predicted the French military might use the Communists' movement as an excuse to execute a military coup, but figured the right-wing Croix de Feu would keep the Communists from stirring up too much trouble. About the Croix de Feu in particular MacGuire wrote, "I recently attended a meeting of this organization and was quite impressed with the type of men belonging," because it consisted of veterans of the World War rather than politicians. MacGuire told the Committee he had attended this assembly by pure chance. As he sat at Mass in Notre Dame, these fellows gathered outside. He saw their rally when emerged from the cathedral.[3]

The McCormack-Dickstein Committee finished off its hearings in New York by interviewing Clark's lawyer, Albert Christmas. The two congressmen drilled him on matters financial at first, getting into the minutiae about various bank transactions that could well drive an accountant to the brink of insanity. After quite a bit of this line of questioning, they turned to the more tantalizing aspects of their investigation. They asked for details about Christmas's involvement with the Committee for a Sound Dollar. Christmas said Clark had nothing to do with its activities other than he had financed it; Clark left the details to Christmas and MacGuire. MacGuire came up with the idea of asking Butler to make a speech in favor of the gold standard at the American Legion's Chicago convention, and went to see him for this reason. Christmas did not know if MacGuire gave Butler the gold standard speech, but he verified its existence.[4]

Christmas acknowledged he and Clark had sent MacGuire to Europe to check the general economic conditions there. McCormack read excerpts from some of MacGuire's letters to Christmas. One reported on the number of storm troopers in Italy, especially those stationed along the railroad lines and on the trains themselves. Another noted the German influence in Holland and how German Nazis had backed a home-grown fascist movement. German interference in the country had made "trade conditions ... extremely poor." McCormack intimated that MacGuire concerned himself with the political activities of paramilitary organizations in order to find a model upon which he could form such a group in America. He noted that since MacGuire usually addressed most letters to "Gentlemen" or to "Christmas" instead of "Clark," this suggested a cabal of men had backed MacGuire's trip. Christmas replied that the letters had come directly to him, and he had passed them on to Clark when he found them interesting; no one else saw them.[5]

MacGuire's letters offered no real evidence he had in mind to create an American paramilitary group based on the ones he had seen in Europe. A

more practical if mundane reason explains his interest: by including information on the various militant groups in Europe, MacGuire simply did his job.
Such organizations had already taken over Italy and Germany, so it made sense
this could happen elsewhere. Thus, had MacGuire *not* reported on the paramilitary movements in the countries he visited, he would have failed in his
task. After all, investors only want to put their money in stable places, not
those with a potential to be toppled by coups, especially communist ones.

Upon the conclusion of the McCormack-Dickstein Committee's hearings,
a journalist named John L. Spivak used his contacts in Washington, D.C., to
inquire into the matter of the plot. He pushed the McCormack-Dickstein
Committee to release the transcript of the Butler hearings, which it did. When
he read the result, he found it odd that some of the names mentioned in
French's article, such as Al Smith and Hanford MacNider, had not appeared
anywhere in the testimony. Probing deeper, he found a source who revealed
to him that the Committee had deleted portions of it.[6]

Spivak tried and failed to get the redacted material released. Still, he
figured he could extract a few articles out of the entirety of the testimony the
Special Committee on Un-American Activities had unearthed during its existence (this encompassing far more than just the Butler material). He asked
Representative Dickstein about obtaining copies. Dickstein agreed and introduced Spivak to the Committee's secretary, Frank P. Randolph. The overworked Randolph accidentally gave Spivak testimony that included the deleted
portions from the Butler hearings.[7]

Spivak decided to make this public. He would do so as part of an article
he planned to write for a magazine called *New Masses,* started by muckrakers
in 1911, that had initially printed fiction and art but had evolved into a communist mouthpiece over the years. No communist himself, Spivak had little
interest in the ideological side of the story: "I cared little if the magazine's primary interest was to show that big business in the United States, which was
ready to finance a fascist coup as big business had done in Italy and Germany,
was thus an enemy of democracy and the people. Americans were entitled to
know that a committee of the Congress was suppressing testimony without
even checking it out."[8]

Spivak phoned Butler, whom he had never before met nor spoken to, and
asked him if he knew that some of his testimony had not made it into the publicly released transcript. He did not. When Spivak told Butler he planned to
write an article about this for *New Masses,* Butler seemed unconcerned about
the magazine's communist associations. He invited Spivak to his house to discuss the matter. Spivak trudged up to Butler's Newtown Square house the day
after a heavy snowstorm. Butler opened the door before the journalist could
knock, and the two discussed the matter. As the conversation progressed Spi-

vak found, to his surprise, Butler liked to use an excessive number of "four-letter words." Moreover, Butler only wanted to talk about how he and the Marines had fought for the benefit of American corporations and Wall Street. He planned to write an autobiography detailing all this and asked Spivak if he would collaborate. He declined. Spivak wondered if Butler quite understood that *New Masses* proselytized communism, so he repeated this point. Butler replied that he did not care, adding, "There wouldn't be a United States if it wasn't for a bunch of radicals.... I once heard of a radical named George Washington. As a matter of fact from what I read he was an extremist — a goddamn revolutionist!"[9]

When Spivak's *New Masses* piece appeared, it varied considerably from what he had planned to compose — perhaps his editor had a heavy hand in the writing process. The resulting two-part article contained a vast conspiracy theory that went well beyond simply asking why the McCormack-Dickstein Committee had deleted testimony and had not questioned all the people allegedly involved. Spivak opened his article's first part by declaring he had written it mainly for the purpose of exposing anti–Semitism in America. The son of Orthodox Jews, he had of late become interested in anti–Semitic activities in America, and had taken to investigating them. He did not help his cause with this statement: "The anti–semetic [*sic*] character of Nazism has been abundantly demonstrated in these pages; nevertheless this article, and succeeding ones, will reveal Jewish financiers working with fascist groups which, if successful, would unquestionably heighten the wave of Hate-the-Jew propaganda."[10]

Spivak concocted a conspiracy theory so complex he had to include a detailed chart chock-full of the names of the businesses, organizations and people he accused of engineering it. At its simplest, Spivak's theory named the J.P. Morgan banking empire as the prime mover behind the fascist plot. Others who worked with Morgan included the McCormack-Dickstein Committee itself, the American Jewish Committee, the Crusaders ("a monetary reform group"), Kuhn-Loeb (a powerful banking house), the American Liberty League, the Remington Arms Company, and, not surprisingly, William Randolph Hearst.[11]

Spivak also included verbatim the entirety of Butler and French's redacted testimony. Butler's deleted statements included his accusation that big business had often used the American Legion as a strike-breaking outfit, that MacGuire told him FDR, born into the American upper class, would one day "come back" into the fold, that Al Smith had personal connections with MacGuire, and that if Butler did not agree to head the half-million-man army, then those whom MacGuire represented would instead ask either Hanford MacNider or Douglas MacArthur. French's deleted testimony included his recollection of

MacGuire's claim that he could get his financing for his fascist army from John W. Davis of National City Bank, and that he would get its weapons from the Remington Arms Company with credit from the DuPont family.[12]

Spivak obsessed on one group in particular that he connected to the conspiracy: the American Liberty League. This organization had its genesis in March 1934 when an irate R.R.M. Carpenter, a retired vice-president of DuPont, started writing a series of letters to John J. Raskob, a one-time chairman of the Democratic Party and also a DuPont vice-president, complaining about the New Deal's treatment of the American upper class. Carpenter railed against the fact that his staff of black servants had all quit to take better-paying New Deal-created government jobs (never, one presumes, considering giving them raises to induce them to stay). Raskob suggested Carpenter do something about it. So he did. He and two friends, Pierre and Irénée DuPont, founded the American Liberty League. It incorporated in Washington, D.C., on August 15, 1934. With DuPont and General Motors as its chief financiers, it had the purpose of teaching people to "respect property" as well as promote the right to ownership.[13]

Grayson M.-P. Murphy served as the League's treasurer.[14] Others associated with it included three names mentioned in parts of the missing Butler and French testimony: Al Smith, John W. Davis, and William Randolph Hearst. The League's philosophy embraced the idea of rugged individualism, of helping oneself without depending on others. It opposed unions and lacked any concern for the social issues created by the Depression. Its founders could not understand why this philosophy failed to attract the average worker, although the League did gain the support of the National Lawyers Committee, an association made up of corporate attorneys. The League had hoped to obtain a membership of four to five million people. Despite the fact it had no fee for joining nor annual membership dues, it attracted a mere 75,000 members in its first seventeen months. It peaked at 150,000 members and died in obscurity in 1940, having affected no significant government policies.[15]

Butler had nothing to say about the League. When he made a public statement about the deleted testimony on radio station WCAU, he said, "Like most committees, it has slaughtered the little and allowed the big to escape. The big shots weren't even called to testify. They were all mentioned in the testimony. Why was all mention of these names suppressed from the testimony?" Dickstein, in a separate interview, replied, "The testimony given by General Butler was kept confidential until such time as the names of the persons who were mentioned could be checked upon and verified. This accounts for the fact that when the results of the hearings were made public, references were omitted."[16]

A journalist friend of Butler's, Morris A. Bealle, informed Butler just who had done the deleting: Democratic Congressman Charles Kramer, who bragged about having done so, along "with a dirty crack about" Butler. Altering the Congressional record as Kramer had done constituted, in Bealle's informed opinion, an infringement of a federal law which, according to an article he wrote, violated Title 18, Section 72 of the Criminal Code of the United States. Those found guilty of doing so for a fraudulent purpose faced a maximum of ten years in jail.[17]

Spivak's article only muddled up the truth, already strained by the fact that MacGuire's testimony contradicted much of what French, Butler and Christmas had stated. Still, the matter has a simpler explanation than one might at first expect. We know for certain that Clark helped to finance the Committee for a Sound Dollar, and that he wanted Butler to make a speech on returning to the gold standard to rally the support of former enlisted soldiers to this cause.[18] After Clark told MacGuire to leave Butler alone, the bond salesman never again approached the general on the Committee's behalf.

The proposal that Butler lead an army of half a million men could have come from no one other than MacGuire himself. No evidence of it beyond his own words exists to say otherwise. To give his scheme a bit of plausibility, he had dipped into the money he received both for the Committee for a Sound Dollar and the purchase of stocks and bonds. His trip to Europe as well as his reports on the various paramilitary groups there added a whiff of believability to his fantasy of creating a super-organization of American veterans led by Smedley Butler.

In a series of interviews with the press, MacGuire's delusions became apparent. He insisted he gave Butler advice on a regular basis. Once he said, "The thing was General Butler was always coming around to me with books and letterheads from all these crackpot organizations, and I would keep telling him: 'General, you're a — damn fool to fall for all those outfits.'… I've kept him out of plenty of trouble and this is what he does to show his gratitude. Everybody told me not to trust him, that he would pull his publicity stunts on his best friends, but I always thought he was a square shooter."[19] In another variation of this, MacGuire said, "I sent word back to the general to stay on his farm and have a good time.… I told him I thought the veterans' organizations merely wanted to use his name as a means of getting money, members or something."[20] He further claimed, "We were going to the Army-Navy game together next week-end. I haven't telephoned him yet, and I don't know whether I will."[21]

MacGuire told the McCormack-Dickstein Committee that Butler had frequently called him for advice. Once he claimed Butler had introduced him to a man named General Williams, an engineer who wanted money from the Reconstruction Finance Corporation[22] to build a "bridge or viaduct." Williams "needed $100,000 capital to put this deal across to show the R.F.C. that he …

[had] the financial set-up." Butler wanted to know if MacGuire could approach
Clark to obtain a loan from him. Clark had no interest in it. MacGuire produced a letter allegedly written by Butler about this proposal that read:

> Dear Gerry: Enclosed is that stuff about the contracting firm about which I spoke
> to you. Hope to see you soon.
>   Yours truly,
>   S.D. Butler.
> P.S.— When you are through with the enclosed, will you please send it back.—
> S.D.B.

Although McCormack questioned the note's authenticity, MacGuire swore
under oath Butler had written it in his own hand.[23]

MacGuire's reasons for saying and doing what he did went with him to
the grave. He died of pneumonia not too many months after the hearings
ended. His obituary appeared in the *New York Times* on March 26, 1935. In it
his brother William blamed Jerry's death on the strain caused by the
McCormack-Dickstein Committee's accusations. Since the hearings, William
said, Jerry's blood pressure had gone up to dangerous levels and his heart and
kidneys weakened. His friends and family vehemently denied his connections
to any fascist plots. William also said Jerry's personal physician, Dr. Lawrence
Renehan of Stamford, "specifically states that this last illness can be directly
attributed to the unjust charges launched by Congressman McCormack's committee." When MacGuire died at Grace Hospital, the attending physician, Dr.
Frank E. Toole, stated he thought the pressure from the previous year's ordeal
had indeed contributed to MacGuire's untimely death.[24] Interestingly, William
had played fast and loose with the truth just like his brother. After he told the
New York Times his brother's personal physician, Dr. Renehan, said Jerry died
because of the strain caused by the hearings, Dr. Renehan refuted this claim:
"I made no such statement because I knew nothing of Mr. Macguire's [*sic*]
affair." To which William replied he said this only "to clear up the injustice
done to Mr. Macguire [*sic*] and his family."[25]

Those still convinced that a cabal of American corporate tycoons plotted
to oust FDR might benefit from looking at this matter from a different perspective. For the sake of argument let us say a secret group of powerful businessmen and American corporations decided they wanted to replace FDR's
administration with a fascist government, and they planned to front it with a
well-known military man to control their private army. If so, why would they
choose Butler as their man when he had a philosophy ideologically opposed
to theirs? On the day of his retirement, for example, he had publicly proposed
a tax of fifty percent on the wealthiest Americans.[26] For our supposed conspirators to choose Butler to head their private army, a man known for his
anti–corporate stance on issues, they would have had to suffer from sheer

incompetence on an epic level. Spivak agreed, opining years after his original article appeared that the more he learned about Butler, "the more I was convinced that the conspirators were incredibly incompetent in picking him."[27] Never mind, too, that trying to control a man like Butler would prove impossible, as the Nicaraguan and Mussolini controversies showed.

Moreover, Hanford MacNider and Douglas MacArthur, the two alternatives these conspirators had in mind if Butler refused, would have made far more suitable generals to lead a private army. MacNider, a loyal Republican, had served in the National Guard and, during the Great War, the Army. Known for insubordination, he nonetheless distinguished himself during his military service and received almost as many decorations as General Pershing. As national commander of the American Legion in 1921, he led the charge for the veterans' World War bonus, which passed Congress in 1925. He served as the assistant secretary of war under President Coolidge and as the American minister to Canada under President Hoover. His work in the private sector involved the banking industry. Once, for example, he ran a major holding company of banks. Most importantly, he opposed the New Deal.[28]

Our theoretical conspirators would have done even better than MacNider by selecting General MacArthur as their man. He was deeply concerned about the possibility of communist takeovers, making him perfect for the role. In fact, FDR considered him one of the two most dangerous men in America,[29] fearing that during the current economic crisis the American people might turn to "strong men" (such as powerful industrialists) who could use MacArthur as a fulcrum to rally the masses behind them. FDR based his assessment in part on MacArthur's handling of the Bonus Army, during which the general demonstrated his willingness to act with an iron fist. More chillingly, many right-wingers admired how MacArthur had executed the Bonus Army's dispersal.[30]

The McCormack-Dickstein Committee never charged anyone with a crime, not even MacGuire for perjury. When Spivak asked Dickstein why it had not investigated the alleged connections of the American Liberty League with the plot or even called Murphy as a witness, the congressman answered that the Committee had lacked the time and money to do so. Spivak also tried to interview McCormack on this matter, but when he learned the journalist had a copy of the redacted sections of the hearing, he abruptly ended the interview. He agreed to respond to Spivak's questions in a letter, answering only those he wanted.[31] Spivak also unearthed a report written by the Committee to the House stating it had found evidence someone had proposed the plot, but it did not discover anyone had acted upon it.[32]

12

Cassandra

In February 1931, shortly after his official reprimand for insulting Mussolini, Butler made a speech on crime at the University Club in Buffalo, New York. Here he said, "There is no doubt that crime is organized on a national scale.... The headquarters are in New York. That is where the master-minds are who direct the operations of various bands of criminals throughout the country. That is where the criminals dispose of their loot. That is where they go for advice and protection."[1]

Butler wrote two articles on the subject of fighting organized crime for *Forum* magazine, titled "Making War on the Gangs" and "Wipe Out the Gangsters!" In the former he observed that police forces lacked the equipment, training, and ability to work together in any meaningful way to fight organized crime. He called for modeling state-run police forces on the military, with men moved from post to post every year to keep communities from compromising them. (Earlier in the year he had helped to organize Oregon's new state police.) He called for "an American Scotland Yard," or a "Federal crime bureau,"[2] although one already existed — the United States Bureau of Investigation, officially designated as the Division of Investigation. This possessed all the powers Butler thought such an agency ought to have. On July 1, 1935, it took on a new name: Federal Bureau of Investigation.[3]

His second article, "Wipe Out the Gangsters!," suggested former soldiers serve as agents of law enforcement because they had combat training. He wanted to take away the rights of monstrous criminals such as "baby killers." In that same uncompromising line of thought, he suggested America also needed its own version of Devil's Island, the notorious French penal colony where that country sent its worst offenders.[4]

At this time most American law enforcement officials as well as the government refused to recognize the size and threat of organized crime. In 1950 Senator Carey Estes Kefauver, a Democrat from Tennessee, held televised hearings on its most famous example, the Mafia. He also produced the first government report to officially acknowledge the Mafia's existence. The FBI, under J. Edgar Hoover's stubborn leadership, continued to refuse to acknowledge the Mafia's presence in America despite the fact that a New York state trooper had stumbled into a meeting of its leaders from across the country at Appalachian. As late as August 1960 the Justice Department denied the Mafia had anything more coherent than a few loose connections. Attorney General Robert F. Kennedy forced Justice both to recognize the Mafia's existence and to do something about it. The FBI submitted its first official report on the subject to him in 1962.[5]

Had someone in the Justice Department listened to Butler's warning in 1931, organized crime in general and the Mafia in particular might have suffered an earlier loss of its power and influence in America long before the implementation of the Racketeer Influence and Corrupt Organizations Act, or RICO — the anti–racketeering law that started this process in 1970. During his years of retirement Butler made many observations and predications of problems America faced, then proposed possible solutions only implemented by later generations. In this way he found himself in a situation like that of Cassandra, the daughter of the mythic King Priam of Troy. The god Apollo had given her the gift of prophecy, but when she rejected his love, he punished her by causing those who heard her predictions to never believe them.[6]

Butler often drew on his experience as a soldier and policeman for the subject matter of his speeches, magazine and newspaper articles. During his last year as commandant of Quantico, he received an offer allowing him to do so in a format unrestrained by space or time. Writer and radio personality Lowell Thomas proposed they collaborate on a boys' adventure book based on Butler's life.[7] At first nothing came of it. In January 1931 Louis Alger, Butler's booking agent, wrote to the general that he would try to arrange the business details for this venture. Butler replied with skepticism; he thought Thomas had "ditched" him, although he would love the chance to tell his story.[8] Thomas had not abandoned the venture. The book evolved into a true memoir rather than a boys' adventure book.

Lowell Thomas's own celebrity dwarfed Butler's. Everyone in America knew him from his national radio show, broadcast out of New York City, as well as his books and filmmaking. Thomas's daily radio show featured the news of the day. He began each show with "Good evening, everyone," and ended with "So long, until tomorrow." Thomas had received his break in the entertainment business while filming in the Middle East during the First World War. There he noticed a fellow named Colonel Thomas Edward Lawrence rallying the Arabs to overthrow their Turkish masters. Lawrence had gone native, wearing the local garb and riding camels like his Arab compatriots. Thomas filmed him in action, and, after the war, did a popular lecturing tour using this material, promoting his subject as Lawrence of Arabia. He also wrote two books about him.[9]

Butler dictated his autobiography to one of Thomas's secretaries, sent to Quantico for that purpose. Thomas wrote the final draft.[10] While Thomas received full writing credit, much of the prose likely came straight from Butler's mouth rather than Thomas's pen. One of Butler's friends, James Harbord, recognized this discrepancy. Harbord wondered why Thomas had gotten all the writing credit because he could see from the book's "charm" that Butler had a heavy hand in the storytelling.[11] Thomas and Butler contracted with publisher Farrar & Rinehart, Inc. One of the publisher's co–owners, Stanley M. Rinehart, erroneously told Butler that he and Thomas would each receive half of the $2,000 advance. It turned out Thomas would collect the entire $2,000 and Butler would earn the first $1,000 in royalties. Thomas generously forwarded $500 of his advance to Butler so he had something after all.[12] Upon the manuscript's receipt, Farrar & Rinehart did not go to print immediately; the firm decided to wait for better economic times.[13]

Butler suggested his publisher market the book to former soldiers and police departments in general and organizations such as the American Legion and V.F.W. in particular. Farrar & Rinehart asked him if he planned to make a speaking tour to promote the book, and told him a prominent Philadelphia radio station with "a national hook-up" wanted him to come do so.[14] The publisher released *Old Gimlet Eye: The Adventures of Smedley D. Butler as Told to Lowell Thomas* on August 25, 1933.[15] To promote it, Thomas asked Butler if he would have lunch in New York City at Circus, Saints and Sinners, a club whose members included mainly "explorers, military men, political leaders [and] writers." After this they would go to the Wanamakers bookstore to sign autographs, then do a quick stint on Thomas's radio show that evening. The two did all this on December 30, 1933.[16] *Old Gimlet Eye* made the *New York Times* best seller list for the city of Philadelphia for two weeks.[17] The *Times* gave it a favorable review, noting that of the autobiographies Thomas had ghostwritten, he had "done none quite the equal of this in some of its qualities, none with quite such a fascinating combination of fantastic, even ludicrous, incidents and concomitants with breath-taking dangers, daredevil courage and grisly necessities."[18]

In February 1934 Butler wrote a bitter letter to Farrar & Rinehart complaining his book had not sold well because the publisher failed to promote it. This was a strange thing to bemoan, considering that in 1933 alone it sold 4,125 copies out of 4,965 printed, for a total royalty of $1,704.25[19]— not a bad showing for a book released in the middle of the Great Depression. Butler hoped to have it serialized since this would mean a bit more money. Stanley Rinehart personally tried to make such a deal with the Hearst papers and the *Saturday Evening Post,* but nothing came of it. To help ease Butler's disappointment, Thomas wrote to him: "All who have had much to do with book publishing are convinced that it is a bigger gamble than Monte Carlo."[20]

Old Gimlet Eye offered details and insights about Butler's life and military career found nowhere else to this day. Much of the material in it paralleled that found in his letters, and external primary sources verify some of its more outrageous escapades. Although the book is long out of print, its lively prose makes for good reading, and those able to find a copy may wish to indulge. It included whimsical illustrations done by artist Paul Brown. After its publication, Farrar & Rinehart's art editor wrote Butler to inform him Brown had offered to give the general the original art if he would like them. Delighted at this prospect, Butler accepted, promising to frame these illustrations.[21]

Beyond his writing ventures, Butler continued his lecture touring without any particular scruples as to whom he spoke. In 1933 he addressed a gathering of the Ku Klux Klan in Delaware for a fee of $100 with the topic "Communism Will Not Be Tolerated." The Grand Dragon told him a humorist would warm the audience up, and one wonders just what sort of comedy amused that crowd.[22] In 1935 Butler committed himself to a series of eleven lectures on behalf of the Socialist Party of Milwaukee,[23] the KKK's ideological opposite. When he made any speech, he did so extemporaneously to give it a more natural feel, although he did use notes.[24]

Despite his willingness to speak to whomever could pay, Butler still held his own strong political convictions. When the Economy Act of 1933, a bill pushed through Congress by FDR, passed in March, Butler turned on the man for whom he had once campaigned. The bill "cut federal expenditures through a 400-million-dollar reduction in veteran pensions and benefits." In bread and butter terms, this "removed 501,777 veterans and their dependents from the pension roll" and reduced disability from twenty-five to eight percent. FDR did this despite his support of the Bonus Army the year before. Along with other veterans' groups, the V.F.W. went into action to have it repealed. Already believing Wall Street and big business had caused both the World War and the Great Depression, the veterans saw this bill as another example of such power and interests getting their way.[25]

V.F.W. leader James Van Zandt recruited a willing Butler to lead a public campaign to get Congress to repeal the offensive bill. Van Zandt made speeches on NBC and CBS, sometimes week after week. He and Butler embarked on a ten-city tour in eleven days using the title of Butler's first speech on the matter, "You've Got to Get Mad," as its slogan. Butler railed against big business and launched into the sort of populist messages he would use throughout the rest of his speaking career. In New Orleans he spoke alongside Louisiana's one-time firebrand governor and current senator, Huey Long. There Butler, who blamed the passing of the Economy Act on American big business, proposed

A press photograph used by the *Tribune* showing General Smedley D. Butler speaking at a national V.F.W. convention on the subject of war as a racket (date unknown, but probably taken in 1934). From the Smedley D. Butler Collection, courtesy of the Marine Corps Archives and Special Collections Department at the Gray Research Center, Quantico.

just who he thought should finance veterans' benefits: "I believe in making Wall Street pay for it — taking Wall Street by the throat and shaking it up."[26] Butler presumably impressed Long because the Louisiana senator later stated that if elected president, he would name Butler as his secretary of war. When asked about this, Butler considered it "the greatest compliment ever paid me."[27] The pressure put on Congress by the V.F.W. and similar groups prompted it to pass two Independent Offices Bills, the second of which, enacted in March 1934, voided the Economy Act in all but name. FDR vetoed the latter bill but Congress overrode him.[28]

Butler's populist message caught the attention of the Veterans National Rank and File Committee, asking him to endorse the upcoming "Congress Against War and Fascism" meeting in Chicago. Sponsored by the American League Against War and Fascism, this event called for the immediate payment of the veterans' bonus, the repeal of the Economy Act, and the introduction of a system of workers' unemployment and social insurance.[29] Although the American League Against War served as front organization of the American Communist Party,[30] Butler addressed its third annual "Congress Against War and Fascism" meeting in 1936, where he predicted the coming of a second world war and said that the United States must resist being drawn into it. Not all of his predictions came true. He thought, "There's not a chance of war with Japan."[31]

Butler took his populist message to the radio. During his campaign against the Economy Act, for example, he recited a five-minute piece written by the V.F.W. on NBC out of Chicago.[32] As we have already seen, radio station managers sometimes got nervous at what he had to say, cutting him off the air when he became offensive in their opinion. Such an incident occurred in October 1934 during a speech to a V.F.W. convention in Lexington, Kentucky, that was broadcast over local NBC affiliate station WAVE. The station shut Butler off when he uttered the phrases "turning food into fertilizer" (in reference to the Agricultural Adjustment Administration's practice of slaughtering hogs to raise prices) and "marines making whoopee in the red-light district." Butler spoke for another four and a half minutes after this, never realizing that only the men at the convention itself could hear him. When asked about the incident later, he made it into a political statement, the sort that had endeared him to veterans: "People are allowed to say what they like in abusing our soldiers, but when a man takes their part, he is cut off." Although the V.F.W.'s leadership approved WAVE's decision,[33] judging by the vast amount of mail Butler received about this matter from its members, the bulk of them did not.[34]

Despite incidents such as these, Butler acquired his own radio program. Broadcasting from Philadelphia's WCAU, he received $150 to transmit a minimum of two times and no more than four times a week. He also had free reign as to what he wished to speak about, and he would not have to deal with the advertisers. Pep Boys became his sponsor. He usually talked about matters political.[35] Once, for example, he spoke about the "Forgotten Man."[36] The fan mail poured in.[37]

On October 29, 1934, he made a speech to the V.F.W. in which he said veterans such as himself needed to unite and outlaw war. Only munitions makers profited from it.[38] He expanded on this theme in an article titled "War Is a Racket," which appeared in *Forum* magazine. In it he wrote he had come to the realization that those who profited most from war, large industries and Wall Street, had started to gear up for another one. He warned, "War, like any other racket, pays high dividends to the very few."[39]

Although he filled this piece with statistics of dubious value,[40] he nonetheless made predictions and observations not properly addressed to this day. He

noted, "The soldiers, of course, pay the biggest part of the bill." Having just visited eighteen government hospitals, he had seen firsthand the thousands of "destroyed men"—about 50,000 in his estimate—who suffered from physical and emotional scars not yet healed from the Great War. He called them the "living dead." The government had trained them to kill, then expected them to do an "about face" and return to civilian life with no problems. Since soldiers did not receive adequate pay, the government compensated them by offering pretty awards instead. To stop another international conflict, the people of the

Butler's 1938 press photograph. From the Smedley D. Butler Collection, courtesy of the Marine Corps Archives and Special Collections Department at the Gray Research Center, Quantico.

world's nations needed to take "the profit out of war." Instead of conscripting the masses, the military should draft the owners of the industries who banked the most from war, then pay them the same meager $30 a month the enlisted soldiers made.[41]

The U.S. Congress had periodically investigated allegations similar to Butler's starting as far back as the American Revolution, but it had never found firm evidence that those who had benefited financially from war ever pushed the United States into one. In the early 1930s the idea that American industrialists had driven the U.S. into the Great War so they could make obscene profits by selling war materials gained popular support. In response to these charges, Congress created the Munitions Investigating Committee, headed by Republican senator Gerald Prentice Nye of North Dakota, to look into the matter. Tainted by accusations of bullying witnesses and seeking unnecessary publicity, Nye's Committee nonetheless found no evidence that any American companies had helped to thrust America into the Great War.[42]

Butler's article offered a solution he thought would keep America out of war for once and all. He called for a constitutional amendment which would forbid Congress to declare war unless the majority of people voted for it on a national ballot.[43] Here he repeated a failed proposal made in 1917 by Senator Thomas P. Gore, a Democrat from Oklahoma. In 1938, Representative Louis Ludlow, also a Democrat from Oklahoma, reintroduced this same measure to the Judicial Committee. Backed by a petition filled with thousands of signatures from pacifists and other antiwar people, he forced a vote to get it removed to the floor for debate, something FDR opposed. It failed to receive the require two-thirds majority it needed.[44]

"War Is a Racket" elicited a positive reaction. A motion picture company, Eureka Productions, told Butler it had a movie of the same name in production and wanted to consult Butler about it.[45] Publisher Dorrance & Company offered to print it as a pamphlet or booklet, giving Butler a royalty of five cents per copy.[46] Although Butler did not take this offer, he did business with another publisher, Roundtable Press, which produced an expanded version of the original article in a booklet form in 1935. Although Butler's frequent collaborator E.Z. Dimitman had a hand in the writing,[47] Butler dictated the booklet to his wife after dinner every night, during which he elaborated on points made in the original article.[48]

Butler's status as a prominent retired military officer sometimes drew him back to Washington, D.C. On February 5, 1935, he received a telegram from Senator Hugo L. Black, a Democrat from Alabama, asking him to appear before the Senate Naval Affairs Committee on February 8.[49] The Committee planned to hold a confirmation hearing in which it would consider making John H. Russell a major general and thus the permanent commandant of the Marine Corps, a position he had taken upon General Fuller's departure the previous year.[50] Butler agreed to come.[51] He hated Russell with a passion, as evidenced by his many letters on the subject.

Born at Mare Island, California, in 1872, Russell came from a military family. His father had served in the Union Army during the Civil War, and he himself attended the Naval Academy, an appointment he received from President Grover Cleveland. After taking a two-year cruise as a cadet, he graduated from the Academy in 1894 but did not receive a naval appointment due to a lack of open positions. He instead took a commission as a second lieutenant in the Marines.[52]

In 1917 he took command of the Provisional Marine Brigade in Port-au-Prince. Although he did not fight in France during the Great War, he served on the 1919 Retention Board set to deal with the downsizing of the Corps from 75,000 to 20,000 men. The Board had to select the officers who would remain. Russell recommended keeping officers who had attended the Naval Academy over those with combat experience who had come up from the ranks. The controversy this sparked caused the dismissal of all of the Board's suggestions. Butler, no fan of most officers who came out of the Naval Academy anyway, never forgave Russell for this. In January 1922, Russell began his controversial nine-year civilian position as American High Commissioner of Haiti and Ambassador Extraordinaire. Upon his return to the Corps proper, he took command of Quantico as Butler's replacement in 1931.[53]

The Senate Naval Committee divided itself on the matter of Russell's nomination. Senators Black and William Henry King led the charge against him. King disliked Russell on the grounds that when he had gone to Hispaniola on a fact-finding mission, Russell and the Haitian president had both signed a document barring King from entry in the country. Senators Park Trammell, a Democrat from Florida, and Hiram Warren Johnson, a Republican from California, both defended Russell on the grounds that he had only carried out his orders.[54]

During his testimony, Butler stated that Russell favored graduates from the Naval Academy over those who came from the ranks, which, of course, he had done back in 1919. Butler gave an example of Russell's doing so in the present. He cited the fate of an officer with whom he had served, Captain Cukela. "I know this man," he said. "To be sure his table manners are not good, but it was my impression that we were not running a knitting society." Russell said he had nothing to do with the fact that in the last two years the Promotion Board had denied Cukela an advancement in rank, although he admitted he had approved the decision. Russell further refuted the claim he had ever favored men from the Naval Academy over those who came up from the ranks.[55]

In hope of swaying Senator Johnson's opinion, Butler wrote him a private letter in which he said Russell often terrorized his men. Butler gave as an example an incident that happened while he gave his testimony in front of the committee: "One of the young men sitting on the lounge almost directly opposite me had been one of my close associates in the Marine Corps for years. He is a boy I care for very greatly, and yet he was afraid to look, let alone speak to me, in the presence of his Commandant and the Assistant Secretary of the Navy." He continued, "If you permit this group of social parasites to retain its hold on the Marine Corps, our dear, old Corps will lose something that many men have given their whole lives to build up." In another letter, this one to a friend, Butler described Russell as "a perfect dumb-ball.... Not only is he dumb but malicious and above all — infinitely selfish."[56]

Senator Black took what Butler had to say about Russell's influence over the Promotion Board and its discrimination against certain officers as fact. He promised to "continue his fight to block" Russell's confirmation. Butler's letter to Senator Johnson failed to make an impression; he persisted in supporting Russell.[57] Russell received the confirmation and thus became the permanent head of the Corps. During his tenure he pushed through a revised version of officer promotions similar to what the Navy had used for years, then focused on other things such as developing the Fleet Marine Force. After his retirement at the age of sixty-four he became a newspaper columnist who wrote about military affairs.[58]

With this fight lost, Butler continued his antiwar crusade and his theme of war as a racket. In November 1935 he produced one of his most oft-quoted pieces, "'In Time of Peace': The Army." It appeared in a socialist-sympathizing magazine called *Common Sense*. In it he declared, "I was a racketeer for capitalism." He called himself "a high-class muscle man for Big Business, for Wall Street and for the bankers." Although the piece was filled with some inaccuracies and outright exaggerations, its most poignant paragraph did summarize much of what he and his Marines had done during his career:

> Thus I helped make Mexico and especially Tampico safe for American oil interests in 1914. [He had gone to Veracruz, not Tampico, and then only to seize its customs house, not any oil fields.] I helped make Haiti and Cuba a decent place for the National City Bank boys to collect revenues in. I helped in the raping of half a dozen Central American republics for the benefit of Wall Street. The record of racketeering is long. I helped purify Nicaragua for the international banking house of Brown Brothers in 1909–12. I brought light to the Dominican Republic for American sugar interests in 1916. [He had done no such thing.] I helped make Honduras "right" for the American fruit companies in 1903. [These businesses had nothing to do with this conflict, one fought over a disputed election in which both presidential candidates just wanted power for themselves.] In China in 1927 I helped see to it that Standard Oil went its way unmolested.[59]

The article further accused the War Department of planning for offensive instead of defensive wars despite its claims to the contrary. Butler believed that to say the United States only fought defensive wars flew in the face of American history: the unprovoked attacks on the American Indians, Filipinos, Mexicans and Spanish demonstrated that. Butler accused the Army of creating plans to launch an attack against Russia from Alaska, and of drawing up invasion plans for Canada (quite true). Butler went on to say that the military used its domestic intelligence units to go on "Red-hunting" expeditions, often with the cooperation of right-wing businessmen like William Randolph Hearst or groups such as the American Vigilantes. Military intelligence units planted their own men in these organizations to keep a closer eye on them,[60] tactics used by the FBI and other government agencies during the anti–communist atmosphere of the 1950s.

The War Department created dummy orders for materials in case of war in order to gain the support of the industries that stood to make money off armed conflict. Industries themselves refused to provide any materials to America's armed forces if Congress imposed a price cap on what they could charge. Butler suggested that to solve all these problems, the Army and its Air Corps must dedicate themselves exclusively to defensive plans rather than offensive ones.[61] While his rhetoric would evolve over the next few years, this summed up most what he had to say on the matter.

On June 20, 1936, his mother died at the age of 80. Because of his closeness to her, he experienced the same emptiness he felt when his father had passed away. His mother left most of her estate of $28,800 to her three sons. The remaining amount went into a trust for her grandchildren. She had passed away at the home of Samuel Butler, her middle son.[62] The value of her estate appeared in the papers. This attracted the attention of at least one criminal desperate enough to try to get a piece of it for himself. The criminal in question wrote "a note" to Sam Butler demanding $3,000, or else he would kidnap Sam's two children. Sam immediately sent his children to the safety of relatives living in West Chester, Pennsylvania, then contacted the police. To make the payment, Sam had "to board an eastbound Texas & Pacific passenger train and at some point [he] would be notified to drop the satchel of money from the observation coach." At a stop in Cisco, a man instructed him to throw the bag of money out a window when he received a predetermined signal.[63]

"Between Eastland and El Paso" Sam saw the signal and threw it from the train. A state policeman immediately fired a flare out of a window, but this spooked the extortionist, and he failed to show. Undeterred, law enforcement officials searched for the fellow.[64] They arrested Frederick E. Mahan, a thirty-eight-year-old unemployed laborer. A judge set his bail for $1,000. Mahan declared his innocence and could not understand why the police had picked on him: "When those federals went to work on the case, they had to strike at somebody. I don't see why it had to be me."[65]

Butler's politics continued to evolve as his retirement lengthened. Despite German and Japanese aggression, he advocated isolationism, a position often criticized in historic hindsight but one supported by the majority of Americans before the bombing of Pearl Harbor.[66] Butler opposed overseas wars because he did not believe Americans should throw their lives away for conflicts in which they had no personal interest. He saw neither the Germans nor the Japanese as a real threat to U.S. interests.[67] He reckoned that even if Germany conquered all of Europe, it still lacked the ability to invade America. To pull such a thing off, Germany would need a minimum of one million men. Each man would require seven tons of baggage. Without 400,000 vehicles plus the gasoline to fuel them, they could go nowhere. A lack of harbors would force the Germans to operate 1,500 miles from their home bases, an impossibility. Nor would establishing bases in South America do them any good: this would increase the number of miles they had to cross to reach the United States, not reduce them. No airplane had the capability to fly from Germany to America and back, and even if one existed, America's air forces would stop it.[68] By now Butler had become a dedicated pacifist and his desire for isolationism came solely from this conviction, although he had no problem with fighting in self-defense; he once said that if the Germans did manage to land on America's beaches, he would be the first one there defending them.[69]

Not all isolationists had such noble sentiments. Charles Lindbergh, the aviator who had made the first solo flight across the Atlantic, believed going to the defense of Europeans would open up attacks from non–white races and possibly lead to the usurping of white dominance of the world. Fortunately for the Europeans, the most powerful man in America, President Roosevelt, opposed isolationism despite having campaigned in 1938 to preserve American neutrality. After winning reelection on this platform, he pushed through legislation such as the Lend-Lease Act that set America on the path toward interventionism.[70]

In 1938, when Congress considered a billion-dollar spending bill to build up the Navy, Butler opposed it. He said the Navy's size did not need increasing. If Japan, for example, decided to attack America, we should abandon Alaska and Puerto Rico, then blow up the Panama Canal. If the United States formed a cordon around its coasts complete with 20,000 tons of battleships and submarines, the Japanese navy would have no chance of reaching American shores. The Navy did not need those ships: "I have a feeling," he testified, "that this bill does not represent a consensus of opinion among naval officers. I have a feeling that it is a grand bluff.... I cannot prove it, but I believe it is proposed for the purpose of doing somebody else's business"—the war profiteers and their racket.[71]

In an article he wrote titled "Amendment for Peace" for *Women's Home Companion*—an appropriate venue, for here he wanted to appeal to mothers nervous about sending their sons off to war — he proposed another constitutional amendment, this one forbidding "the removal of members of the land armed forces from within the continental limits of the United States and the Panama Canal Zone" save for missions of mercy. Nor could U.S. naval vessels go any farther than five hundred miles from the American coast. That went for military aircraft of any sort as well. In this piece, he changed his mind about giving up Hawaii and Alaska; since they had territorial status, the United States had an obligation to defend them.[72]

Butler never stopped his personal crusade for what he believed. Going to the far left, he voted for Norman Thomas of the Socialist Party for president in 1936.[73] In 1940 he continued lecturing despite ill health. At the end of his last lecture tour he stopped in Texas to visit his brother Sam, who became increasingly worried as he watched his brother "popping aspirin like candy" to stave off intense internal pain. Sam wrote a letter to brother Horace urging him to get Smedley to go to a hospital for an examination. Smedley did so on May 26, checking into the Naval Hospital at Philadelphia "for a general check up." Although no one ever told him, he had pancreatic cancer,[74] a disease often

fatal even in our era of high-tech medicine. Butler had no warning as to its coming. It strikes fast and its symptoms of weight loss, possible jaundice, abdominal pain, nausea, vomiting and "unexpected depression" show up only after it has spread to other parts of the body.[75]

He died on June 21, 1940, just over a month short of his fifty-ninth birthday, with his wife and children beside him. The family had his body removed to his Newtown Square house. They placed his open coffin, "buried in hundreds of floral tributes sent from all over the country and from abroad," in the study. Several Marines stood as an honor guard.

A 1938 press photograph of General Smedley D. Butler testifying before the Senate Naval Affairs Committee in which he said that the newly proposed navy should not be built. From the Smedley D. Butler Collection, courtesy of the Marine Corps Archives and Special Collections Department at the Gray Research Center, Quantico.

Two of them, one standing at the coffin's head and other at its foot, closed the casket. The pallbearers, who included Butler's sons, his son-in-law, his brother Sam, a brother-in-law and several cousins, took the coffin into the great hall, which the family decorated with all his memorabilia including his two Blessing Umbrellas, complete with streamers. The family stood on the balcony above to view the service held below. Many of his old friends attended, including Vandegrift and thirty Philadelphia police officers. The Rev. Doctor Frederick

R. Griffin, a Unitarian minister, and Doctor William T. Sharpless, "a laymember [*sic*] of the Society of Friends" from West Chester, gave eulogies. The family had the coffin taken to Oakland Cemetery in West Chester to a plot beside his parents and other relatives. They buried him "at the foot of an ancient oak" and held a brief private ceremony for family members.[76] He left a estate worth $2,000.[77]

Chapter Notes

Abbreviations:
SDB: Smedley Darlington Butler
TSB: Thomas Stalker Butler — Smedley's Father
MMB: Maud Mary (Darlington) Butler — Smedley's Mother
ECB: Ethel Conway (Peters) Butler — Smedley's Wife

Databases: In days past finding old newspaper, magazine, and journal articles often involved going through reels of microfilm. In our modern age much of this material has moved into databases. Those I used are listed immediately below, along with their home page URL's:

EBSCO databases: http://www.ebscohost.com
Newspaper AccessARCHIVE database: http://access.newspaperarchive.com
ProQuest Historical Newspapers: The New York Times (1851–2005) database:
http://proquest.umi.com
LexisNexis database: https://www.lexisnexis.com

Preface

1. SDB, "'In Time of Peace:' The Army," *Common Sense*, November 1935, 8.

Chapter 1

1. C.W. Heathcote, Sr., and Lucile Shenk, ed., *A History of Chester County, Pennsylvania* (Harrisburg, PA: National Historical Association, 1932), 1.

2. "Latest News," *Chester Daily Times*, July 30, 1881, 1, in *Newspaper AccessARCHIVE* database (accessed August 26, 2009).

3. Edith Wehle, telephone conversation with author, May 15, 2010.

4. Patrick Hanks, ed., *Dictionary of American Family Names, O–Z*, vol. 3 (Oxford & New York: Oxford University Press, 2003), 366.

5. Butler Family Association, *The Butler Family: Noble Butler of Pennsylvania, Ancestors & Descendents* (self-published, 1982), 204.

6. An example: Letter from Fred Lewis to SDB, October 2, 1933, Box 31, folder 9, Smedley D. Butler Papers, Marine Corps Archives and Special Collections, Gray Research Center, Quantico, Virginia.

7. "Smedley Butler of Marines Dead," *The New York Times*, June 22, 1940, 34, in *ProQuest* database (accessed March 31, 2008); *The Butler Family* lists Maud Mary Darlington's birth date as July 3, 1855, and Thomas's as November 4, 1854 (which contradicts the one listed in several obituaries), 204.

8. Butler Family Association, *The Butler Family*, 205.

9. Heathcote and Shenk, ed., *A History of Chester County, Pennsylvania*, 69.

10. Butler Family Association, *The Butler Family*, 302–303.

11. "Texas Auto Crash Toll 4," *The New York Times*, February 15, 1930, in *ProQuest* database (accessed March 31, 2008).

12. Butler Family Association, *The Butler Family*, 302.

13. "Fisherman Finds Bodies Beside Lake," *The Abilene Reporter-News*, October 16, 1947, 1, in *Newspaper AccessARCHIVE* database (accessed August 27, 2009).

14. "Two Oil Men Shot to Death," *Evening Journal*, October 16, 1947, 1, in *Newspaper*

AccessARCHIVE database (accessed August 27, 2009).

15. "T.S. Butler Dies in Capital Hotel," *The New York Times*, May 27, 1928, 3, in *ProQuest* database (accessed March 31, 2008); "House Veteran Dies, Victim of Heart Disease," *Decatur Herald*, May 27, 1928, 1, in *Newspaper AccessARCHIVE* database (accessed August 17, 2008).

16. William Wistar Comfort, *Quakers in the Modern World* (New York: Macmillan, 1949), 54–55.

17. High Barbour and J. William Frost, *The Quakers* (Westport, CT: Greenwood Press, 1988), 175, 186.

18. Lowell Thomas, *Old Gimlet Eye: The Adventures of Smedley D. Butler as Told to Lowell Thomas* (New York: Farrar & Rinehart, 1933), 4–5.

19. Comfort, *Quakers in the Modern World*, 80, 124, 130.

20. Erza Kempton Maxfield, "Quaker 'Thee' and Its History," *American Speech*, 1:12 (September 1926): 638, 641, in *JSTOR* database (accessed June 29, 2008).

21. Thomas, *Old Gimlet Eye*, 3–4.

22. See, for example, *Congressional Record*, 64th Cong., vol. 53, part 3, 1st sess., 1916, 2241–2243.

23. Molly Swanton, e-mail to author, September 5, 2009.

24. Comfort, *Quakers in the Modern World*, 196.

25. Swanton, e-mail to author, September 5, 2009.

26. Eunice M. Lyon, "The Unpublished Papers of Major General Smedley Darlington Butler, United States Marine Corps: A Calendar" (PhD diss., Catholic University of America, 1962), 5.

27. "T.S. Butler Dies in Capital Hotel," *The New York Times*, 3.

28. Butler Family Association, *The Butler Family*, 298.

29. Thomas, *Old Gimlet Eye*, 5.

30. Samuel McCoy, "Philadelphia at War Over General Butler," *The New York Times*, July 27, 1924, XX3, in *ProQuest* database (accessed March 31, 2008).

31. Hans Schmidt, *Maverick Marine: General Smedley Darlington Butler and the Contradictions of American Military History* (Lexington: University of Kentucky Press, 1987), 7.

32. Thomas, *Old Gimlet Eye*, 5–6.

33. John L. Offner, *An Unwanted War: The Diplomacy of the United States and Spain Over Cuba, 1895–1898* (Chapel Hill: University of North Carolina Press), 122–123.

34. Ivan Musicant, *Empire by Default: The Spanish-American War and the Dawn of the American Century* (New York: Henry Holt, 1998), 143.

35. Quoted in Musicant, *Empire by Default*, 144.

36. "The *Maine*," *The New York Times*, February 17, 1898, 6, in *ProQuest* database (accessed August 23, 2009).

37. Graham A. Cosmas, "From Order to Chaos: The War Department, The National Guard, and Military Policy, 1898," *Military Affairs*, 29:3 (Autumn 1965): 105, in *JSTOR* database (accessed December 14, 2008).

38. Thomas, *Old Gimlet Eye*, 7.

39. Offner, *An Unwanted War*, 116–117, 122–123.

40. Adam Scher, "Remembering America's 'Splendid Little War': Spanish-American War Collections at the Minnesota Historical Society," *Minnesota History*, 56:3 (Fall 1998): 130, in *JSTOR* database (accessed June 13, 2010).

41. Louis A. Pérez, Jr., "The Meaning of the *Maine*: Causation and the Historiography of the Spanish-American War," *The Pacific Historical Review*, 58:3 (August 1989): 303, in *JSTOR* database (accessed June 13, 2010).

42. Scher, "Remembering America's 'Splendid Little War,'" 131.

43. "Spain to Use Privateers," *The New York Times*, April 25, 1898, 1, and William McKinley, "The Declaration of War," *The New York Times*, April 26, 1898, 3, in *ProQuest* database (accessed June 13, 2010).

44. Stanley Karnow, *In Our Image: America's Empire in the Philippines* (New York: Random House, 1989), 88.

45. Offner, *An Unwanted War*, 2.

46. Karnow, *In Our Image*, 88.

47. Offner, *An Unwanted War*, 3.

48. Karnow, *In Our Image*, 88.

49. Julius W. Pratt, "American Business and the Spanish-American War," *The Hispanic American Historical Review*, 14:2 (May 1934): 163–164, in *JSTOR* database (accessed July 31, 2008).

50. Pratt, "American Business and the Spanish-American War," 173, 175, 178 ("a memorial on…," 175).

51. Offner, *An Unwanted War*, 117.

52. "Smedley Butler of Marines Dead," *The New York Times*, 34.

53. United States Department of Commerce, *Historical Statistics of the United States: Colonial Times to 1970*, Bicentennial Edition, part 2 (Washington, D.C.: U.S. Government Printing Office, 1976), 1141; Thomas, *Old Gimlet Eye*, 7.

54. Thomas, *Old Gimlet Eye*, 7–8.

55. "Military History of Smedley D. Butler, U.S. Marine Corps, Retired," November 8, 1933, Military Personnel File, National Archives, St. Louis, MO.

56. "T.S. Butler Dies in Capital Hotel," *The New York Times*, May 27, 1928, 3.

57. Jack Murphy, *History of the US Marines* (North Dighton, MA: JG Press, 2002), 47.

58. Marrill L. Bartlett and Jack Sweetman, *Leathernecks: An Illustrated History of the U.S. Marine Corps* (Annapolis: Naval Institute Press, 2008), 143–144.

59. Michael Blow, *A Ship to Remember: The Maine and the Spanish-American War* (New York: William Morrow, 1992), 291, 293; Avery Chenoweth with Brooke Nihart, *Semper Fi: The Definitive Illustrated History of the U.S. Marines* (New York & London: Sterling, 2005), 89; *The War of 1898 and U.S. Interventions, 1989–1934*, "Battle of Guantánamo Bay, Cuba," ed. Benjamin R. Beede (New York & London: Garland, 1994), 210.

60. Thomas, *Old Gimlet Eye*, 10, 12–14; "Military History of Smedley D. Butler," Military Personnel File.

61. Thomas, *Old Gimlet Eye*, 15.

62. Ibid., 16–21.

63. Ibid., 22.

64. Jerry Keenman, *Encyclopedia of the Spanish-American and Philippine-American Wars* (Santa Barbara, CA: ABC-CLIO, Inc., 2001), 237–238.

65. Thomas, *Old Gimlet Eye*, 22.

66. Ibid., 25–26.

67. Order from Charles Heywood, commandant of the Marines, to SDB, October 19, 1898, Box 4, folder 4, Smedley D. Butler Papers.

68. "Military History of Smedley D. Butler," Military Personnel File.

69. David T. Zabecki, "Paths to Glory: Medal of Honor Recipients Smedley Butler and Dan Daly," *Military History*, January/February 2008, http://www.historynet.com/paths-to-glory-medal-of-honor-ricipients-smedley-butler-and-dan-daly.htm (accessed May 29, 2008); Bartlett and Sweetman, *Leathernecks*, 151.

70. "Military History of Smedley D. Butler," Military Personnel File.

71. John Tebbel, *America's Great Patriotic War with Spain: Mixed Motives, Lies and Racism in Cuba and the Philippines, 1898–1915* (Manchester Center, VT: Marshall Jones, 1996), 326–237.

72. David J. Silbey, *A War of Frontier and Empire: The Philippine-American War, 1899–1902* (New York: Hill and Wang, 2007), 13–15.

73. Emilio Aguinaldo with Vincent Albano Pacis, *A Second Look at America* (New York: Robert Speller & Sons, 1957), 28–29.

74. Correspondence of the *Baltimore Sun*, "In Manila a Month Ago," *The New York Times*, July 11, 1898, 4, in *ProQuest* database (accessed June 13, 2010).

75. Karnow, *In Our Image*, 110–111.

76. Aguinaldo with Pacis, *A Second Look at America*, 31–34.

77. Karnow, *In Our Image*, 111–112.

78. Aguinaldo with Pacis, *A Second Look at America*, 35–39.

79. Ibid., 57, 60, 100.

80. Tebbel, *America's Great Patriotic War With Spain*, 328.

81. Aguinaldo with Pacis, *A Second Look at America*, 107.

82. Brian M. Linn, "Provincial Pacification in the Philippines, 1900–1901: The First District Department of Northern Luzon," *Military Affairs*, 51: 2 (April 1987): 62–64, in *JSTOR* database (accessed July 3, 2008).

83. "Military History of Smedley D. Butler," Military Personnel File.

84. Thomas, *Old Gimlet Eye*, 29–31 ("quartered in the…," 30; "whose chief occupation…," 31).

85. Letter from SDB to MMB, August 8, 1899, Box 4, unmarked folder, Smedley D. Butler Papers.

86. Thomas, *Old Gimlet Eye*, 32.

87. Ibid., 31–34.

88. Brian McAllister Linn, *The Philippine War, 1899–1902* (Lawrence, KS: University Press of Kansas, 2000), 142–143.

89. "Gen. Schwan's Expedition," *The New York Times*, October 13, 1899, 7, in *ProQuest* database (accessed September 5, 2009).

90. Lt. Col. G.F. Elliott, action report, October 12, 1899, Box 4, unmarked folder, Smedley D. Butler Papers, 1.

91. "Marines Gain a Victory," *The New York Times*, October 9, 1899, 7, in *ProQuest* database (accessed September 5, 2009).

92. Captain H.C. Haines, action report, October 11, 1899, Box 4, unmarked folder, Smedley D. Butler Papers, 1.

93. Thomas, *Old Gimlet Eye*, 34.

94. Letter from Eva Jane Price to "Home Folks," February 14, 1900, and August 1, 1900, reprinted in *China Journal, 1889–1900: An American Missionary Family During the Boxer Rebellion with the Letters and Diaries of Eva Jane Pierce*, ed. Robert H. Felsing (New York: Charles Scribner's Sons, 1989), 216, 235–236 ("If only foreign…," 236).

95. Robert H. Felsing, ed., editorial commentary, *China Journal, 1889–1900*, 238–239.

96. Wehle, telephone conversation with author, May 15, 2010.

97. Thomas, *Old Gimlet Eye*, 39–40.

98. Ibid., 36.

99. Anne Cipriano Venzon, "Littleton Waller Tazewell Waller," in *Leaders of Men: Ten Marines Who Changed the Corps* (Lanham, MD: Scarecrow Press, 2008), 39–46.

100. Thomas, *Old Gimlet Eye*, 41–43 ("Godforsaken island," 41).

Chapter 2

1. "Solace Sails from Manila," *The New York Times*, June 14, 1900, 2, in *ProQuest* database (accessed September 7, 2009).

2. Chester M. Biggs, Jr., *The United States Marines in North China, 1894–1942* (Jefferson, NC: McFarland, 2003), 40–41.

3. "China's Two Great Cities," *The Oxford Mirror*, June 21, 1900, 7, in *Newspaper AccessARCHIVE* database (accessed August 17, 2008).

4. Thomas F. Millard, "A Comparison of the Armies in China," *Scribner's*, July 1, 1914, 79.

5. "The Taku Fortifications," *The New York Times*, June 18, 1900, 3, in *ProQuest* database (accessed September 7, 2009).

6. Jonathan D. Spence, *The Search for Modern China* (New York: W.W. Norton, 1990), 233.

7. Ibid., 233–234.

8. Diana Preston, *The Boxer Rebellion: The Dramatic Story of China's War on Foreigners That Shook the World in the Summer of 1900* (New York: Walker, 1999, 2000), 344.

9. SDB, "Dame Rumor: The Biggest Liar in the World," *The American Magazine*, June 1931, 24.

10. Chester C. Tan, *The Boxer Catastrophe* (New York: Columbia University Press, 1955), 36.

11. Spence, *The Search for Modern China*, 233.

12. Jerome Ch'ên, "The Nature and Characteristics of the Boxer Movement — A Morphological Study," *Bulletin of the School of Oriental and African Studies*, 23:2 (1960): 291, 293, in *JSTOR* database (accessed July 31, 2008); Tan, *The Boxer Catastrophe*, 35.

13. Preston, *The Boxer Rebellion*, xxi–xxii, 29.

14. Tan, *The Boxer Catastrophe*, 11, 33 ("floods, famine, and…," 33); Diana Preston, "The Boxer Rising," *Asian Affairs*, 31:1 (February 2000): 27, in *EBSCO* databases (accessed September 12, 2009).

15. Ch'ên, "The Nature and Characteristics of the Boxer Movement," 295.

16. Tan, *The Boxer Catastrophe*, 47–48, 55.

17. Spence, *The Search for Modern China*, 233.

18. Preston, "The Boxer Rising," 29, 31.

19. Ibid., 31–32.

20. Preston, *The Boxer Rebelliion*, 90.

21. Edward H. Bayly, journal entry, June 10, 1900, reprinted in *China 1900: The Eyewitnesses Speak: The Experience of Westerners in China During the Boxer Rebellion, as Described by Participants in Letters, Diaries and Photographs*, ed. Frederic A. Sharf and Peter Harrington (Mechanicsburg, PA: Stackpole Books, 2000), 102.

22. Preston, "The Boxer Rising," 31–32.

23. "Admiral Seymour's Report," *The New York Times*, June 30, 1900, 1, in *ProQuest* database (accessed September 9, 2009).

24. Ibid.

25. SDB, "Dame Rumor," 24.

26. Ibid.

27. "China's Two Great Cities," *The Oxford Mirror*, 7.

28. Biggs Jr., *The United States Marines in North China*, 47.

29. Herbert Hoover, *The Memoirs of Herbert Hoover: Years of Adventure, 1874–1920*, (London: Hollis & Carter, 1952), 35–37.

30. Ibid., 48; Preston, *The Boxer Rebellion*, 107.

31. Hoover, *The Memoirs of Herbert Hoover*, 35–37.

32. Biggs Jr., *The United States Marines in North China*, 47.

33. Waller, reports, June 22, 1900 and June 28, 1900, Box 4, folder 1, Smedley D. Butler Papers.

34. Waller, report, June 28, 1900.

35. Letter from SDB to MMB, July 2, 1900, reprinted in *General Smedley Darlington Butler: The Letters of a Leatherneck*, ed. Anne Cipriano Venzon (New York & Westport, Connecticut & London: Praeger, 1992), 19.

36. Waller, report, June 22, 1900; SDB to MMB, July 2, 1900, reprinted in *The Letters of a Leatherneck*, 19–20; the complete list of names of those who participated in the rescue of Private Carter came form a footnote in *The Letters of a Leatherneck*, 20.

37. Letter from SDB to MMB, July 2, 1900, 20.

38. Thomas, *Old Gimlet Eye*, 49–50.

39. Biggs, Jr., *The United States Marines in North China*, 42–43.

40. Ibid., 43.

41. Letter from SDB to MMB, July 2, 1900, 18.

42. Thomas, *Old Gimlet Eye*, 51–52 ("on the honor…," 51; "barber's itch … howling toothache," 52).

43. Ibid., 52–53 ("'You ought to …,'" 53).

44. "The Relief Force Enters Tien-Tsin," *The New York Times*, June 26, 1900, 1, in *ProQuest* database (accessed September 9, 2009).

45. Preston, *The Boxer Rebellion*, 101–102 ("who tied him…," 102).

46. Thomas, *Old Gimlet Eye*, 56–57.

47. Spence, *The Search for Modern China*, 219.

48. Letter from SDB to MMB, July 5, 1900, reprinted in *The Letters of a Leatherneck*, 21–22.

49. Thomas, *Old Gimlet Eye*, 58–59.

50. Biggs, Jr., *The United States Marines in North China*, 55, 57; Preston, *The Boxer Rebellion*, 184–185 ("canals, irrigation channels…," 185).

51. Hoover, *The Memoirs of Herbert Hoover*, 53.

52. Preston, *The Boxer Rebellion*, 184.

53. Biggs Jr., *The United States Marines in North China*, 57.

54. Ibid., 57–58.

55. Letter from SDB to MMB, July 23, 1900, reprinted in *The Letters of a Leatherneck*, 24.

56. A.R.F. Dorward, letter to Commander of All U.S. Forces, July 15, 1900, Box 1, folder 1, Smedley D. Butler Papers.

57. Robert B. Asprey, *Once a Marine: The Memoirs of General A.A. Vandegrift as Told to Robert B. Asprey* (New York: W.W. Norton, 1964), 30.

58. Thomas, *Old Gimlet Eye*, 63–65.

59. "Defeat at Tientsin," *The Anaconda Standard*, July 19, 1900, 1, in *Newspaper AccessARCHIVE* database (accessed September 13, 2009).

60. Joseph Mulvaney, "The Fightin'est Marine Passes," *The San Antonio Light*, July 7, 1940, 37, in *Newspaper AccessARCHIVE* database, (accessed March 31, 2008); Thomas, *Old Gimlet Eye*, 64–65.

61. "Military History of Smedley D. Butler" and "Synopsis of Military History of Brigadier General Smedley D. Butler, Marine Corps," March 5, 1921, Military Personnel File, National Archives, St. Louis, MO.

62. Preston, *The Boxer Rebellion*, 186.

62. "Scene Was Fearful," *Des Moines Daily News*, August 29, 1900, 1, in *Newspaper AccessARCHIVE* database (accessed September 14, 2009).

64. "Defeat at Tientsin," *The Anaconda Standard*, 1.

65. Ibid.

66. Michael H. Hunt, "The Forgotten Occupation: Peking, 1900–1901," *The Pacific Historical Review*, 48:4 (November 1979): 503–504, in *JSTOR* database (accessed September 9, 2009).

67. Paul A. Varg, "The Foreign Policy of Japan and the Boxer Revolt," *The Pacific Historical Review*, 15:3 (September 1946): 279, 285, in *JSTOR* database (accessed September 9, 2009).

68. Letter from SDB to MMB, August 4, 1900, reprinted *The Letters of a Leatherneck*, 25–26.

69. Millard, "A Comparison of the Armies in China," 79.

70. Letter from SDB to MMB, August 4, 1900, reprinted *The Letters of a Leatherneck*, 25–26; Thomas, *Old Gimlet Eye*, 69.

71. Millard, "A Comparison of the Armies in China," 83, 81.

72. Biggs Jr., *The United States Marines in North China*, 123.

73. Millard, "A Comparison of the Armies in China," 80.

74. Preston, *The Boxer Rebellion*, 4–10.

75. Ibid., 228–299.

76. Ibid., 241.

77. W.P. Biddle, letter and report, August 20, 1900, and Waller, report, August 20, 1900, Box 1, folder 1, Smedley D. Butler Papers.

78. Letter from SDB to MMB, August 19, 1900, reprinted in *The Letters of a Leatherneck*, and Venzon, editorial note, 28; Thomas, *Old Gimlet Eye*, 73–74.

79. Waller, report, August 20, 1900.

80. Letter from SDB to MMB, August 19, 1900, 27; Thomas, *Old Gimlet Eye*, 73–74.

81. Felsing, editorial notes, *China Journal, 1889–1900*, 241.

82. "Still Fighting in Peking," *The New York Times*, August 20, 1900, 1, in *ProQuest* database (accessed September 17, 2009).

83. "European Barbarism in China," *The New York Times*, October 2, 1900, 8, in *ProQuest* database (accessed October 18, 2008).

84. "Looting in Peking," *The New York Times*, September 1, 1900, 2, in *ProQuest Historical* database (accessed September 17, 2009).

85. Thomas, *Old Gimlet Eye*, 76.

86. "European Barbarism in China," *The New York Times*, 2.

87. Thomas, *Old Gimlet Eye*, 78–79.

88. Jacqueline L. Longe, ed., *The Gale Encyclopedia of Medicine: T–Z, Organizations General Index*, vol. 5, 3rd ed. (Detroit, et al.: Thomas Gale, 2006), 3825.

89. SDB, "Dame Rumor," 26; Jules Archer, *The Plot to Seize the White House: The Shocking True Story of the Conspiracy to Overthrow FDR* (New York: Hawthorn Books, 1973), 47.

Chapter 3

1. This description is based on photos, a variety of contemporary accounts, and information provided by SDB's granddaughter, Molly Swanton.

2. Letter from SDB to Charles Hunt, August 12, 1916, and letter from SDB to Colonel Cyrus S. Radford, November 8, 1921, reprinted in "The Unpublished Papers of Major General Smedley Darlington Butler," 156.

3. Wehle, telephone conversation with author, May 15, 2010.

4. Letter from Andrew Schoader to SDB, November 15, 1934, Box 34, folder 4, Smedley D. Butler Papers.

5. Letter from SDB to Chester E. Linden, September 13, 1933, Box 31, folder 9, Smedley D. Butler Papers.

6. Thomas, *Old Gimlet Eye*, 83, 78.

7. Bartlett and Sweetman, *Leathernecks*, 143.

8. Venzon, "Henry Clay Cochrane," in *Leaders of Men*, 38.

9. Thomas, *Old Gimlet Eye*, 84–85 ("shirts, underclothes and socks," 84).

10. Ibid., 86–93.

11. Venzon, editorial commentary, *The Letters of a Leatherneck*, 31.

12. T. Cuyler Smith, "The Charleston Exposition," *The Independent*, January 16, 1902, 142–144.

13. Venzon, editorial commentary, *The Letters of a Leatherneck*, 32.

14. Thomas, *Old Gimlet Eye*, 94–95.

15. Letter from SDB to MMB, November 29, 1902, reprinted in *The Letters of a Leatherneck*, 33–34.

16. Thomas, *Old Gimlet Eye*, 95–96, 98.

17. Ibid., 99; letter from SDB to MMB, December 14, 1902, reprinted in *The Letters of a Leatherneck*, 35.

18. *Mosby's Medical Dictionary*, 7th ed. (St. Louis, Missouri: Mosby/Elsevier, 2006), 351.

19. Thomas, *Old Gimlet Eye*, 100–101 ("raised hell with…," 101).

20. Letter from SDB to MMB, December 14, 1902, reprinted in *The Letters of a Leatherneck*, 35.

21. Thomas, *Old Gimlet Eye*, 102, 104.

22. "Honduran Muddle Worse," *The New York Times*, January 30, 1903, 6, and untitled article, *The New York Times*, February 4, 1903, 1, in

ProQuest database (accessed September 20, 2009).

23. "The War in Honduras: Bonilla's Forces Have Every Fort on East Coast," *Davenport Daily Republican*, March 28, 1903, 1, in *Newspaper AccessARCHIVE* database (accessed August 17, 2008).

24. Letter from SDB to MMB, March 20, 1903, reprinted in *The Letters of a Leatherneck*, 39.

25. "Bonilla Defeats Sierra," *Eau Claire Leader*, March 27, 1903, 1, in *Newspaper AccessARCHIVE* database (accessed September 20, 2009).

26. Thomas, *Old Gimlet Eye*, 112–113.

27. SDB, "'In Time of Peace:' The Army," 12.

28. Alison Acker, *Honduras: The Making of a Banana Republic* (Boston: South End Press, 1988), 62–64, 60.

29. Schmidt, *Maverick Marine*, 32.

30. Venzon, "Smedley Darlington Butler," in *Leaders of Men*, 152.

31. Roy Porter, *The Greatest Benefit to Mankind: A Medical History of Humanity* (New York: W.W. Norton, 1998), 294.

32. Albert S. Lyons and R. Joseph Petrucelli, *Medicine: An Illustrated History* (New York: H.N. Abrams, 1978), 503, 561.

33. Ibid., 503, 561.

34. For a discussion of this, see Elihu Thomson, "The Progress of the Isthmian Canal," *Proceedings of the American Philosophical Society*, 46:185 (January–April 1907): 133–134, in *JSTOR* database (accessed April 1, 1910).

35. Ovidio Diaz Espino, *How Wall Street Created a Nation: J.P. Morgan, Teddy Roosevelt, and the Panama Canal* (New York & London: Four Walls Eight Windows, 2001), 11–12.

36. Lars Schoultz, *Beneath the United States: A History of U.S. Policy Toward Latin America* (Cambridge, MA: Harvard University Press, 1998), 164, 160.

37. Espino, *How Wall Street Created a Nation*, 51.

38. Ibid., 51–52.

39. Schoultz, *Beneath the United States*, 166–169.

40. Henry J. Hendrix II, "TR's Plan to Invade Colombia," *Naval History*, 20:6 (December 2006), in *EBSCO* databases (accessed November 14, 2008).

41. John A. Garraty and Mark C. Carnes, ed., "John Archer Lejeune," *American National Biography*, vol. 13 (New York: Oxford University Press, 1999), 461.

42. "Synopsis of Military History of Brigadier General Smedley D. Butler," Military Personnel File.

43. SDB, "Dame Rumor," 26.

44. Ibid.

45. "Synopsis of Military History of Brigadier General Smedley D. Butler," Military Personnel File.

46. Venzon, "Smedley Darlington Butler," in *Leaders of Men*, 153.

47. Schmidt, *Maverick Marine*, 33.

48. Swanton, e-mail to author, September 5, 2009 ("it was well…"); Venzon, "Smedley Darlington Butler," in *Leaders of Men*, 155; Butler Family Association, *The Butler Family*, 300.

49. G.F. Elliott to SDB, order, May 4, 1905, Box 4, folder 4, Smedley D. Butler Papers.

50. Venzon, "Smedley Darlington Butler," in *Leaders of Men*, 153.

51. Letter from SDB to MMB, October 5, 1905, reprinted in *Letters of a Leatherneck*, 50–51 ("modern buildings and…," 50; "the prettiest place…," 51).

52. "Why Congress Should Rush Work on a Stronghold in the Philippines," *The Washington Post*, January 12, 1908, Magazine Section, 1, in *Newspaper AccessARCHIVE* database (accessed September 22, 2009).

53. Thomas, *Old Gimlet Eye*, 114–116.

54. Letter from SDB to unnamed superior, November 21, 1906, Box 4, folder 3, Smedley D. Butler Papers.

55. Thomas, *Old Gimlet Eye*, 116–117.

56. SDB to U.S. Patent Office, 1907, Smedley D. Butler Papers, 1–2.

57. "Rush Work on Forts," *The Daily Times*, July 6, 1907, 6, in *Newspaper AccessARCHIVE* database (accessed September 22, 2009).

58. Thomas, *Old Gimlet Eye*, 118–119.

59. Ibid., 119–120.

60. Ibid., 120–121 ("high altitude and…," 121).

61. G.F. Elliott to SDB, order, January 9, 1908, Box 4, folder 4, Smedley D. Butler Papers.

62. Thomas, *Old Gimlet Eye*, 120–121.

63. Charles Smith, *Fire Creek: A New River Gorge Mining Community* (Glen Jean, WV: Gem, 1999), ii, 8, 64.

64. "Smedley Butler of Marines Dead," *The New York Times*, 34.

65. Thomas, *Old Gimlet Eye*, 121–122.

66. Ibid., 122–123 ("might as well…," 123).

67. Elliott to SDB, order, September 24, 1908, Box 4, folder 4, Smedley D. Butler Papers.

68. "Military History of Smedley D. Butler," Military Personnel File.

69. Mulvaney, "The Fightin'est Marine Passes," 37.

70. Letter from C.J. Stokes to SDB, November 28, 1911, Box 4, folder 10, Smedley D. Butler Papers.

71. SDB, "Organization of Camp Management and Sanitation in Effect at the Marine Barracks, Camp Eliott," April 15, 1910–February 26, 1912, Box 5, folder 1, Smedley D. Butler Papers.

72. Asprey, *Once a Marine*, 37–38, 42 ("the value of … not by words…," 42; "he scratched his…," 37).

73. SDB, reports, Box 4, folders 4 and 10, Smedley D. Butler Papers.

74. Thomas, *Old Gimlet Eye*, 135–137.

75. "How the Canal Zone is Governed," *Lowell Sun*, July 22, 1912, 21, in *Newspaper AccessARCHIVE* database (accessed August 17, 2008).
76. Venzon, "Littleton Waller Tazewell Waller," in *Leaders of Men*, 57.
77. Bartlett and Sweetman, *Leathernecks*, 158–159.
78. Michael D. Haydock, "Marine Scapegoat," *Military History*, 18:6 (February 2002): 51, in *EBSCO* databases (accessed September 5, 2009).
79. Ibid.
80. Ibid., 52.
81. "Taft Quits Zone for His Home," *Daily Gazette*, December 26, 1912, 1, in *Newspaper AccessARCHIVE* database (accessed September 24, 2009).
82. Thomas, *Old Gimlet Eye*, 134–135 ("took care of...," 135).
83. "Will Smedley Butler Sniff More Powder in China?" *The Literary Digest*, April 2, 1927, 42.
84. "How the Canal Zone is Governed," *Lowell Sun*, 21.
85. Thomas, *Old Gimlet Eye*, 134.
86. Beverly Rae Kimes, *Standard Catalog of American Cars, 1805–1942*, 3rd ed. (Iola, WI: Krause, 1996), 33–34 ("'A Car for ...,'" quoted on 34; "Unfortunately there weren't...," 34).
87. Thomas, *Old Gimlet Eye*, 134.
88. Butler Family Association, *The Butler Family*, 451, 301.

Chapter 4

1. SDB, "'In Time of Peace:' The Army,'" *Common Sense*, 8.
2. Anna I. Powell, "Relations Between the United States and Nicaragua, 1898–1916," *The Hispanic American Historical Review*, 8:1 (February 1928): 45, in *JSTOR* database (accessed July 31, 2008).
3. Michael Gismondi and Jeremy Mouat, "Merchants, Mining, and Concessions on Nicaragua's Mosquito Coast: Reassessing the American Presence, 1895–1912," *Journal of Latin American Studies*, 34:4 (November 2002): 849–850, in *JSTOR* database (accessed March 22, 2008).
4. Powell, "Relations Between the United States and Nicaragua," 45.
5. Gismondi and Mouat, "Merchants, Mining, and Concessions on Nicaragua's Mosquito Coast," 854–855.
6. Ibid., 855–856.
7. Stephen Kinzer, *Overthrow: America's Century of Regime Change from Hawaii to Iraq* (New York: Henry Holt, 2006), 64–67 ("to Knox's surprise...," 65).
8. Ibid., 66–67.
9. Powell, "Relations Between the United States and Nicaragua," 48.
10. Ibid., 48–49.
11. Thomas, *Old Gimlet Eye*, 126.
12. Letter from SDB to MMB and TSB, January 2, 1910, and letter from SDB to ECB and his children, January 22, 1910, reprinted in *The Letters of a Leatherneck*, 66–67.
13. SDB, report on El Realejo-Chinendeya Road, January 7, 1910, Box 4, folder 6, Smedley D. Butler Papers.
14. Letter from SDB to ECB, January 22, 1910, reprinted in *The Letters of a Leatherneck*, 67–68 ("Good looking native...," 67).
15. Ibid., 67–68 (mental notes ... extreme innocence ... apologized profusely," 68).
16. Letter from SDB to ECB, February 7, 1910, reprinted in *The Letters of a Leatherneck*, 69–70.
17. Ibid., 70–71 ("who ... Spanish like a...," 70).
18. Ibid., 71–72 ("canvas bunks and...," 71).
19. Ibid., 72–74 ("vile lunch ... the most desirable...," 72).
20. Letter from SDB to MMB and TSB, January 2, 1910, reprinted in *The Letters of a Leatherneck*, 65–66.
21. Letter from SDB to MMB and TSB, March 1, 1910, reprinted in *The Letters of a Leatherneck*, 75–78 ("What makes me...," 75–76; "The whole game...," 77).
22. Gismondi and Mouat, "Merchants, Mining, and Concessions on Nicaragua's Mosquito Coast," 867.
23. Captain R.M. Gilson, intelligence report on Bluefields, Nicaragua, 1910, Box 4, folder 7, Smedley D. Butler Papers.
24. "Our Conflict with Nicaragua," *Current Literature*, October 1912, 378.
25. "Official Decree From Nicaragua Forbidding Vessels Enter Bluefield," *Lowell Sun*, June 2, 1910, 24, in *Newspaper AccessARCHIVE* database (accessed August 17, 2008).
26. Letter from SDB to MMB, June 4, 1910, reprinted *The Letters of a Leatherneck*, 82; Thomas, *Old Gimlet Eye*, 127.
27. Letter from SDB to MMB, June 4, 1910, reprinted in *The Letters of a Leatherneck*, 84–85.
28. Letters from SDB to TSB, June 10, 1910, and June 14, 1910, reprinted in *The Letters of a Leatherneck*, 86–88 ("to stop this...," 86).
29. "'Death to 'Yankees': Mobs Menace Americans in Capital of Nicaragua," *The Washington Post*, August 22, 1910, 1, in *Newspaper AccessARCHIVE* database (accessed August 17, 2008).
30. Thomas, *Old Gimlet Eye*, 131–132.
31. "No Indictments: No One Accused of Burning of Antonio Rodriguez at Rock Springs," *Advocate*, December 24, 1910, 1, in *Newspaper AccessARCHIVE* database (accessed August 18, 2008).
32. Frederick C. Turner, "Anti-Americanism in Mexico, 1910–1913," *The Hispanic American Historical Review*, 47:4 (November 1967): 505–506, in *JSTOR* database (accessed July 31, 2008).
33. "Nicaragua Fuss Grows Serious," *The Ana-*

conda Standard, August 29, 1912, 4, in Newspaper AccessARCHIVE database (accessed September 28, 2009).

34. "Our Conflict with Nicaragua," Current Literature, 377–378.

35. "Estrada a Fugitive," The New York Times, May 11, 1911, 1 (accessed June 27, 2010); "Aid for Nicaragua Asked by Estrada," The New York Times, September 10, 1912, 4, in ProQuest database (accessed September 27, 2009).

36. "Another Nicaragua Revolt," The New York Times, August 1, 1912, 5, in ProQuest database (accessed September 27, 2009).

37. Michel Gobat, Confronting the American Dream: Nicaragua Under U.S. Imperial Rule (Durham & London: Duke University Press, 2005), 111, 117, 113.

38. SDB, report on his battalion's activities in Nicaragua, August 10–September 5, 1912, Box 5, folder 4, Smedley D. Butler Papers, 1.

39. Letter from SDB to MMB, August 11,1912, reprinted in The Letters of a Leatherneck, 99–100.

40. SDB, report, August 10–September 5, 1912, 2.

41. Letter from SDB to MMB, August 11, 1912, reprinted The Letters of a Leatherneck, 100–101.

42. SDB, report, August 10–September 5, 1912, 2.

43. Gobat, Confronting the American Dream, 112.

44. Thomas, Old Gimlet Eye, 140–141.

45. Ibid., 141–142.

46. Letter from SDB to MMB, August 11, 1912, reprinted The Letters of a Leatherneck, 103.

47. Gobat, Confronting the American Dream, 113.

48. Letter from SDB to MMB, August 11, 1912, 104.

49. Letter from SDB to ECB, August 28, 1912, reprinted in The Letters of a Leatherneck, 105–106; Asprey, Once a Marine, 38.

50. Asprey, Once a Marine, 40.

51. Letter from SDB to ECB, August 28, 1912, 106.

52. Thomas, Old Gimlet Eye, 145–146; Vandegrift witnessed this — see Asprey, Once a Marine, 41.

53. Asprey, Once a Marine, 40–41.

54. Letter from SDB to ECB, August 28, 1912, 107–108.

55. Footnote, Venzon, The Letters of a Leatherneck, 107.

56. Letter from SDB to ECB, August 28, 1912, 108–110.

57. Thomas, Old Gimlet Eye, 149–150.

58. "Hitler? Butler Says It's He Who'll Get Slapped," The San Antonio Light, October 18, 1938, 2-A, in Newspaper AccessARCHIVE database (accessed July 3, 2008).

59. Letter from SDB to ECB, September 18, 1912, reprinted The Letters of a Leatherneck, 110–112.

60. Ibid., 113.

61. Ibid., 114.

62. Letter from SDB to Luis Mena, September 21, 1912; letter from Mena to SDB, September 21, 1912; letter from SDB to Mena, September 22, 1912; and letter from Mena to SDB, September 23, 1912, Box 5, folder 3, Smedley D. Butler Papers.

63. Butler, "Dame Rumor," 26.

64. Letter from SDB to ECB, September 30, 1912, reprinted in The Letters of a Leatherneck, 118; Dorland's Illustrated Medical Guide, 31st ed. (Philadelphia: Saunders Elsevier, 2007), 536.

65. Ibid., 117; Thomas, Old Gimlet Eye, 163.

66. Letter from SDB to ECB, September 30, 1912, reprinted in The Letters of a Leatherneck, 118.

67. Thomas, Old Gimlet Eye, 157–158.

68. "Smedley Butler of Marines Dies," The New York Times, June 22, 1940, 34.

69. "The Fightin'est Marine Passes," San Antonio Sunday Light, 37.

70. Letter from SDB to ECB, September 30, 1912, 118–119.

71. Gobat, Confronting the American Dream, 114.

72. "Yankee Marines in Nicaragua Are Killed in a Battle," Waterloo Reporter, October 5, 1912, 1, in Newspaper AccessARCHIVE database (accessed October 2, 2009).

73. "Nicaraguans Kill Yankee Marines," Daily Herald, October 11, 1912, 2, in Newspaper AccessARCHIVE database (accessed October 2, 2009).

74. Letter from SDB to ECB, October 5, 1912, reprinted in The Letters of a Leatherneck, 121.

75. Letter from SDB to ECB, October 5, 1912, 122–123.

76. "Rebels Crushed, Our Marines Die," The New York Times, October 6, 1912, 1, in ProQuest Historical Newspapers: The New York Times (1851–2005) database (accessed October 2, 2009).

77. Letter from SDB to ECB, October 5, 1912, reprinted in The Letters of a Leatherneck, 121–122.

78. "Rebels Crushed, Our Marines Die," The New York Times, 7.

79. Gobat, Confronting the American Dream, 118.

80. Thomas Walker, Nicaragua: Land of the Sandino (Boulder, CO: Westview Press, 1991), 21–22.

81. Ibid., 39–42.

82. David M. Abshire, Saving the Reagan Presidency: Trust Is the Coin of the Realm (College Station, TX: Texas A&M University Press, 2005), 5.

83. Thomas, Old Gimlet Eye, 168; "Military History of Smedley D. Butler," and Synopsis of Military History of Brigadier General Smedley D. Butler," Military Personnel File.

Chapter 5

1. "Military History of Smedley D. Butler," Military Personnel File.

2. Thomas, *Old Gimlet Eye*, 171, 175.

3. W. Dirk Raat, "US Intelligence Operations and Covert Action in Mexico, 1900–47: Intelligence Services During the Second World War, Part 2," *Journal of Contemporary History*, 22:4 (October 1987): 616–617, 619, in *JSTOR* database (accessed July 31, 2008).

4. Robert L. Scheina, *Latin America's Wars: The Age of the Professional Soldier, 1900–2001*, vol. 2 (Washington, D.C.: Brassey's, 2003), 11–12.

5. Enrique Krauze, *Mexico, Biography of Power: A History of Modern Mexico, 1810–1996*, trans. Hank Heifetz (New York: HarperCollins, 1997), 245, 251, 255.

6. Ibid., 255.

7. Scheina, *Latin America's Wars*, 16, 18. Although Wilson had no solid proof of Huerta's culpability, he believed the general had done the deed, prompting his machinations to oust Huerta from office; see George J. Rausch Jr., "The Exile and Death of Victoriano Huerta," *The Hispanic American Historical Review*, 42:2 (May 1962): 133, in *JSTOR* database (accessed June 14, 2010).

8. Turner, "Anti-Americanism in Mexico," 506–507, 512, 514–515 ("Death to the ... Down with Gringos ... Kill Díaz and...," 515).

9. Thomas, *Old Gimlet Eye*, 171–172.

10. "Will Smedley Butler Sniff More Powder in China?" *The Literary Digest*, 42.

11. Thomas, *Old Gimlet Eye*, 173.

12. "Gen. Butler, As Spy, Met Huerta," *The New York Times*, May 7, 1931, 28, in *ProQuest* database (accessed November 26, 2008).

13. Thomas, *Old Gimlet Eye*, 173–175.

14. SDB and Arthur J. Burks, *Walter Garvin in Mexico* (Philadelphia: Dorrance and Company, 1927).

15. "Marines Ready to Seize Road to Mexico City," *The New York Times*, April 21, 1914, 1, in *ProQuest* database (accessed October 4, 2009).

16. Michael C. Meyer, "The Arms of the Ypiranga," *The Hispanic American Historical Review*, 50:3 (August 1970): 556, in *JSTOR* database (accessed April 1, 2010).

17. "President Ordered Occupation to Prevent Landing of Munitions," *The New York Times*, April 22, 1914, 1 ("a large supply"), in *ProQuest* database (accessed October 4, 2009); Meyer, "The Arms of the Ypiranga," 555–556.

18. "150 Mexicans Slain in Seizure of Mexican Port," *Waterloo Evening Courier*, April 22, 1914, 1, in *Newspaper AccessARCHIVE* database (accessed August 17, 2008).

19. Thomas, *Old Gimlet Eye*, 178–179.

20. Venzon, "Wendell Cushing Neville," in *Leaders of Men*, 83–84, 87–88, 93 ("'marrying governor,'" 87; "even tempered ... the loudest of...," 93).

21. Thomas, *Old Gimlet Eye*, 179.

22. SDB, *Dame Rumor*, 156.

23. Meyer, "The Arms of the Ypiranga," 552–553, 554–556 ("The shipment was...," 555).

24. Rausch, Jr., "The Exile and Death of Victoriano Huerta," 133.

25. J. Arthur McFall, "After 33 Years of Marine Service, Smedley Butler Became An Outspoken Critic of U.S. Foreign Policy," *Military History*, 19:6 (February 2003): 16–17, in *EBSCO* databases (accessed September 27, 2008).

26. Letter from SDB to John McClay, August 8, 1933, Box 31, folder 3, Smedley D. Butler Papers; letter from SDB to the Navy Department, February 23, 1916, and letter from Josephus Daniels to SDB, August 3, 1916, reprinted in Lyon, "The Unpublished Papers of Major General Smedley Darlington Butler," 65, 67.

27. Letter from the Department of the Navy to SDB, August 3, 1916, and letter from SDB to McClay, August 8, 1933, Smedley D. Butler Papers.

28. Paul H. Douglas, "The Political History of the Occupation," in *Occupied Haiti: Being The Report of a Committee of Six Disinterested Americans Representing Organizations Exclusively American, Who, Having Personally Studied Conditions in Haiti in 1926, Favor the Restoration of the Independence of the Negro Republic*, ed. Paul H. Douglas (New York: Writers, 1927), 20.

29. Walter H. Posner, "American Marines in Haiti, 1915–1922," *The Americas*, 20:3 (January 1964): 231–233, in *JSTOR* database (accessed April 4, 2010).

30. Douglas, "The Political History of the Occupation," 15–18, in *Occupied Haiti*, and "The American Occupation of Haiti I," *Political Science Quarterly*, 42:2 (June 1927): 232, 235–236, in *JSTOR* database (accessed June 14, 2010); Posner, "American Marines in Haiti," 235–236.

31. George Marvin, "Assassination and Intervention in Haiti," *The World's Work*, February 1916, 404–405 ("in charge of...," 405).

32. Ibid., 404–406 ("jumped on his ... emptied his revolver...," 406).

33. Douglas, "The Political History of the Occupation," in *Occupied Haiti*, 20.

34. Robert Deb Heinl Jr. and Nancy Gordon Heinl, revised and expanded by Michael Heinl, *Written in Blood: The Story of the Haitian People 1492–1995* (Lanham, MD: University Press of American, Inc., 1996), 337.

35. Thomas K. Adams, "Intervention in Haiti: Lessons Relearned," *Military Review*, 76:5 (September/October 1996): 45–57, in *EBSCO* databases (accessed October 4, 2009).

36. George W. Brown, "Haiti and the United States," *The Journal of Negro History*, 8:2 (April 1923): 136–137, 143, 149, in *JSTOR* database (accessed October 9, 2009).

37. Mary A. Renda, *Taking Haiti: Military Occupation and the Culture of U.S. Imperialism,*

1915–1940 (Chapel Hill: University of North Carolina Press, 2001), 30–31.

38. Beede, ed., *The War of 1898 and U.S. Interventions, 1898–1934*, "Philippe Sudre Dartiguenave (1863–1926)," 157–158 ("a double game," 157); Heinl and Heinl, *Written in Blood*, 405.

39. Renda, *Taking Haiti*, 31.

40. Douglas, "The Political History of the Occupation," in *Occupied Haiti*, 22.

41. Adams, "Intervention in Haiti."

42. Testimonies of Smedley D. Butler and Littleton W.T. Waller, Senate Select Committee on Haiti and Santo Domingo, *Inquiry into Occupation and Administration of Haiti and Santo Domingo*, 60th Cong., 1st sess., 1921, S. Res 112, 511, 607, 611–613.

43. Letter from SDB to TSB, October 15, 1915, reprinted in *The Letters of Leatherneck*, 155–156 ("where to get…," 155).

44. Letter from SDB to TSB, October 15, 1915, 155–156; Thomas, *Old Gimlet Eye*, 186.

45. Adams, "Intervention in Haiti."

46. Testimonies of Waller and Eli K. Cole, *Inquiry into Occupation and Administration of Haiti and Santo Domingo*, 613, 680; SDB, "The 'Fightingest' Man I Know," *The American Magazine*, September 1931, 84.

47. Thomas, *Old Gimlet Eye*, 189, 191, 193.

48. SDB, report, October 19–November 27, 1915, Box 1, folder 1915 "B," Smedley D. Butler Papers, 3.

49. SDB, "The 'Fightingest' Man I Know," 82, 84; *Old Gimlet Eye*, 193, 196.

50. Ibid., 35.

51. Zabecki, "Paths to Glory."

52. McFall, "After 33 Years of Marine Service, Smedley Butler Became An Outspoken Critic of U.S. Foreign Policy," 16, 24 ("Come on, you…," 24).

53. Letter from F.E. Smith to SDB, and telegram from SDB to Smith, Box 25, folder 10, Smedley D. Butler Papers.

54. SDB, "The 'Fightingest' Man I Know," 84.

55. SDB, report, October 19–November 27, 1915, 3.

56. Letter from SBD to TSB, October 31, 1915, reprinted in *The Letters of a Leatherneck*, 158–159 ("120 miles in…," 158).

57. Thomas, *Old Gimlet Eye*, 198.

58. Franklin Delano Roosevelt, "Trip to Haiti and Santo Domingo, 1917," 1917, Box 41, Franklin D. Roosevelt Papers, Franklin D. Roosevelt Presidential Library, Hyde Park, New York, 9.

59. SDB, report, October 19–November 27, 1915, 8.

60. Zabecki, "Paths to Glory."

61. Testimony of Cole, *Inquiry into Occupation and Administration of Haiti and Santo Domingo*, 681.

62. SDB, report, October 19–November 27, 1915, 7–8.

63. Roosevelt, "Trip to Haiti and Santo Domingo, 1917," 9.

64. Thomas, *Old Gimlet Eye*, 205.

65. Roosevelt, "Trip to Haiti and Santo Domingo, 1917," 9.

66. Zabecki, "Paths to Glory"; SDB, report, October 19, 1915–November 27, 1915, 8 ("rifles, clubs … stones").

67. Roosevelt, "Trip to Haiti and Santo Domingo, 1917," 10.

68. "Stand Taken: Americans Capture Fort Riviere Last Haytian Rebel Stronghold," *The Gleaner*, November 27, 1915, 8, in *Newspaper AccessARCHIVE* database (accessed October 8, 2009).

69. SDB, report, October 19–November 27, 1915, 9.

70. "Haitians Class Gen. Butler as Very Imaginative," *Clearfield Progress*, April 21, 1931, 1, 5, ("In Haiti we…," 5), in *Newspaper AccessARCHIVE* database (accessed April 6, 2008).

71. Testimony of Cole, *Inquiry into Occupation and Administration of Haiti and Santo Domingo*, 683–685.

72. Senate Select Committee on Haiti and Santo Domingo, *Inquiry into Occupation and Administration of Haiti and Santo Domingo*, 78.

73. Testimony of SDB, *Inquiry into Occupation and Administration of Haiti and Santo Domingo*, 511

74. "Military History of Smedley D. Butler," Military Personnel File.

75. Thomas, *Old Gimlet Eye*, 209.

76. Testimony of SDB, *Inquiry into Occupation and Administration of Haiti and Santo Domingo*, 517–518 ("It is instinctive…," 534; "The Haitian people … took … as a joke…," 517; "a first–class…," 518).

77. Letter from SDB to Mr. Mann, April 4, 1916, Box 1, Folder "M," 2; Senate Select Committee on Haiti and Santo Domingo, report, *Inquiry into Occupation and Administration of Haiti and Santo Domingo*, 82.

78. Thomas, *Old Gimlet Eye*, 191, 240 ("a hideous, ungainly…," 191).

79. Comfort, *Quakers in the Modern World*, 183–188.

80. Elliott M. Rudwick, "The National Negro Committee Conference of 1909," *The Phylon Quarterly*, 18:4 (4th Quarter, 1957): 413–419, in *JSTOR* database (accessed September 20, 2009).

81. "Gendarmerie Agreement," Box 6, folder 8, Smedley D. Butler Papers, 3.

82. Testimony of SDB, 533, 514, and Senate Select Committee on Haiti and Santo Domingo, report, *Inquiry into Occupation and Administration of Haiti and Santo Domingo*, 81.

83. Testimony of SDB, 530, 532, and Senate Select Committee on Haiti and Santo Domingo, report, *Inquiry into Occupation and Administration of Haiti and Santo Domingo*, 82–83.

84. Letter from SDB to Mr. Mann, April 4, 1916, 2.

85. Letter from SDB to ECB, March 2, 1916, reprinted in *The Letters of a Leatherneck*, 165.

86. Letter from SDB to Waller, May 16, 1916, and letter from SDB to John A. Lejeune, July 13, 1916, reprinted in *The Letters of a Leatherneck*, 175, 182.

87. Letter from SDB to ECB, July 16, 1916, reprinted in *The Letters of a Leatherneck*, 186.

88. Letter from SDB to ECB, July 18, 1916, October 1, 1916, reprinted in *The Letters of a Leatherneck*, 186–187.

89. Letter from R.L. Farnharn to SDB, December 1917, reprinted in "The Unpublished Papers of Major General Smedley Darlington Butler," 117.

90. Letter from SDB to TSB, October 1, 1916, and editor's footnote, reprinted in *The Letters of a Leatherneck*, 189–190 ("a little nest egg...," from Butler's letter, 190).

91. "Gendarmerie Agreement," Box 6, folder 8, 2; letter from SDB to Treasury Department, Box 1, folder 1916 "M," Smedley D. Butler Papers

92. SDB, rental agreement, 1916, Box 1, folder "G," Smedley D. Butler Papers.

93. Letter from SDB to Lt. Col. Cyrus S. Radford, January 1917, and note from the U.S. Naval Radio Service to SDB, January 28, 1917, Box 1, Folder "R," Smedley D. Butler Papers.

Chapter 6

1. Letter from SDB to TSB, December 23, 1915, reprinted in *The Letters of a Leatherneck*, 59.

2. Testimony of Waller, *Inquiry into Occupation and Administration of Haiti and Santo Domingo*, 616–617.

3. Order from President Dartiguenave to SDB, August 30, 1916, Box 6, folder 8, and report from Butler to President Dartiguenave, October 18, 1916, Box 1, folder 1916 "D," Smedley D. Butler Papers.

4. Letter from SDB to TSB, October 1, 1916, and editor's footnote, reprinted in *The Letters of a Leatherneck*, 188.

5. Bruce J. Calder, "Caudillos and Gavilleros Versus the United States Marines: Guerrilla Insurgency During the Dominican Intervention, 1916–1924," *The Hispanic American Historical Review*, 58:4 (November 1978): 650, 652, 657, in JSTOR database (accessed August 31, 2009).

6. Letter from SDB to TSB, October 1, 1916, reprinted in *The Letters of a Leatherneck*, 188–189 ("176 miles ... in 5 days," 189).

7. SDB, "Dame Rumor," 26, 155.

8. Letter from SDB to TSB, October 1, 1916, reprinted in *The Letters of a Leatherneck*, 188.

9. FDR at this time could still walk since the polio that disabled him would not strike him until 1921.

10. Livingston Davis, "Log of the Trip to Haiti and Santo Domingo," February 15, 1917, Box 41, Franklin D. Roosevelt Papers, Franklin D. Roosevelt Presidential Library, Hyde Park, New York, 1, 3–4.

11. Roosevelt, "Trip to Haiti and Santo Domingo, 1917," 3.

12. Ibid., 4, 5–6.

13. Davis, "Log of the Trip to Haiti and Santo Domingo," 6.

14. Davis recollected that this occurred at San Raphaël.

15. Roosevelt, "Trip to Haiti and Santo Domingo, 1917," 8.

16. Davis, "Log of the Trip to Haiti and Santo Domingo," 7.

17. Roosevelt, "Trip to Haiti and Santo Domingo, 1917," 10.

18. Davis, "Log of the Trip to Haiti and Santo Domingo," 8.

19. Letter from George Barnett to SDB, February 10, 1917, reprinted in *The Letters of a Leatherneck*, 190–191.

20. Douglas, "The Political History of the Occupation," in *Occupied Haiti*, 24; James A. Padgett, "Diplomats to Haiti and Their Diplomacy," *The Journal of Negro History*, 25:3 (July 1940): 310, in *JSTOR* database (accessed October 14, 2009).

21. Testimony of Cole, *Inquiry into Occupation and Administration of Haiti and Santo Domingo*, 698–699, 701.

22. Testimony of SDB, *Inquiry into Occupation and Administration of Haiti and Santo Domingo*, 536.

23. Ibid., 537.

24. Douglas, "The Political History of the Occupation," in *Occupied Haiti*, 26.

25. Testimony of SDB, *Inquiry into Occupation and Administration of Haiti and Santo Domingo*, 536.

26. Letter from SDB to TSB, May 16, 1917, reprinted in *Letters of a Leatherneck*, 192.

27. Letter from T. Eyre to SDB, 1917; letter from John McIlhenny, undated [c. 1917], reprinted in "The Unpublished Papers of Major General Smedley Darlington Butler," 113, 108.

28. Letter from SDB to MMB and TSB, October 6, 1917, and letter from SDB to Franklin D. Roosevelt, December 28, 1917, reprinted in *Letters of a Leatherneck*, 196, 198.

29. Testimony of Cole, *Inquiry into Occupation and Administration of Haiti and Santo Domingo*, 685, 688–689.

30. Letter from SDB to Lejeune, reprinted in "The Unpublished Papers of Major General Smedley Darlington Butler," 106.

31. Letter from SDB to MMB and TSB, October 6, 1917, 196.

32. Order to SDB, April 10, 1918, reprinted in "The Unpublished Papers of Major General Smedley Darlington Butler," 23.

33. Letter from SDB to MMB, March 2, 1918, 201.

34. Swanton, e-mail to author, September 23, 2009.

35. Charles A. Fleming, Robin L. Austin, and Charles A. Bradley, *Quantico: Crossroads of the Marine Corps* (Washington, D.C.: United States Marine Corps, History and Museums Division, 1978), 22, 24.

36. Ibid., 27, 28, 31.

37. Letter from M.R. Thacher to H.A. Peatross, October 8, 1931, and "Military History of Smedley D. Butler," Military Personnel File, National Archives, St. Louis, Missouri.

38. "Synopsis of Military History of Brigadier General Smedley D. Butler" and "Military History of Smedley D. Butler," Military Personnel File; Thomas, *Old Gimlet Eye*, 243–244.

39. Christine M. Kreiser, "The Enemy Within," *American History*, December 2006, in *EBSCO* databases (accessed November 14, 2008), 24–25 ("miles northwest of...," 25); John F. Brundage and G. Dennis Shanks, "Deaths from Bacterial Pneumonia During 1918–19 Influenza Pandemic," *Emerging Infectious Diseases*, 14:8 (August 2008): 1197–1198, http://www.ncbi.nlm.nih.gov/pmc/articles/PMC2600384/pdf/07–1313_finalHR.pdf (accessed February 21, 2010).

40. Brundage and Shanks, "Deaths from Bacterial Pneumonia During 1918–19 Influenza Pandemic," 1197–1198.

41. Letter from SDB to TSB and ECB, October 5, 1918, and letter from SDB to ECB, October 27, 1918, reprinted in *Letters of a Leatherneck*, 206–207, 209; "Synopsis of Military History of Brigadier General Smedley D. Butler" and "Military History of Smedley D. Butler," Military Personnel File.

42. "Military History of Smedley D. Butler," Military Personnel File.

43. Guy L. Edie, et al., "Camp Pontanezen, Brest, France," *The Military Surgeon: Journal of the Association of Military Surgeons of the United States*, XLVI (1920), 301–303.

44. Ibid., 303–304.

45. Thomas, *Old Gimlet Eye*, 247.

46. Ibid., 248, 250 ("shovels axes, picks...," 250).

47. "Will Smedley Butler Sniff More Powder in China?" *The Literary Digest*, 42.

48. Letter from SDB to ECB, January 5, 1919, and editor's footnote, reprinted in *Letters of a Leatherneck*, 216, 213–214 (Last night I...," from SDB's letter, 216).

49. Letter from James E. Harbord to SDB, August 24, 1933, Smedley D. Butler Papers, Box 33, folder unknown.

50. Jan Cohn, *Improbably Fiction: The Life of Mary Roberts Rinehart* (Pittsburgh: University of Pennsylvania, 1980), 123.

51. Mary Roberts Rinehart, *My Story* (New York: Farrar & Rinehart, Inc., 1931), 278–279 ("a blistering report ... high rubber boots ... that dynamo of ... no red tape ... double rations of ... hot soup all...," 278).

52. Edie, et al., "Camp Pontanezen, Brest, France," 303–304 ("taxed to their...," 304).

53. Letter from SDB to ECB, January 15, 1919, 218–219 ("produce the best...," 218).

54. Zabecki, "Paths to Glory"; letter from SDB to ECB, February 1, 1919, reprinted in *Letters of a Leatherneck*, 221 ("weak ... insincere").

55. Letters from SDB to ECB, January 9, 1919, February 1, 1919, February 7, 1919, March 14, 1919, March 24, 1919, and April 9, 1919, reprinted in *Letters of a Leatherneck*, 217, 220–224, 225.

56. Letter from SDB to ECB, June 5, 1919, reprinted in *Letters of a Leatherneck*, 227–228; "Synopsis of Military History of Brigadier General Smedley D. Butler," Military Personnel File.

57. "Nation Voted Dry; 38 States Adopt the Amendment," *The New York Times*, January 17, 1919, 1, in database (accessed October 17, 2009).

58. Venzon, editorial commentary, *The Letters of a Leatherneck*, 227.

59. Letter from SDB to Lejeune, February 23, 1935, Box 35, folder 1, 1.

60. Bartlett and Sweetman, *Leathernecks*, 211–212.

61. Order, June 30, 1920, reprinted in "The Unpublished Papers of Major General Smedley Darlington Butler," 38.

62. Order, August 31, 1920, reprinted in "The Unpublished Papers of Major General Smedley Darlington Butler," 29.

63. Calder, "Caudillos and Gavilleros Versus the United States Marines," 662–663.

64. Bartlett and Sweetman, *Leathernecks*, 207.

65. Ibid., 208–210.

66. "Daniels Orders Haitian Inquiry," *Newport Mercury*, October 23, 1920, 5, in *Newspaper AccessARCHIVE* database (accessed August 17, 2008).

67. Letter from SDB to ECB, September 4, 1920, reprinted in *The Letters of a Leatherneck*, 233–236; Lejeune, report of the military situation in Haiti, published in *Inquiry into Occupation and Administration of Haiti and Santo Domingo*, 140.

68. Letter from SDB to MMB, October 1, 1920, reprinted in *The Letters of a Leatherneck*, 238.

69. Senate Select Committee on Haiti and Santo Domingo, *Inquiry into Occupation and Administration of Haiti and Santo Domingo*, 84–85 ("convened a court...," 84; "isolated ... indiscriminate killing of...," 85).

70. Order, October 3, 1921, reprinted in "The Unpublished Papers of Major General Smedley Darlington Butler, United States Marine Corps," 38.

71. In his article "James Weldon Johnson and Haiti," Rayford W. Logan called the Mayo Court's conclusion a "whitewash," noting that Warren G. Harding used its distorted conclusions as a part of his campaign platform; Rayford W. Logan, "James Weldon Johnson and Haiti," *The Phylon Quarterly*, 32:4 (4th Quarter, 1971): 401, in *JSTOR* database (accessed March 7, 2010); see Calder,

"Caudillos and Gavilleros Versus the United States Marines," for details on the American atrocities against the Dominican people.

72. "Failure in Haiti," *The Nation*, December 18, 1929, 739.

73. Mark Blumenthal, *Images of America: Quantico* (Charleston, NC: Arcadia, 2003), 19.

74. Asprey, *Once a Marine*, 62.

75. Fleming, Austin, and Bradley, *Quantico: Crossroads of the Marine Corps*, 62.

76. Ibid., 43.

77. Ibid., 57.

78. Blumenthal, photo, *Images of America: Quantico*, 37.

79. Letter from D.C. Gurney to SDB, November 22, 1922, reprinted in "The Unpublished Papers of Major General Smedley Darlington Butler," 184.

80. Fleming, Robin, and Bradley, *Quantico: Crossroads of the Marine Corps*, 42.

81. Lyon, "The Unpublished Papers of Major General Smedley Darlington Butler," 8.

82. Aprey, *Once a Marine*, 63.

83. Letter from SDB to John G. Muir, July 19, 1923, reprinted in "The Unpublished Papers of Major General Smedley Darlington Butler," 218.

Chapter 7

1. SDB, "Dame Rumor," 26.

2. Samuel McCoy, "Philadelphia at War Over General Butler," *The New York Times*, July 27, 1924, XX3, in *ProQuest* database (accessed March 31, 2008).

3. Thomas, *Old Gimlet Eye*, 264–265.

4. McCoy, "Philadelphia at War Over General Butler," XX3.

5. Ibid.

6. Letter from Dr. McIntire to SDB, June 1923 [undated note], and, letter from SDB to W. Freeland Kendrick, June 18, 1923, reprinted in "The Unpublished Papers of Major General Smedley Darlington Butler," 213, 260.

7. Letter from SDB to John Marston, December 27, 1923; letter from SDB to Thomas Holcomb, December 27, 1923; letter from SDB to H.L. Roosevelt, reprinted in "The Unpublished Papers of Major General Smedley Darlington Butler," 260.

8. "General Butler's Value to Philadelphia," *The New York Times*, July 18, 1924, 12, in *ProQuest* database (accessed March 31, 2008).

9. "Butler Gives $2,000 of Pay to Widow," *The New York Times*, September 18, 1924, 11, in *ProQuest* database (accessed October 22, 2009).

10. Fred D. Baldwin, "Smedley D. Butler and Prohibition Enforcement in Philadelphia, 1924–1925," *The Pennsylvania Magazine of History and Biography*, 84:3 (July 1960): 354–355 ("In a uniform ... blue with gold...," 354), in *JSTOR* database (accessed July 19, 2009).

11. "Philadelphia Raids Close 973 Saloons," *The New York Times*, January 12, 1924, 1, 3, in *ProQuest* database (accessed March 31, 2008).

12. This law gave teeth to the Eighteenth Amendment.

13. Philip Klein and Ari Hoogenboom, *A History of Pennsylvania*, Second and Enlarged Edition (University Park & London: Pennsylvania State University Press, 1980), 441, 446.

14. "Philadelphia Raids Close 973 Saloons," *The New York Times*, 1.

15. Arthur P. Dudden, "The City Embraces 'Normalcy,' 1919–1929," in *Philadelphia: A 300-Year History*, ed. Russell F. Weigley (New York & London: W.W. Norton, 1982), 577.

16. Thomas, *Old Gimlet Eye*, 271.

17. "Arms Firemen in Philadelphia," *The New York Times*, January 17, 1924, 19, in *ProQuest* database (accessed March 31, 2008).

18. Thomas Raeburn White, "The Philadelphia System," *Forum*, May 1927, 678, 681.

19. Thomas A. Reppetto, *The Blue Parade* (New York: The Free Press, 1978), 144.

20. Samuel Walker, *A Critical History of Police Reform: The Emergence of Professionalism* (Lexington, MA: Lexington Books, 1977), 62.

21. Imogen B. Oakley, "Two Dictatorships," *Outlook*, December 22, 1926, 527.

22. Oliver H.P. Garrett, "Why They Cleaned Up Philadelphia," *New Republic*, February 27, 1924, 11–12 ("deliver votes," 11; "the lobby ... fashionable ... respectable ... Midnight Club ... crazy ... a poor sport," 12).

23. Walker, *A Critical History of Police Reform*, 63–64, 66 ("regular physical exercise ... boxing, wresting ... ceremonial occasions ... written and oral," 66).

24. Baldwin, "Smedley D. Butler and Prohibition Enforcement in Philadelphia, 1924–1925," 359.

25. Maxwell Hyde, "Philadelphians Fail on Crusade on Vice," *Charleston Daily Mail*, April 6, 1924, 35, in *Newspaper AccessARCHIVE* database (accessed November 27, 2008).

26. Ibid.

27. Thomas, *Old Gimlet Eye*, 268.

28. Baldwin, "Smedley D. Butler and Prohibition Enforcement in Philadelphia, 1924–1925," 363–364.

29. "Butler to Punish Officers," *New York Times*, April 9, 1924, 24, in *ProQuest* database (accessed October 22, 2009).

30. McCoy, "Philadelphia at War Over General Butler," XX3.

31. Archer, *The Plot to Seize the White House*, 87.

32. C.K.T., "Baiting a Marine: A Special Correspondence from Philadelphia," *Outlook*, October 8, 1924, 199.

33. "Kendrick Prepares to Oust Gen. Butler," *The New York Times*, July 21, 1924, 4, in *ProQuest* database (accessed October 23, 2009).

34. "'Big Storm Coming,' Butler Tells Force," *The New York Times*, July 17, 1924, 4, in *ProQuest* database (accessed October 22, 2009).

35. Dudden, "The City Embraces 'Normalcy,'" in *Philadelphia: A 300-Year History*, 577–578.

36. "General Butler's Value to Philadelphia," *The New York Times*, 12.

37. "Gen. Butler's Leave Extended One Year," *The New York Times*, December 10, 1924, 7, in *ProQuest* database (accessed October 22, 2009).

38. Reppetto, *The Blue Parade*, 145.

39. "General Butler's Job," *The New York Times*, September 7, 1925, 10, in *ProQuest* database (accessed March 31, 2008).

40. "Pinchot Requests Coolidge to Grant Butler More Time," *New Castle News*, October 19, 1925, 8, in *Newspaper AccessARCHIVE* database (accessed November 27, 2008).

41. "President Refuses Butler More Leave," *The New York Times*, November 4, 1925, 25, in *ProQuest* database (accessed October 23, 2009).

42. Baldwin, "Smedley D. Butler and Prohibition Enforcement in Philadelphia, 1924–1925," 363–364.

43. "Philadelphia Mayor Fires Gen. Butler," *Logansport Pharos-Tribune*, December 22, 1925, 1, in *Newspaper AccessARCHIVE* database (accessed November 27, 2008).

44. Thomas, *Old Gimlet Eye*, 275.

45. Walker, *A Critical History of Police Reform*, 67.

46. Reppetto, *The Blue Parade*, 145.

47. Dudden, "The City Embraces 'Normalcy,'" in *Philadelphia: A 300-Year History*, 577–578.

48. "More Police Heads in Philadelphia Net," *The New York Times*, October 8, 1928, 9, in *ProQuest* database (accessed March 31, 2008).

49. "Philadelphia's Whiskey Ring," *The Literary Digest*, September 15, 1928, 11.

50. Klein and Hoogenboom, *A History of Pennsylvania*, 446–447, 441.

51. See "The Unpublished Papers of Major General Smedley Darlington Butler," 266–275, for copies of many of these; letter from William M. Betts to SDB, December 23, 1925; letter from Universal Pub. Syndicate to W. Freeland Kendrick, copied to SDB, December 25, 1925 ("a street cleaning job," 266); letter from W.B. Shafer, Jr. to SDB, December 23, 1925; letter from Lincoln W. Dygert to SDB, December 1925; and letter from SDB to Nathan H. Davis, April 29, 1926, reprinted in "The Unpublished Papers of Major General Smedley Darlington Butler," 266, 265, 320.

52. Schmidt, *Maverick Marine*, 161.

53. "Munitions Ship Blown to Bits in Chinese War," *Nevada State Journal*, October 18, 1926, 1, in *Newspaper AccessARCHIVE* database (accessed October 27, 1926).

54. "General Butler and His Family Sail for San Diego," *The Evening Bulletin*, January 2, 1926.

55. Thomas, *Old Gimlet Eye*, 277.

56. Letter from SDB to MMB, March 14, 1926, reprinted in *The Letters of a Leatherneck*, 245.

57. Ibid., 245–247.

58. "Gen. Butler's Rum Charges Arouses Ire," *Logansport Pharos-Tribune*, March 11, 1926, 1, 5, in *Newspaper AccessARCHIVE* database (accessed November 27, 2008).

59. "Rally to Defense of Col. Williams," *The New York Times*, March 12, 1926, 2, in *ProQuest* database (accessed March 31, 2008).

60. Letter from SDB to E.Z. Dimitman, April 24, 1926; letter from SDB to Dr. George Burke, April 20, 1926; letter from SDB to John Stevens, April 29, 1926, reprinted in "The Unpublished Papers of Major General Smedley Darlington Butler," 316–317, 321.

61. SDB, "Dame Rumor," 25.

62. Letter from SDB to Admiral Phillip Andrews, May 24, 1926, reprinted in "The Unpublished Papers of Major General Smedley Darlington Butler," 326.

63. The Rev. Floy Thornton Barkman, "Men of the U.S. Navy at San Diego," *Missionary Review of the World*, March 1925, 197–198 ("government ships … destroyers…," 197).

64. SDB, "Dame Rumor," 25.

65. "Whether Colonel Was Drunk or Just Sick Subject of Inquiry," *Ogden Standard-Examiner*, April 16, 1926, 3, in *Newspaper AccessARCHIVE* database (accessed November 27, 2008).

66. "Declare Williams Suffered From Drug," *The New York Times*, April 15, 1926, 2, in *ProQuest* database (accessed October 24, 1926).

67. "Cocktail Colonel Convicted," *Oakland Tribune*, April 19, 1926, 1, in *Newspaper AccessARCHIVE* database (accessed October 24, 2009).

68. "Col. Williams Reduced 4 Numbers in Grade," *The New York Times*, May 22, 1926, 19, in *ProQuest* database (accessed October 24, 2009).

69. Asprey, *Once a Marine*, 67.

70. Thomas, *Old Gimlet Eye*, 277.

71. Venzon, "Smedley Darlington Butler," in *Leaders of Men*, 166.

72. Letter from Lejeune to SDB, February 7, 1927, reprinted in *My Dear Smedley: Personal Correspondence of John A. Lejeune and Smedley D. Butler, 1927–1928*, ed. J. Michael Miller (Quantico, VA: Marine Corps Research Center, 2002), 2.

73. "Marines Ordered to Guard U.S. Mails," *Portsmouth Daily Times*, October 16, 1926, 1, in *Newspaper AccessARCHIVE* database (October 25, 2009).

74. "Mail Guards Will Use Gas," *The Salt Lake Tribune*, November 13, 1926, 24, in *Newspaper AccessARCHIVE* database (accessed October 25, 2009).

75. Letter from SDB to MMB, January 9, 1927, reprinted in *The Letters of a Leatherneck*, 255.

76. "More Marines Taken from Mail Guard

Duty," *The New York Times*, January 25, 1927, 10, in *ProQuest* database (accessed October 25, 2009); letter from Lejeune to SDB, February 21, 1927, reprinted in *My Dear Smedley*, 3.

77. Letter from SDB to MMB, November 30, 1926, and December 30, 1926, reprinted in *The Letters of a Leatherneck*, 250–253.

78. Letter from SDB to MMB and TSB, February 27, 1927, reprinted in *The Letters of a Leatherneck*, 256.

79. "Butler on the Job But Father Isn't Cheering," *The News*, April 16, 1927, 1, in *Newspaper AccessARCHIVE* database (accessed April 6, 2008).

Chapter 8

1. "Guns of U.S. Battleships Roar as Americans Are Slain by Rebel Cantonese," *Jefferson City Tribune-Post*, March 24, 1927, 1, 2, in *Newspaper AccessARCHIVE* database (accessed October 28, 2009).

2. C. Stanley Smith, "Five Days," *Atlantic Monthly*, December 1927, 838, 840–846; "Guns of U.S. Battleships Roar as Americans Are Slain by Rebel Cantonese," *Jefferson City Tribune-Post*, 2.

3. Venzon, "Smedley Darlington Butler," *Leaders of Men*, 167.

4. Letter from SDB to MMB, April 13, 1927, reprinted in *The Letters of a Leatherneck*, 266–267.

5. James Porter Davis, "Shanghai: A City Ruled by Five Nations," *Current History*, August 1926, 747.

6. Ibid., 747–749; "Shanghai's Fall and China's Future," *The Literary Digest*, April 2, 1927.

7. Letter from SDB to Lejeune, February 7, 1927, reprinted in *My Dear Smedley*, 11–13.

8. Ibid. 13.

9. Letter from SDB to MMB, April 13, 1927, reprinted in *The Letters of a Leatherneck*, 266–267 ("little open fires … dry and comfortable," 266).

10. Stanley High, "Shanghai: Where Fear Breeds Hates" *New Republic*, May 4, 1927, 294.

11. Letter from SDB to Lejeune, April 1, 1927, reprinted in *My Dear Smedley*, 17.

12. Letter from SDB to Lejeune, April 1, 1927, 25.

13. George F. Hofmann and Donn A. Starry, ed., *The History of U.S. Armored Forces* (Lexington, KY: The University of Kentucky, 1999), 68, 71–73, 75.

14. Letter from SDB to Lejeune, April 1, 1927, 15, 18, 25 ("I have never…," 15).

15. Letter from SDB to MMB, May 8, 1927, reprinted in *The Letters of a Leatherneck*, 270.

16. High, "Shanghai: Where Fear Breeds Hate," 294.

17. Ibid., 294–295.

18. Letter from SDB to Lejeune, May 12, 1927, and, letter from SDB to Lejeune, March 31, 1927, reprinted in *My Dear Smedley*, 64, 69.

19. J.A.G. Roberts, *A Concise History of China* (Cambridge, MA: Harvard University Press, 1999), 202. 206.

20. E.R. Hooton, *The Greatest Tumult: The Chinese Civil War 1936–49* (London: Brassey's (UK), 1991), xxv, xxvii.

21. Stephen Haw, *A Traveller's History of China* (New York & Northampton: Interlink Books, 1995, 1998, 2001), 182.

22. Hooton, *The Greatest Tumult*, xxvii–xxviii.

23. Letter from SDB to Lejeune, May 31, 1927, reprinted in *My Dear Smedley*, 76, 80.

24. Russell D. Buhite, "Nelson Johnson and American Policy Toward China, 1925–1928," *The Pacific Historical Review*, 35:4 (November 1966): 355, 460, in *JSTOR* database (accessed November 3, 2009).

25. Letter from SDB to Lejeune, April 1, 1927, and letter from SDB to Lejeune, May 31, 1927, reprinted in *My Dear Smedley*, 78.

26. Davis, "Shanghai: A City Ruled by Five Nations," 295.

27. Letter from SDB to Lejeune, May 31, 1927, 71, and letter from SDB to Lejeune, June 25, 1927, reprinted in *My Dear Smedley*, 87, 89, 96, 91.

28. Letter from SDB to Lejeune, July 16, 1927, reprinted in *My Dear Smedley*, 103, 107–108.

29. Asprey, *Once a Marine*, 73; Vandegrift only mentioned these planes by their nickname "Jennies." The details about their make and type came from the following article: Ernest B. Furgurson, "Amelia Earhart's Brazen Cohorts," *American History*, February 2010, 56.

30. Letter from SDB to Lejeune, August 11, 1927, reprinted in *My Dear Smedley*, 116.

31. Ibid., 118–119.

32. Asprey, *Once a Marine*, 72.

33. Nickel-plated bayonets will not do in a combat situation because they glare when exposed to bright light, giving away a soldier's position.

34. Letter from Lejeune to SDB, August 22, 1927, reprinted in *My Dear Smedley*, 128.

35. Letter from SDB to Lejeune, September 29, 1927, reprinted in *My Dear Smedley*, 138.

36. Letter from Lejeune to ECB, August 29, 1927; letter from ECB to Lejeune, September 27, 1927; letter from Lejeune to SDB, November 16, 1927, reprinted in *My Dear Smedley*, 131, 136, 173.

37. Venzon, footnote, *The Letters of a Leatherneck*, 285.

38. Letter from SDB to Lejeune, September 29, 1927, reprinted *My Dear Smedley*, 143–144.

39. Letter from SDB to Lejeune, November 2, 1927, reprinted in *My Dear Smedley*, 164.

40. Archer, *Plot to Seize the White House*, 98.

41. Letter from SDB to Lejeune, October 2, 1928, reprinted in *My Dear Smedley*, 280.

42. Swanton, e-mail to author, September 5, 2009.

43. Wehle, telephone conversation with author, May 15, 2010.

44. "General Butler Led the United Fire Forces Which Saved Most of Oil Plant at Tien-Tsin," *The New York Times*, December 26, 1927, 1, in *ProQuest* database (accessed October 18, 2008).

45. Noel H. Pugach, "Standard Oil and Petroleum Development in Early Republican China," *The Business History Review*, 45:4 (Winter 1971): 452, in *JSTOR* database (accessed November 3, 2009).

46. David A. Wilson, "Principles and Profits: Standard Oil Responds to Chinese Nationalism, 1925–1927," *The Pacific Historical Review*, 46:4 (November 1977): 630, in *JSTOR* database (accessed November 3, 2009).

47. SDB, "'In Time of Peace:' The Army," 8.

48. Letter from SDB to Lejeune, December 27, 1927, reprinted *My Dear Smedley*, 204, 206.

49. Ibid., 204.

50. Ibid.., 204–206 ("a big Red…," 206).

51. "Mussolini's Fine Rule in Italy Sketched by William Hervey at Masonic Dinner Meeting," *The Oxnard Daily Courier*, December 22, 1927, 4, in *Newspaper AccessARCHIVE* database (accessed November 7, 2009).

52. Letter from SDB to TSB, February 7, 1928, reprinted *The Letters of a Leatherneck*, 285.

53. Letter from SDB to Lejeune, January 21, 1928, and letter from Lejeune to SDB, March 7, 1928, reprinted in *My Dear Smedley*, 221, 231.

54. "T.S. Butler Dies in Capital Hotel," *The New York Times*, 3.

55. *The New York Times* reported that Horace, Butler's other brother, also stood at his father's deathbed, but Lejeune made no mention of this in his letter to SDB.

56. Letters from Lejeune to SDB, May 2, 11, and June 13, 1928, reprinted in *My Dear Smedley*, 247, 254, 263.

57. Letter quoted in Archer, *The Plot to Seize the White House*, 102.

58. Swanton, e-mail to author, November 30, 2009.

59. Letter from SDB to Lejeune, October 2, 1928, reprinted in *My Dear Smedley*, 283–285 ("fiddled around for…," 283).

60. "'Umbrella of Blessings' Conferred on Gen. Butler," *The New York Times*, October 21, 1928, 147, in *ProQuest* database (accessed November 7, 2009).

61. Paul Yeung, Cultural Program Director, Chinese Cultural Centre Museum, e-mail to author, July 17, 2009.

62. Letter from SDB to Lejeune, October 2, 1928, 282–283.

63. Thomas, *Old Gimlet Eye*, 297.

64. Letter from SDB to MMB, November 4, 1928, reprinted in *The Letters of a Leatherneck*, 293.

65. "Chinese Sell Children to Get Food in Famine," *The New York Times*, January 9, 1928, 4 ("three years of…") (accessed October 3, 2008); "10,000,000 Suffer in Chinese Famine," *The New York Times*, January 12, 1928, 6, in *ProQuest* database (accessed October 31, 2008).

66. Letter from SDB to MMB, November 25, 1928, reprinted in *The Letters of a Leatherneck*, 294.

67. Letter from SDB to Lejeune, October 22, 1928, reprinted in *My Dear Smedley*, 284, 286 ("somebody to oppose…," 286).

68. Venzon, "Smedley Darlington Butler," in *Leaders of Men*, 169.

69. Order, January 8, 1929, reprinted in "The Unpublished Papers of Major General Smedley Darlington Butler, 59.

70. Letter from A.C. Dearing to SDB, January 7, 1933, Box 30, folder 1, Smedley D. Butler Papers.

71. "Neville Will Take Post as Marine Head," *The Evening Tribune*, February 8, 1929, 1, in *Newspaper AccessARCHIVE* database (accessed August 17, 2008).

72. "Smedley Butler Is Major General," *Kingsport Times*, July 14, 1929, 6, in *Newspaper AccessARCHIVE* database (accessed November 7, 2009).

Chapter 9

1. Archer, *The Plot to Seize the White House*, 106, 118, 120.

2. Letter from SDB to E.Z. Dimitman, January 12, 1931, and letter from Lieutenant L.C. Witaker to Dimitman, January 17, 1931, Box 16, folder 2; letter from Dimitman to SDB, January 21, 1931, Box 16, folder 3, Smedley D. Butler Papers.

3. Sinclair Lewis, "Devil-Dog Rule," a letter to the editor of *The Nation*, December 18, 1921, 751.

4. "Asks Gen. Butler to Explain Speech," *The New York Times*, December 15, 1929, 1, in *ProQuest* database (accessed August 17, 2009).

5. "Accepts Butler's Version," *The New York Times*, December 22, 1929, 26, in *ProQuest* database (accessed August 17, 2009).

6. Thomas, *Old Gimlet Eye*, 300.

7. "Want General Butler as Keystone Governor," *The New York Times*, September 4, 1929, 6, in *ProQuest* database (accessed March 31, 2008).

8. Letter from SDB to MMB, December 1929, reprinted in *The Letters of a Leatherneck*, 297.

9. Venzon, "Wendell Cushing Neville," in *Leaders of Men*, 102–103.

10. Letter from SDB to MMB and TSB, February 27, 1927, reprinted in *The Letters of a Leatherneck*, 256–257.

11. Letter from SDB to Samuel Butler, July 28,

1930, reprinted in *The Letters of a Leatherneck*, 298–300 ("cool, and even…," 300).

12. Asprey, *Once a Marine*, 76.

13. Merrill L. Bartlett, "Ben Hebard Fuller and the Genesis of a Modern United States Marine Corps, 1891–1934," *The Journal of Military History*, 69:1 (January 2005): 75–76 ("served in such…," 75), in *JSTOR* database (accessed July 31, 2008).

14. Ibid.., 79, 81–85.

15. Letter from SDB to SB, July 28, 1930, reprinted in *The Letters of a Leatherneck*, 304, 303 ("block every Naval … to make any…," 304; an Interdepartmental Board…," 303).

16. In truth Butler had spent $5,000 of Corps funds on cement.

17. Thomas, *Old Gimlet Eye*, 301–302 ("'one of … damned follies,'" 301).

18. "General Butler Sends 700 Marines on Leave As Drought Depletes Quantico Water Supply," *The New York Times*, August 1, 1930, 4, in *ProQuest* database (accessed March 31, 2008).

19. "General Butler Wins Second Battle for Civic Law and Order," *Olean Times*, October 1, 1929, 19, in *Newspaper AccessARCHIVE* database (accessed August 17, 2008).

20. "Italian Envoy Protests Gen. Butler's Talk Calling Mussolini an 'Embryo' War Starter," *The New York Times*, January 27, 1931, 1, 2, ("An eel which … Right now there…," 2), in *ProQuest Historical Newspapers: The New York Times (1851–2005)* database (accessed November 10, 2009).

21. "When a Marine Tells It," *The Literary Digest*, February 14, 1931, 7.

22. "Our Comic-Opera Court-Martial," *The Literary Digest*, February 28, 1931, 10.

23. "When a Marine Tells It," *The Literary Digest*, 7.

24. United States, State Department, *Papers Relating to the Foreign Relations of the United States, 1931*, vol. II, Washington: Government Printing Office, 1946, in *LexisNexis* database (accessed April 26, 2008), 640–642 ("never driven around…," 640).

25. Letter from C.F. Adams to SDB, January 24, 1931, Box 16, folder 3, Smedley D. Butler Papers.

26. "The Genial General," *Outlook*, May 6, 1931, 5.

27. Letter from SDB to Adams, January 31, 1931, reprinted in *The Letters of a Leatherneck*, 307–308.

28. Letter from Ben Fuller to SDB, January 29, 1931, and letter from SDB to Samuel Butler, January 31, 1931, Box 16, folder 5, Smedley D. Butler Papers.

29. "U.S. Apologizes to Italy for Gen. Butler's Remarks About Premier Mussolini," *Moberly Weekly Monitor*, January 29, 1931, 1, in *Newspaper AccessARCHIVE* database (accessed April 6, 2008).

30. Letter from SDB to Louis J. Alger, January 30, 1931, Box 16, folder 5, Smedley D. Butler Papers.

31. "Finds Vanderbilt Met Mussolini 5 Years Ago," *The New York Times*, February 2, 1931, 11, in *ProQuest* database (accessed August 17, 2009).

32. "The Press: Vanderbilt Truth," *Time*, February 13, 1931, http://www.time.com/time/magazine/article/0,9171,930365,00.html (accessed November 12, 2009).

33. Cornelius Vanderbilt, Jr., *Man of the World: My Life on Five Continents* (New York: Crown, 1959), 52–53 ("jumped at the…," 54).

34. Ibid 53–55 ("a hand … right knee … Never look back…," 55).

35. "Public Hearing in Butler Case Heflin Demand," *Mason City Globe-Gazette*, February 4, 1931, 1, in *Newspaper AccessARCHIVE* database (accessed April 6, 2008).

36. John P. Diggins, "The Italo-American Anti-Fascist Opposition," *The Journal of American History*, 54:3 (December 1967): 580, 583–584, 581 ("the writings of … nervous…," 580), in *JSTOR* database (accessed November 11, 2009).

37. See Box 16 for the bulk of the letters in the Smedley D. Butler Papers collection; letter from E.L. Stevenson to SDB, January 22, 1931, and letter from the Order of the Sons of Italy to SDB, January 28, 1931, Box 16, folder 3, Smedley D. Butler Papers.

38. Telegrams from SDB to Josephus Daniels, and from Daniels to SDB, January 30, 1931; telegram from Franklin D. Roosevelt to SDB, January 31, 1931, Box 16, folder 5, Smedley D. Butler Papers.

39. "Name the Naval Board to Hear Butler Case," *The Chillicothe Constitution-Tribune*, January 31, 1931, 1, in *Newspaper AccessARCHIVE* database (accessed March 31, 2008); letter from SDB to Fuller, January 31, 1931, Box 16, folder 5, Smedley D. Butler Papers; Thomas, *Old Gimlet Eye*, 307–308.

40. Thomas, *Old Gimlet Eye*, 306.

41. "Butler's Counsel Wrote Reprimand," *The New York Times*, February 15, 1931, 22, in *ProQuest* database (accessed August 17, 2009).

42. Ibid.

43. "Gen. Butler to Quit Marines to Lecture," *The New York Times*, February 19, 1931, 3, in *ProQuest* database (accessed March 31, 2008).

44. SDB, "To Hell with the Admirals," *Liberty: A Weekly for Everyone*, December 5, 1931, 14–15, 18, 20, 23 ("The opinions or…," 23).

45. "Smedley Butler Leaves Marines," *Lowell Sun*, September 30, 1931, 17, in *Newspaper AccessARCHIVE* database (accessed February 11, 2010).

46. "Gen. Butler Hauls Down His Flag," *The New York Times*, October 1, 1931, 25, in *ProQuest* database (accessed November 12, 2009).

47. Molly Swanton, phone conversation with author, August 30, 2009; letter from C.C. Eddleman to Edwards and Hoffman, Architects, to SDB, June 4, 1931, reprinted in "The Unpublished

Papers of Major General Smedley Darlington Butler," 559; letter from Melville M. Parker to SDB, 1931, Box 4, folder 4, Smedley D. Butler Papers.

48. Lyon, Speaking Engagements, "The Unpublished Papers of Major General Smedley Darlington Butler," 577–580.

49. Smedley D. Butler Papers, see especially Boxes 25, 30, 31 and 32.

50. "Butler Is Fiery When Radio Manager Says 'Hell' Is Obscenity," *San Antonio Express*, April 27, 1931, 1, 3, ("We are sorry…," 1), in *Newspaper AccessARCHIVE* database (accessed April 6, 2008).

51. Ibid.

52. "Gen. Butler Speaks Freely In Baltimore," *The New York Times*, May 13, 1931, 27, in *ProQuest* database (accessed August 17, 2009).

53. "General Butler Plans Relief Lecture Tour," *The New York Times*, February 21, 1931, 18, in *ProQuest* database (accessed March 31, 2008).

54. "Gen. Butler Maps Prosperity by Tax," *The New York Times*, October 2, 1931, 51, in *ProQuest* database, (accessed November 12, 2009).

55. Ibid.

56. "Butler 'Would Like' to Be a Senator," *The New York Times*, April 9, 1931, 26, and "Gen. Butler As Dry Seeks Senate Seat," *The New York Times*, March 3, 1932, 2 ("I enter this…"), in *ProQuest* database (accessed November 26, 2008).

57. Wehle, telephone conversation with author, May 15, 2010.

58. Letter from Marshall Keck to SDB, January 5, 1932, Box 25, folder 1, Smedley D. Butler Papers.

59. "Gen. Butler on Stump Says He Will 'Clean Up' the Senate," *The New York Times*, April 7, 1932, 2, in *ProQuest* database (accessed November 26, 2008).

60. "Davis Downs Butler 2 to 1 in State for Seat in U.S. Senate," *Chester Times*, April 27, 1932, 1, in *Newspaper AccessARCHIVE* database (accessed April 6, 2008).

61. "Smedley Butler Joins Roosevelt Backers," *San Antonio Express*, July 8, 1932, 1, in *Newspaper AccessARCHIVE* database (accessed August 17, 2008); "Gen. Butler to Stump," *The New York Times*, September 8, 1932, 2, in *ProQuest* database (accessed November 26, 2008).

62. Wright Patman and Ogden L. Mills, "Should the World War Veterans' Service Certificates Be Paid in Cash?" *Congressional Digest*, 11:5 (November 1932): 270, 273.

63. Donald Lisio, *The President and Protest: Hoover, MacArthur, and the Bonus Riot* (New York: Fordham University Press, 1994), 71–73.

64. "Butler for 'Real' Bonus," *The New York Times*, April 24, 1932, 16 (accessed August 17, 2009) and "Gen. Butler Urges Bonus Army to Stick," *The New York Times*, July 20, 1932, 2 ("You have as…"), in *ProQuest Historical* database (ac-

cessed November 3, 2008); "Smedley Butler Tells Bonus Army Hang Together," *The Times Recorder*, July 20, 1932, 1 ("took off his…") (accessed August 17, 2008), and "Gen. Smedley Butler Roars 'Hells' to the Bonus Vets," *The Emmetsburg Democrat*, July 21, 1932, 1, in *Newspaper AccessARCHIVE* database (accessed July 3, 2008).

65. F. Raymond Daniels, "Gen. Butler Advises B.E.F. to Disperse," *New York Times*, August 2, 1932, 2, in *ProQuest* database (accessed November 13, 2009).

66. Lisio, *The President and Protest*, 74, 76, 191–193.

67. Howard Zinn, *A People's History of the United States: 1492–Present* (New York: Harper-Perennial, 1980, 1995), 382.

68. Geoffrey Perret, *Old Soldiers Never Die: The Life of Douglas MacArthur* (Holbrook, Massachusetts: Adams Media, 1996), 159–161.

69. "Miss Ethel Butler Engaged to Marry: Daughter of Major Gen. and Mrs. D. Butler to Wed Lieut. John Wehle," *The New York Times*, January 4, 1932, 25 (accessed March 31, 2008); "Miss Ethel P. Butler Bride of Lieut. Wehle," *The New York Times*, March 6, 1932, N5, in *ProQuest* database (accessed November 26, 2008).

70. Letter from SDB to John Wehle, November 21, 1932, Box 4, folder 4, Smedley D. Butler Papers; Swanton, e-mail to author, November 29, 2009.

71. Swanton, e-mail to author, November 29, 2009.

Chapter 10

1. Butler could not recall Jack Quinn's last name at the hearing. Reporter Morris A. Bealle from *Plain Talk Magazine* later discovered it, which Butler verified, as revealed in letters from Bealle to SDB, February 9, 1935, and SDB to Bealle, February 11, 1935, Box 36, folder 5, Smedley D. Butler Papers.

2. Testimony of SDB, Special Committee on Un-American Activities, *Investigation of Nazi Propaganda Activities and Investigation of Certain Other Propaganda Activities, Part 1*, 73rd Cong., 2nd sess., 1935, No. 73-D, C-6, 9.

3. Ibid., 9–10 ("the royal family…," 9).

4. Ibid., 10.

5. Ibid., 10–11 ("Make a speech…," 10; "How can you…" and "smelled a rat … Wounded soldiers do…," 11).

6. Ibid., 11–12 ("Well, I knew…," 11).

7. "G.M.-P. Murphy, 58, Financier, Is Dead," *The New York Times*, October 19, 1937, 25, in *ProQuest* database (accessed March 31, 2008).

8. Testimony of SDB, *Investigation of Nazi Propaganda Activities*, 12.

9. Richard Seelye Jones, *A History of the American Legion* (Indianapolis: Bobbs-Merrill, 1946), 24; William Pencak, *For God & Country:*

The American Legion, 1919–1941 (Boston: Northeastern University Press, 1989), 317 ("any major position").

10. Testimony of SDB, *Investigation of Nazi Propaganda Activities*, 12.

11. Ibid.

12. Ibid., 13.

13. "Sterling Clark, Art Patron, Dies," *The New York Times*, December 30, 1956, 32, in *ProQuest* database (accessed April 1, 2008).

14. Testimony of SDB, *Investigation of Nazi Propaganda Activities*, 13.

15. Ibid 13–14 ("They wrote a..." and "That speech cost...," 13); testimony of Albert Grant Christmas, *Investigation of Nazi Propaganda Activities*, 146.

16. Elmus Wicker, "Roosevelt's 1933 Monetary Experiment," *The Journal of American History*, 57:4 (March 1971): 864; James W. Angell, "Gold, Banks and the New Deal," *Political Science Quarterly*, 49:4 (December 1934): 484–488, in *JSTOR* database (accessed October 18, 2008).

17. Angell, "Gold, Banks and the New Deal," 493.

18. Special Committee on Un-American Activities, *Investigation of Nazi Propaganda Activities and Investigation of Certain Other Propaganda Activities: Public Statement*, 73rd Cong., 2nd sess., 1935, 10.

19. Testimony of SDB, *Investigation of Nazi Propaganda Activities*, 15.

20. Ibid.

21. Ibid.

22. Ibid.

23. Ibid.

24. Letter from James E. Van Zandt to SDB, November 8, 1933, Box 32, folder 1, Smedley D. Butler Papers.

25. Testimony of SDB, *Investigation of Nazi Propaganda Activities*, 15–16 (I believe that...," 16).

26. Letter from Hanson Cleveland Coxe to SDB, early 1926, reprinted in "The Unpublished Papers of Major General Smedley Darlington Butler," 267 ("a device to..."); letter from William Night to SDB, November 22, 1934, Box 34, folder 4; letter from John H. Skaley to SDB, December 15, 1934, Box 34, folder 5, Smedley D. Butler Papers.

27. Letter from J.E. Shields to SDB, January 19, 1934 [erroneously dated as 1930], Box 34, folder 1, Smedley D. Butler Papers.

28. Testimony of SDB, *Investigation of Nazi Propaganda Activities*, 15–16 ("super organization to...," 16).

29. Ibid., 16.

30. Postcard from Gerald MacGuire to SDB, May 30, 1934, Box 34, folder 5, Smedley D. Butler Papers.

31. Testimony of SDB, *Investigation of Nazi Propaganda Activities*, 16–17. Butler could not recall the Croix de Feu's name in the testimony.

32. William D. Irvine, "Fascism in France and the Strange Case of the Croix de Feu," *The Journal of Modern History*, 63:2 (June 1991): 271–272 ("veiled allusions to ... massive, disciplined, and...," 271), in *JSTOR*, database (accessed December 18, 2008).

33. Testimony of SDB, *Investigation of Nazi Propaganda Activities*, 17–18 ("What do you ... 'support the President,'" 17).

34. Ibid., 18.

35. Ibid., 18–19.

36. Paul Comly French, "Gen. Butler Charges Fascist Plot," *Philadelphia Record*, November 21, 1934, 1–2 ("man on a...," 2).

37. Testimony of SDB, *Investigation of Nazi Propaganda Activities*, 19.

38. Ibid.

39. John Spivak, "Wall Street's Fascist Conspiracy: Testimony That the Dickstein Committee Suppressed," *New Masses*, January 29, 1935, 11, 14, 15.

40. Letter from Daniel Frysinger to Carl S. Miller, Mennonite Church USA, Historical Committee, reprinted in "Comments About Paul Comly French," http://www.mcusa-archives.org/Archives/scannedphotos/Mennonite%20Central%20Committee,%201920-%20(IX)/Civilian%20Public%20Service%20(CPS)%20Photos,%201941–47%20(IX-13-2-2)/General,%20Paul%20C%20French%20(1–2a)/French,%20Paul%20Comly%20-%200D2%20-%201944.pdf (accessed July 7, 2009).

41. Testimony of Paul Comly French, *Investigation of Nazi Propaganda Activities*, 20.

42. Ibid., 2.

43. French, "Gen. Butler Charges Fascist Plot," 1.

44. Clayton Cramer, "An American Coup d'etat?" *History Today* 45:11 (November 1995): 46, in *ProQuest* database (accessed March 31, 2008).

45. "Gen. Butler Bares 'Fascist Plot' to Seize Government by Force," *The New York Times*, November 21, 1934, 1, 5 ("Gen. Butler Bares...," 1), in *ProQuest* database (accessed March 31, 2008).

46. "Plot Without Plotters," *Time*, December 3, 1934, http://www.time.com/time/magazine/article/0,9171,929957,00.html (accessed September 7, 2008).

47. "Gen. Butler Bares 'Fascist Plot' to Seize Government by Force," *The New York Times*, 1

48. "Plot Without Plotters," *Time*.

49. Letter from Fred D. Irving to SDB, November 22, 1934, Box 34, folder 4.

50. Letter from Richard St. Clair to SDB, January 3, 1935, Box 34, folder 4.

51. "Smedley Butler Quizzed About Dictatorship," *The Charleston Gazette*, November 21, 1934, 1, in *Newspaper AccessARCHIVE* database (accessed April 6, 2008).

52. Charles E. Schamel, et al., *Guide to the Records of the United States House of Representatives at the National Archives, 1789–1989*, Bicen-

tennial Edition (Washington, D.C.: National Archives and Records Administration, 1989), http://www.archives.gov/legislative/guide/house/chapter-22-select-propaganda.html (accessed November 19, 2009).

53. "Butler's 'Fascist' Coup Labeled Publicity Stunt," *Kingsport Times*, November 21, 1934, 6, in *Newspaper AccessARCHIVE* database (accessed February 23, 2010).

54. Letter from Chas M. Kelley to SDB, February 2, 1935, Box 36, folder 1.

55. "Butler's 'Fascist' Coup Labeled Publicity Stunt," 1, 6; *Investigation of Nazi Propaganda: Public Hearings*, 8–162.

56. "G.C. M'Guire Dies; Accused of 'Plot,'" *The New York Times*, May 26, 1935, 13, in *Pro-Quest* database (accessed April 1, 2008).

57. "Call MacGuire Cashier of Dictatorship Plot," *The Sheboygan Press*, November 21, 1934, 1, 8, in *Newspaper AccessARCHIVE* database (accessed April 6, 2008).

58. "Butler's Charges of Fascist 'Plot' Denied by Broker," *Philadelphia Record*, November 21, 1934, 2.

59. French, "Gen. Butler Charges Fascist Plot," 2.

60. "Butler's Charges of Fascist 'Plot' Denied by Broker," 2; according to Jewel Brassell in a letter to the author (November 20, 2008), no one at the National Archives could locate MacGuire's military record based on the limited information about his naval career.

61. Testimony of SDB, *Investigation of Nazi Propaganda Activities*, 13, 17 ("a silver plate … head," 13; "Now, he is…," 17).

62. Testimony of MacGuire, *Investigation of Nazi Propaganda Activities*, 24.

63. Ibid., 24–25.

64. "Doyle Makes Denial," *The New York Times*, December 1, 1934, 6, in *ProQuest Historical* database (accessed November 26, 2008).

65. Testimony of MacGuire, *Investigation of Nazi Propaganda Activities*, 25–26; "I had always…" 25

66. Ibid., 28–29 ("How did you…," 28).

67. Ibid., 29, 31–35 ("Did he ever…," 31; "No, sir; to…," 32; "General, you are … was just another…," 35).

68. Testimonies of MacGuire and Albert Grant Christmas, *Investigation of Nazi Propaganda Activities*, 23, 29, 30–31, 77–80, 138, 140–143.

Chapter 11

1. Testimony of MacGuire, *Investigation of Nazi Propaganda Activities*, 71–73, 37 ("I had plainly…," 71).

2. Ibid., 85–86, 99–100; Testimony of SDB, *Investigation of Nazi Propaganda Activities*, 16.

3. Testimony of MacGuire, *Investigation of Nazi Propaganda Activities*, 112–113 ("'There is no …,'" 112; "'I recently attended …,'" 113).

4. Testimony of Christmas, *Investigation of Nazi Propaganda Activities*, 139, 145–146.

5. Ibid., 157–159 ("trade conditions…," 159).

6. John L. Spivak, *A Man in His Time* (New York: Horizon Press, 1967), 311, 312–315.

7. Ibid., 317–318.

8. Ibid., 257, 322, 328 ("I cared little…," 322).

9. Ibid., 326–329 ("four letter-words," 328; "There wouldn't be…," 329).

10. Spivak, "Wall Street's Fascist Conspiracy: Testimony That the Dickstein Committee Suppressed," 9, and *A Man in His Time*, 246–247.

11. Spivak, "Wall Street's Fascist Conspiracy: Morgan Pulls the Strings," *New Masses*, February 5, 1935, 9.

12. Ibid., 12.

13. Frederick Rudolph, "The American Liberty League, 1934–1940," *The American Historical Review*, 56:1 (October 1950): 20–21, in *JSTOR* database (accessed October 18, 2008).

14. Mike Thomson, *Document*, "The White House Coup," BBC Radio 4, July 23, 2007, http://www.bbc.co.uk/radio4/history/document/document_20070723.shtml (accessed July 28, 2009).

15. Rudolph, "The American Liberty League," 23–26, 33.

16. Thomson, "The White House Coup," with quotes replayed by BBC Radio 4 broadcast; Butler made his statement on February 17, 1935.

17. Bealle to SDB, February 11, 1935; Bealle, "Falsifying the Congressional Record," *Plain Talk Magazine*, c. 1934–1935, 3, Box 3, folder 5, Smedley D. Butler Papers.

18. Clark admitted this to *Time* magazine; see "Plot without Plotters."

19. "Butler's Charges of Fascist 'Plot' Denied by Broker," *Philadelphia Record*, 1.

20. "Smedley Butler Quizzed About Dictatorship," *The Charleston Gazette*, November 21, 1934, 3, in *Newspaper AccessARCHIVE* database (accessed April 6, 2008).

21. "Butler's Charges of Fascist 'Plot' Denied by Broker," *Philadelphia Record*, 2.

22. Hoover created this government program to give financial aid to businesses; the New Deal adopted it as its own.

23. Testimony of MacGuire, 35, 117 ("bridge or viaduct … needed $100,000 capital …," 35; "DEAR GERRY: Enclosed…," 117); no copy of this note appeared in SDB's collected papers for 1934. SDB made copies much of what he wrote, making MacGuire's letter a probable forgery.

24. "G.C. M'Guire Dies; Accused of 'Plot,'" *The New York Times*, 13.

25. "MacGuire, Linked in Butler Charge of Fascism, Dies," *Alton Evening Telegraph*, March 25, 1935, 2, in *Newspaper AccessARCHIVE* database (accessed August 23, 2008).

26. "Gen. Butler Maps Prosperity By Tax," *The New York Times*, 51.

27. Spivak, *A Man in His Time*, 302.

28. Garraty and Carnes, ed., "Hanford Mac-Nider," *American National Biography*, vol. 14, 280.

29. FDR regarded Huey Long as the other most dangerous man in America.

30. Rexford G. Tugwell, *The Democratic Roosevelt: A Biography of Franklin D. Roosevelt* (Garden City, NY: Doubleday, 1957), 349–350.

31. Spivak, "Wall Street's Fascist Conspiracy: Testimony That the Dickstein Committee Suppressed," 12–13, 10–11.

32. Spivak, *A Man in His Time*, 318.

Chapter 12

1. "Gen. Butler To Quit Marines to Lecture," 3.

2. SDB, "Making War on the Gangs," *Forum*, March 1931, 134–139; "Smedley Butler Organizes Oregon's New State Police," *Logansport Press*, April 25, 1931, 1, in *Newspaper AccessARCHIVE* database (accessed August 17, 2008).

3. Rhodri Jeffreys-Jones, *The FBI: A History* (New Haven, CT: Yale University Press, 2007), 91.

4. SDB, "Wipe Out the Gangsters! A Proposal for an Anti-Crime Legion," *Forum*, October 1931, xvii–xviii.

5. G. Robert Blakey, "Rico: The Genesis of an Idea," *Trends in Organized Crime*, 9:4 (Summer 2006): 9–11, in *EBSCO* databases (accessed November 26, 2009).

6. Edith Hamilton, *Mythology* (New York & Scarborough, Ontario: New American Library, 1940, 1942), 202.

7. Swanton, e-mail to author, November 30, 2009.

8. Letters from SDB to Alger, January 8, 1931, January 8, 1931, and letter from SDB to Alger, January 9, 1931, Box 16, folder 1, Smedley D. Butler Papers.

9. Garraty and Carnes, ed., "Lowell Thomas," *American National Biography*, vol. 21, 518.

10. Schmidt, *Maverick Marine*, 220.

11. Letter from James E. Harboard to SDB, August 24, 1933, Box 21, folder 4, Smedley D. Butler Papers.

12. Letters from Stanley M. Rinehart to SDB, July 22, 1932, and September 8, 1933, Box 31, folder 5, Smedley D. Butler Papers.

13. Letter from SDB to Lejeune, February 20, 1933, Box 30 folder 4, Smedley D. Butler Papers.

14. Letter from SDB to Rinehart, June 12, 1933, Box 30, folder 11; letter from John Farrar to SDB, July 26, 1933, Box 31, folder 2, Smedley D. Butler Papers.

15. Letter from SDB to Lejeune, June 12, 1933, Box 30, folder 11, Smedley D. Butler Papers.

16. Letter from Lowell Thomas to SDB, No-

vember 2, 1933, and letter from SDB to Thomas, November 22, 1933, Box 32, folder 3, Smedley D. Butler Papers.

17. "Best Sellers Here and Elsewhere," *The New York Times*, September 4, 1933, 9, and September 11, 1933, 15, in *ProQuest* database (accessed August 20, 2009).

18. "The Extraordinary Career of Smedley D. Butler," *The New York Times*, August 27, 1933, BR4, in *ProQuest* database (accessed August 20, 2009).

19. Letter from SDB to Rinehart, February 10, 1934, Box 34, folder 2; letter from Rinehart to SDB, January 29, 1934, Box 35, folder 14, Smedley D. Butler Papers.

20. Letter from Thomas to SDB, July 14, 1932, Box 1, folder 1, Smedley D. Butler Papers.

21. Letters from Ruth E. Anderson to SDB, September 25, 1934, and from SDB to Anderson, January 3, 1935, Box 35, folder 2; letter from Anderson to SDB, January 7, 1935, Box 35, folder 3, Smedley D. Butler Papers.

22. Letters from Raymond B. Phillips to SDB, November 8, 1933, Box 32, folder 2; January 20, 1934, Box 34, folder 1; and February 7, 1934, Box 34, folder 2, Smedley D. Butler Papers.

23. Letter from Andrew J. Biemiller to SDB, January 6, 1935, Box 35, folder 14, Smedley D. Butler Papers.

24. Letter from SDB to Joseph Broadman, January 17, 1935, Smedley D. Butler Papers.

25. Stephen R. Ortiz, "The 'New Deal' for Veterans: The Economy Act, the Veterans of Foreign Wars, and the Origins of New Deal Dissent," *The Journal of Military History*, 70:2 (April 2006): 417–418, 424, 421–422 ("cut federal expenditures…," 418; "removed 501,777 veterans…," 424), in *JSTOR* database (accessed November 28, 2009).

26. Ibid., 434–435; Butler quoted saying, "'I believe in …,'" on 435.

27. "General Butler 'Complimented,'" *The New York Times*, September 16, 1935, 3, in *ProQuest* database (accessed March 31, 2008).

28. Ortiz, "The 'New Deal' for Veterans," 435–436.

29. Letter from Veterans National Rank and File Committee to SDB, November 21, 1934, Box 34, folder 4, Smedley D. Butler Papers.

30. Philip J. Jaffe, *The Rise and Fall of American Communism* (New York: Horizon Press, 1975), 36.

31. "Gen. Butler Calls Neutrality Vital," *The New York Times*, January 4, 1936, 5, in *ProQuest* database, (accessed November 28, 2009).

32. Letter from Barney Yankofsky to SDB, September 8, 1934, Box 34, folder 2, Smedley D. Butler Papers.

33. "Gen. Butler Talk Is Cut Off Radio," *The New York Times*, October 4, 1934, 17, in *ProQuest* database (accessed August 17, 2009).

34. As evidenced by the vast number of letters he received from a variety of former soldiers and

other listeners. See Box 34, folder 3 of the Smedley D. Butler Papers.

35. Letter from SDB to Dick Estill, January 4, 1934, Box 35, folder 2; letter from SDB to Mr. Coyle, December 12, 1934, Box 34, folder 5; letter from A. Rosenman to SDB, January 21, 1935, Box 35, folder 10, Smedley D. Butler Papers.

36. Letter from "The Forgotten Man" to SDB, January 3, 1934, Box 34, folder 1, Smedley D. Butler Papers.

37. Box 35, folder 2, of the Smedley D. Butler Papers contains a large sampling of such letters.

38. "Smedley Butler Declares Wars Are 'International Rackets,'" *Frederick Post*, October 29, 1934, 1, in *Newspaper AccessARCHIVE* database (accessed August 24, 2009).

39. SDB, "War is a Racket," *Forum*, September 1934, 140.

40. According to Schmidt, who interviewed Dimitman, the statistics came mainly from the Nye Hearings (236), a senatorial investigation into alleged war profiteering by American industries during World War I, and the possibility they pushed the country into that war. The Nye Committee failed to take into account any foreign statistical data, an error that compromised its conclusions. See Geoffrey S. Smith, "Isolationism, the Devil, and the Advent of the Second World War: Variations on a Theme," *The International History Review*, 4:1 (February 1982): 62, in JSTOR database (accessed November 30, 2009).

41. SDB, "War is a Racket," 140, 142–143 ("the soldiers ... destroyed men," 140; "living dead ... 'about face,'" 142; "the profit out...," 143).

42. Earl A. Molander, "Historical Antecedents of Military-Industrial Criticism," *Military Affairs*, 40:2 (April 1976): 59, 62, in JSTOR database (accessed April 13, 2009).

43. Ibid., 1.

44. Smith, "Isolationism, the Devil, and the Advent of the Second World War," 63–64.

45. Letter from Samuel Cummins to SDB, November 24, 1934, Box 35, folder 4.

46. Letter from Dorrance & Company, Inc., Publishers, to SDB, November 9, 1934, Box 34, folder 4, Smedley D. Butler Papers.

47. Schmidt, *Maverick Marine*, 236.

48. Wehle, telephone conversation with author, May 15, 2010.

49. Telegram from Hugo L. Black to SDB, February 5, 1935, Box 35, folder 1, Smedley D. Butler Papers.

50. R.T. MacPherson, *John H. Russell, Jr., 1872–1947: Register of His Personal Papers* (Washington, D.C.: History and Museum Divisions, 1987), http://www.marines.mil/news/publications/Documents/John%20H.%20Russell,%20Jr.%201872–1947_Register%20of%20his%20personal%20papers%20%20PCN%2019000317300.pdf (accessed August 22, 2009), 4.

51. Telegram from SDB to Black, 6, 1935, Box 35, folder 1, Smedley D. Butler Papers.

52. MacPherson, *John H. Russell, Jr., 1872–1947*, 1.

53. Ibid., 2–4.

54. "Butler Hits 'Favoritism in Marines,'" *The Syracuse Herald*, March 3, 1935, 14, in *Newspaper AccessARCHIVE* database (accessed August 22, 2009).

55. Ibid.

56. Letters from SDB to Hiram Johnson, February 9, 1935, and from SDB to Frank J. Schwable, March 18, 1935, Box 35, folder 1, Smedley D. Butler Papers.

57. "Black Will Press Fight on Russell," *The New York Times*, March 3, 1935, 28, in *ProQuest* database (accessed November 7, 2009).

58. MacPherson, *John H. Russell, Jr., 1872–1947*, 4.

59. "SDB, "'In Time of Peace:' The Army," 8.

60. Ibid., 8–10; a committee known as the Joint Army and Navy Board drew up an invasion plan of Canada in 1930, naming it "Joint Army and Navy Basic War Plan — Red, or *Plan Red*"; see Christopher M. Bell, "Thinking the Unthinkable: British and American Naval Strategies for an Anglo-American War, 1918–1931," *The International History Review*, 19:4 (November 1997): 800, in JSTOR (accessed January 30, 2010).

61. Ibid 11–12.

62. "Mrs. Thomas S. Butler: Widow of Representative and the Mother of General Butler," *The New York Times*, June 22, 1936, 19 (accessed March 31, 2008); "Gen. Butler Legatee of Mother," *The New York Times*, August 4, 1936, 7, in *ProQuest Historical Newspapers: The New York Times (1851–2005)* database (accessed November 3, 2008); Swanton, e-mail to author, November 30, 2009.

63. "Extortion Scheme Is Foiled," *The Abilene Daily Reporter*, August 7, 1936, 1; "Suspect Held For Attempt at Extortion," *Big Spring Daily Herald*, August 28, 1936, 1 (accessed November 29, 2009) in *Newspaper AccessARCHIVE* database (accessed August 21, 2009); Wehle, telephone conversation with author, May 15, 2010.

64. "Suspect Held For Attempt at Extortion," *Big Spring Daily Herald*, 1.

65. "Offer Mahan $1000 Bail at Hearing Here," *The Abilene Daily Reporter*, September 1, 1936, 1, in *Newspaper AccessARCHIVE* database (accessed November 29, 2009).

66. Smith, "Isolationism, the Devil, and the Advent of the Second World War," 63.

67. SDB, "Common Sense Neutrality," reprinted in *War Is a Racket: The Antiwar Classic by America's Most Decorated General, Two Other Anti-interventionist Tracts, and Photographs from the Horror of It* (Los Angeles, CA: Feral House, 2003), 50–51.

68. Ibid., 51–52.

69. Wehle, telephone conversation with author, May 15, 2010.

70. Smith, "Isolationism, the Devil, and the Advent of the Second World War," 71–72, 68–69.

71. "Navy Bill a 'Bluff' to General Butler," *The New York Times*, April 9, 1938, 10, in *ProQuest* database (accessed November 30, 2009);

72. SDB, "Amendment for Peace," reprinted in *War Is a Racket*, 61, 63 ("the removal of...," 61).

73. Schmidt, *Maverick Marine*, 231.

74. "Smedley Butler of Marines Dead," *The New York Times*, 34 ("for a general..."); Wehle, telephone conversation with author, May 15, 2010 ("popping aspirin like...").

75. Michael J. Klag, ed., *Johns Hopkins Family Health Book* (New York: HarperCollins Publishers, 1999), 1063.

76. "Military Leaders Honor Gen. Butler," *The New York Times*, June 25, 1940, 23, in *ProQuest* database (accessed November 3, 2008); Swanton, e-mail to author, November 30, 2009.

77. "General Butler's Estate $2,000," *The New York Times*, July 18, 1940, in *ProQuest* database (accessed November 3, 2008).

Bibliography

Butler Works

Butler, Smedley D. "Amendment for Peace." Reprinted in *War Is a Racket: The Antiwar Classic by America's Most Decorated General, Two Other Anti-interventionist Tracts, and Photographs from the Horror of It*. Los Angeles, CA: Feral House, 2003.

_____. "Common Sense Neutrality." Reprinted in *War Is a Racket*.

_____. "Dame Rumor: The Biggest Liar in the World." *The American Magazine*, June 1931.

_____. "The 'Fightingest' Man I Know." *The American Magazine*, September 1931.

_____. *General Smedley Darlington Butler: The Letters of a Leatherneck*. Edited by Ann Cipriano Venzon. Westport, CT: Praeger, 1992.

_____. "'In Time of Peace:' The Army." *Common Sense*, November 1935.

_____. *My Dear Smedley: Personal Correspondence of John A. Lejeune and Smedley D. Butler, 1927–1928*. Edited by J. Michael Miller. Quantico, VA: Marine Corps Research Center, 2002.

_____. "To Hell with the Admirals." *Liberty: A Weekly for Everyone*, December 5, 1931.

_____. "War Is a Racket." *Forum*, September 1934.

_____. "Wipe Out the Gangsters! A Proposal for an Anti-Crime Legion." *Forum*, October 1931.

Butler, Smedley D., and Arthur J. Burks. *Walter Garvin in Mexico*. Philadelphia: Dorrance, 1927.

Smedley D. Butler Military Personnel File. National Archives. St. Louis, MO.

Smedley D. Butler Papers. Marine Corps Archives and Special Collections. Gray Research Center. Quantico, VA.

Thomas, Lowell. *Old Gimlet Eye: The Adventures of Smedley D. Butler as Told to Lowell Thomas*. New York: Farrar & Rinehart, 1933.

Periodical Articles

Adams, Thomas K. "Intervention in Haiti: Lessons Relearned." *Military Review* 76:5 (September/October 1996): 45–57. In *EBSCO* databases.

"The American Occupation of Haiti I." *Political Science Quarterly*, 42:2 (June 1927): 232, 235–236.

Angell, James W. "Gold, Banks and the New Deal." *Political Science Quarterly* 49:4 (December 1934): 481–505. In *JSTOR* database.

Baldwin, Fred D. "Smedley D. Butler and Prohibition Enforcement in Philadelphia, 1924–1925." *The Pennsylvania Magazine of History and Biography* 84:3 (July 1960): 352–368. In *JSTOR* database.

Barkman, Floy Thornton. "Men of the U.S. Navy at San Diego." *Missionary Review of the World*, March 1925.

Bartlett, Merrill L. "Ben Hebard Fuller and the Genesis of a Modern United States Marine Corps, 1891-1934." *The Journal of Military History* 69:1 (January 2005): 73–91. In *JSTOR* database.

Bealle, Morris A. "Falsifying the Congressional Record." *Plain Talk Magazine*, c. 1934–1935. Found in the Smedley D. Butler papers collection.

Bell, Christopher M. "Thinking the Unthinkable: British and American Naval Strategies for an Anglo-American War, 1918–1931." *The International History Review* 19:4 (November 1997): 789–808. In *JSTOR* database.

Blakey, G. Robert. "Rico: The Genesis of an Idea." *Trends in Organized Crime* 9:4 (Summer 2006): 8–34. In *EBSCO* databases.

Brown, George W. "Haiti and the United States." *The Journal of Negro History* 8:2 (April 1923): 134–152. In *JSTOR* database.

Brundage, John F., and G. Dennis Shanks. "Deaths from Bacterial Pneumonia During 1918–19 Influenza Pandemic." *Emerging Infectious Diseases* 14:8 (August 2008): 1193–1199. The National Center for Biotechnology Information (NCBI) website (www.ncbi.nlm.nih.gov).

Buhite, Russell D. "Nelson Johnson and American Policy Toward China, 1925–1928." *The Pacific Historical Review* 35:4 (November 1966): 451–465. In *JSTOR* database.

Calder, Bruce J. "Caudillos and Gavilleros Versus the United States Marines: Guerrilla Insurgency During the Dominican Intervention, 1916–1924." *The Hispanic American Historical Review* 58:4 (November 1978): 649–675. In *JSTOR* database.

Ch'ên, Jerome. "The Nature and Characteristics of the Boxer Movement — A Morphological Study." *Bulletin of the School of Oriental and African Studies* 23:2 (1960): 287–308. In *JSTOR* database.

C.K.T. "Baiting a Marine: A Special Correspondence from Philadelphia." *Outlook*, October 8, 1924.

Cosmas, Graham A. "From Order to Chaos: The War Department, the National Guard, and Military Policy, 1898." *Military Affairs* 29:3 (Autumn 1965): 105–122. In *JSTOR* database.

Cramer, Clayton. "An American Coup d'Etat?" *History Today* 45:11 (November 1995): 42–47. In *ProQuest* databases.

Davis, James Porter. "Shanghai: A City

Ruled by Five Nations." *Current History*, August 1926.

Diggins, John P. "The Italo-American Anti-Fascist Opposition." *The Journal of American History* 54:3 (December 1967): 579–598. In *JSTOR* database.

Edie, Guy L., et al., "Camp Pontanezen, Brest, France." *The Military Surgeon: Journal of the Association of Military Surgeons of the United States* XLVI (1920).

"Failure in Haiti." *The Nation*, December 18, 1929.

Furgurson, Ernest B. "Amelia Earhart's Brazen Cohorts." *American History*, February 2010.

Garrett, Oliver H.P. "Why They Cleaned Up Philadelphia." *New Republic*, February 27, 1924.

"The Genial General." *Outlook*, May 6, 1931.

Gismondi, Michael, and Jeremy Mouat. "Merchants, Mining, and Concessions on Nicaragua's Mosquito Coast: Reassessing the American Presence, 1895–1912." *Journal of Latin American Studies* 34:4 (November 2002): 845–879. In *JSTOR* database.

Haydock, Michael D. "Marine Scapegoat." *Military History*, 18:6 (February 2002): 51.

Hendrix, Henry J., II. "TR's Plan to Invade Colombia." *Naval History* 20:6 (December 2006). In *EBSCO* databases.

High, Stanley. "Shanghai: Where Fear Breeds Hate." *New Republic*, May 4, 1927.

Hunt, Michael H. "The Forgotten Occupation: Peking, 1900–1901." *The Pacific Historical Review* 48:4 (November 1979): 501–529. In *JSTOR* database.

Irvine, William D. "Fascism in France and the Strange Case of the Croix de Feu." *The Journal of Modern History* 63:2 (June 1991): 271–295. In *JSTOR* database.

Kreiser, Christine M. "The Enemy Within." *American History*, December 2006. In *EBSCO* databases.

Lewis, Sinclair. "Devil-Dog Rule." Letter to the editor. *The Nation*, December 18, 1921.

Linn, Brian M. "Provincial Pacification in the Philippines, 1900–1901: The First District Department of Northern Luzon." *Military Affairs* 51: 2 (April 1987): 62–66. In *JSTOR* database.

Logan, Rayford W. "James Weldon Johnson

and Haiti." *The Phylon Quarterly* 32:4 (4th Quarter, 1971): 396–402. In *JSTOR* database.

Marvin, George. "Assassination and Intervention in Haiti." *The World's Work*, February 1916.

Maxfield, Erza Kempton. "Quaker 'Thee' and Its History." *American Speech* 1:12 (September 1926): 638–644. In *JSTOR* database.

McFall, J. Arthur. "After 33 Years of Marine Service, Smedley Butler Became An Outspoken Critic of U.S. Foreign Policy." *Military History* 19:6 (February 2003): 16, 24. In *EBSCO* databases.

Meyer, Michael C. "The Arms of the Ypiranga." *The Hispanic American Historical Review* 50:3 (August 1970): 543–556. In *JSTOR* database.

Millard, Thomas F. "A Comparison of the Armies in China." *Scribner's*, July 1, 1914.

Molander, Earl A. "Historical Antecedents of Military-Industrial Criticism." *Military Affairs* 40:2 (April 1976): 59–63. In *JSTOR* database.

Oakley, Imogen B. "Two Dictatorships." *Outlook,* December 22, 1926, 527.

Ortiz, Stephen R. "The 'New Deal' for Veterans: The Economy Act, the Veterans of Foreign Wars, and the Origins of New Deal Dissent." *The Journal of Military History* 70:2 (April 2006): 415–438. In *JSTOR* database.

"Our Comic-Opera Court-Martial." *The Literary Digest,* February 28, 1931, 10.

"Our Conflict with Nicaragua." *Current Literature*, October 1912.

Padgett, James A. "Diplomats to Haiti and Their Diplomacy." *The Journal of Negro History* 25:3 (July 1940): 265–330. In *JSTOR* database.

Patman, Wright, and Ogden L. Mills. "Should the World War Veterans' Service Certificates Be Paid in Cash?" *Congressional Digest* 11:5 (November 1932): 270–276.

Pérez, Louis A., Jr. "The Meaning of the *Maine*: Causation and the Historiography of the Spanish-American War." *The Pacific Historical Review* 58:3 (August 1989): 293–322. In *JSTOR* database.

"Philadelphia's Whiskey Ring." *The Literary Digest*, September 15, 1928.

"Plot Without Plotters." *Time*, December 3, 1934. On the Time.com website.

Posner, Walter H. "American Marines in Haiti, 1915–1922." *The Americas* 20:3 (January 1964): 231–266. In *JSTOR* database.

Powell, Anna I. "Relations Between the United States and Nicaragua, 1898–1916." *The Hispanic American Historical Review* 8:1 (February 1928): 43–64. In *JSTOR* database.

Pratt, Julius W. "American Business and the Spanish-American War." *The Hispanic American Historical Review* 14:2 (May 1934): 163–201. In *JSTOR* database.

"The Press: Vanderbilt Truth." *Time*, February 13, 1931. Time.com website.

Preston, Diana. "The Boxer Rising." *Asian Affairs* 31:1 (February 2000): 26–36. In *EBSCO* databases.

Pugach, Noel H. "Standard Oil and Petroleum Development in Early Republican China." *The Business History Review* 45:4 (Winter 1971): 452–473. In *JSTOR* database.

Raat, W. Dirk. "US Intelligence Operations and Covert Action in Mexico, 1900–47: Intelligence Services During the Second World War, Part 2." *Journal of Contemporary History* 22:4 (October 1987): 615–638. In *JSTOR* database.

Rausch, George J., Jr. "The Exile and Death of Victoriano Huerta." *The Hispanic American Historical Review* 42:2 (May 1962): 133–151. In *JSTOR* database.

Rudolph, Frederick. "The American Liberty League, 1934–1940." *The American Historical Review,* 56:1 (October 1950): 20–21.

Rudwick, Elliott M. "The National Negro Committee Conference of 1909." *The Phylon Quarterly* 18:4 (4th Quarter, 1957): 413–419. In *JSTOR* database.

Scher, Adam. "Remembering America's 'Splendid Little War': Spanish-American War Collections at the Minnesota Historical Society." *Minnesota History* 56: 3 (Fall 1998): 129–137. In *JSTOR* database.

"Shanghai's Fall and China's Future." *The Literary Digest*, April 2, 1927.

Smith, C. Stanley. "Five Days." *Atlantic Monthly*, December 1927.

Smith, Geoffrey S. "Isolationism, the Devil, and the Advent of the Second World War: Variations on a Theme." *The Inter-*

national History Review 4:1 (February 1982): 55–89. In *JSTOR* database.

Smith, T. Cuyler. "The Charleston Exposition." *The Independent*, January 16, 1902.

Spivak, John. "Wall Street's Fascist Conspiracy: Morgan Pulls the Strings." *New Masses*, February 5, 1935.

_____. "Wall Street's Fascist Conspiracy: Testimony That the Dickstein Committee Suppressed." *New Masses*, January 29, 1935.

Thomson, Elihu. "The Progress of the Isthmian Canal." *Proceedings of the American Philosophical Society* 46:185 (January–April 1907): 124–137. In *JSTOR* database

Thomson, Mike. *Document*, "The White House Coup," BBC Radio 4, July 23, 2007.

Turner, Frederick C. "Anti-Americanism in Mexico, 1910–1913." *The Hispanic American Historical Review* 47:4 (November 1967): 502–518. In *JSTOR* database.

Varg, Paul A. "The Foreign Policy of Japan and the Boxer Revolt." *The Pacific Historical Review* 15:3 (September 1946): 279–285. In *JSTOR* database.

"When a Marine Tells It." *The Literary Digest*, February 14, 1931.

White, Thomas Raeburn. "The Philadelphia System." *Forum*, May 1927, 678, 681.

Wicker, Elmus. "Roosevelt's 1933 Monetary Experiment." *The Journal of American History* 57:4 (March 1971): 864–879. In *JSTOR* database.

"Will Smedley Butler Sniff More Powder in China?" *The Literary Digest*, April 2, 1927.

Wilson, David A. "Principles and Profits: Standard Oil Responds to Chinese Nationalism, 1925–1927." *The Pacific Historical Review* 46:4 (November 1977): 625–647. In *JSTOR* database.

Zabecki, David T. "Paths to Glory: Medal of Honor Recipients Smedley Butler and Dan Daly." *Military History*, January/February 2008. Historynet website (historynet.com).

Newspaper Articles

All New York Times articles are found in *ProQuest Historical Newspapers: The New York Times (1851–2005)* database. Most of the other articles can be found in the *Newspaper AccessARCHIVE* database.

"Accepts Butler's Version." *The New York Times*, December 22, 1929.

"Admiral Seymour's Report." *The New York Times*, June 30, 1900.

"Aid for Nicaragua Asked by Estrada." *The New York Times*, September 10, 1912.

"Another Nicaragua Revolt." *The New York Times*, August 1, 1912, 5.

"Arms Firemen in Philadelphia." *The New York Times*, January 17, 1924.

"Asks Gen. Butler to Explain Speech." *The New York Times*, December 15, 1929.

"Best Sellers Here and Elsewhere," *The New York Times*, September 4, 1933, and September 11, 1933.

"'Big Storm Coming,' Butler Tells Force." *The New York Times*, July 17, 1924, 4.

"Black Will Press Fight on Russell." *The New York Times*, March 3, 1935.

"Bonilla Defeats Sierra." *Eau Claire Leader*, March 27, 1903.

"Butler for 'Real' Bonus." *The New York Times*, April 24, 1932.

"Butler Gives $2,000 of Pay to Widow." *The New York Times*, September 18, 1924.

"Butler Hits 'Favoritism in Marines.'" *The Syracuse Herald*, March 3, 1935.

"Butler Is Fiery When Radio Manager Says 'Hell' Is Obscenity." *San Antonio Express*, April 27, 1931.

"Butler on the Job But Father Isn't Cheering." *The News*, April 16, 1927.

"Butler to Punish Officers." *New York Times*, April 9, 1924.

"Butler 'Would Like' to Be a Senator." *The New York Times*, April 9, 1931, 26.

"Butler's Charges of Fascist 'Plot' Denied by Broker." *Philadelphia Record*, November 21, 1934.

"Butler's Counsel Wrote Reprimand." *The New York Times*, February 15, 1931.

"Butler's 'Fascist' Coup Labeled Publicity Stunt." *Kingsport Times*, November 21, 1934.

"Call MacGuire Cashier of Dictatorship Plot." *The Sheboygan Press*, November 21, 1934.

"China's Two Great Cities." *The Oxford Mirror*, June 21, 1900.

"Chinese Sell Children to Get Food in Famine." *The New York Times*, January 9, 1928.

"Cocktail Colonel Convicted." *Oakland Tribune*, April 19, 1926.

"Col. Williams Reduced 4 Numbers in

Grade." *The New York Times*, May 22, 1926.

Correspondence of the *Baltimore Sun*. "In Manila a Month Ago." *The New York Times*, July 11, 1898, 4.

Daniels, F. Raymond. "Gen. Butler Advises B.E.F. to Disperse." *New York Times*, August 2, 1932.

"Daniels Orders Haitian Inquiry." *Newport Mercury*, October 23, 1920.

"Davis Downs Butler 2 to 1 in State for Seat in U.S. Senate." *Chester Times*, April 27, 1932.

"Death to 'Yankees': Mobs Menace Americans in Capital of Nicaragua." *The Washington Post*, August 22, 1910.

"Declare Williams Suffered From Drug." *The New York Times*, April 15, 1926.

"Defeat at Tientsin." *The Anaconda Standard*, July 19, 1900.

"Doyle Makes Denial." *The New York Times*, December 1, 1934.

"Estrada a Fugitive." *The New York Times*, May 11, 1911.

"European Barbarism in China." *The New York Times*, October 2, 1900.

"Extortion Scheme Is Foiled." *The Abilene Daily Reporter*, August 7, 1936.

"The Extraordinary Career of Smedley D. Butler." *The New York Times*, August 27, 1933.

"Finds Vanderbilt Met Mussolini 5 Years Ago." *The New York Times*, February 2, 1931.

"Fisherman Finds Bodies Beside Lake." *The Abilene Reporter–News*, October 16, 1947.

French, Paul Comly. "Gen. Butler Charges Fascist Plot." *Philadelphia Record*, November 21, 1934.

"G.C. M'Guire Dies; Accused of 'Plot.'" *The New York Times*, May 26, 1935, 13.

"G.M.-P. Murphy, 58, Financier, Is Dead." *The New York Times*, October 19, 1937.

"General Butler and His Family Sail for San Diego." *The Evening Bulletin*, January 2, 1926.

"Gen. Butler As Dry Seeks Senate Seat." *The New York Times*, March 3, 1932.

"Gen. Butler, As Spy, Met Huerta." *The New York Times*, May 7, 1931.

"Gen. Butler Bares 'Fascist Plot' to Seize Government by Force." *The New York Times*, November 21, 1934.

"Gen. Butler Calls Neutrality Vital." *The New York Times*, January 4, 1936.

"General Butler 'Complimented.'" *The New York Times*, September 16, 1935, 3.

"Gen. Butler Hauls Down His Flag." *The New York Times*, October 1, 1931.

"General Butler Led the United Fire Forces Which Saved Most of Oil Plant at Tien-Tsin." *The New York Times*, December 26, 1927.

"Gen. Butler Legatee of Mother." *The New York Times*, August 4, 1936.

"Gen. Butler Maps Prosperity by Tax." *The New York Times*, October 2, 1931.

"Gen. Butler on Stump Says He Will 'Clean Up' the Senate." *The New York Times*, April 7, 1932.

"General Butler Plans Relief Lecture Tour." *The New York Times*, February 21, 1931.

"General Butler Sends 700 Marines on Leave As Drought Depletes Quantico Water Supply." *The New York Times*, August 1, 1930.

"Gen. Butler Speaks Freely In Baltimore." *The New York Times*, May 13, 1931.

"Gen. Butler Talk Is Cut Off Radio." *The New York Times*, October 4, 1934

"Gen. Butler to Quit Marines to Lecture." *The New York Times*, February 19, 1931.

"Gen. Butler to Stump." *The New York Times*, September 8, 1932.

"Gen. Butler Urges Bonus Army to Stick." *The New York Times*, July 20, 1932.

"General Butler Wins Second Battle for Civic Law and Order." *Olean Times*, October 1, 1929.

"General Butler's Estate $2,000." *The New York Times*, July 18, 1940.

"General Butler's Job." *The New York Times*, September 7, 1925.

"Gen. Butler's Leave Extended One Year." *The New York Times*, December 10, 1924.

"Gen. Butler's Rum Charges Arouses Ire." *Logansport Pharos-Tribune*, March 11, 1926.

"General Butler's Value to Philadelphia." *The New York Times*, July 18, 1924.

"Gen. Schwan's Expedition." *The New York Times*, October 13, 1899.

"Gen. Smedley Butler Roars 'Hells' to the Bonus Vets." *The Emmetsburg Democrat*, July 21, 1932.

"Guns of U.S. Battleships Roar as Americans Are Slain by Rebel Cantonese." *Jefferson City Tribune-Post*, March 24, 1927.

"Haitians Class Gen. Butler as Very Imaginative." *Clearfield Progress*, April 21, 1931.

"Hitler? Butler Says It's He Who'll Get Slapped." *The San Antonio Light*, October 18, 1938.

"Honduran Muddle Worse." *The New York Times*, January 30, 1903.

"House Veteran Dies, Victim of Heart Disease." *Decatur Herald*, May 27, 1928.

"How the Canal Zone is Governed." *Lowell Sun*, July 22, 1912.

Hyde, Maxwell. "Philadelphians Fail on Crusade on Vice." *Charleston Daily Mail*, April 6, 1924.

"Italian Envoy Protests Gen. Butler's Talk Calling Mussolini an 'Embryo' War Starter." *The New York Times*, January 27, 1931.

"Kendrick Prepares to Oust Gen. Butler." *The New York Times*, July 21, 1924.

"Latest News." *Chester Daily Times*, July 30, 1881.

"Looting in Peking." *The New York Times*, September 1, 1900.

"MacGuire, Linked in Butler Charge of Fascism, Dies." *Alton Evening Telegraph*, March 25, 1935.

"Mail Guards Will Use Gas." *The Salt Lake Tribune*, November 13, 1926.

"The *Maine*." *The New York Times*, February 17, 1898, 6.

"Marines Gain a Victory," *The New York Times*, October 9, 1899.

"Marines Ordered to Guard U.S. Mails," *Portsmouth Daily Times*, October 16, 1926.

"Marines Ready to Seize Road to Mexico City." *The New York Times*, April 21, 1914.

McCoy, Samuel. "Philadelphia at War Over General Butler." *The New York Times*, July 27, 1924.

McKinley, William. "The Declaration of War." *The New York Times*, April 26, 1898.

"Military Leaders Honor Gen. Butler." *The New York Times*, June 25, 1940.

"Miss Ethel Butler Engaged to Marry: Daughter of Major Gen. and Mrs. D. Butler to Wed Lieut. John Wehle." *The New York Times*, January 4, 1932.

"Miss Ethel P. Butler Bride of Lieut. Wehle." *The New York Times*, March 6, 1932.

"More Marines Taken from Mail Guard

Duty." *The New York Times*, January 25, 1927.

"More Police Heads in Philadelphia Net." *The New York Times*, October 8, 1928.

"Mrs. Thomas S. Butler: Widow of Representative and the Mother of General Butler." *The New York Times*, June 22, 1936.

Mulvaney, Joseph. "The Fightin'est Marine Passes." *The San Antonio Light*, July 7, 1940.

"Munitions Ship Blown to Bits in Chinese War." *Nevada State Journal*, October 18, 1926.

"Mussolini's Fine Rule in Italy Sketched by William Hervey at Masonic Dinner Meeting." *The Oxnard Daily Courier*, December 22, 1927.

"Name the Naval Board to Hear Butler Case." *The Chillicothe Constitution-Tribune*, January 31, 1931.

"Nation Voted Dry; 38 States Adopt the Amendment." *The New York Times*, January 17, 1919.

"Navy Bill a 'Bluff' to General Butler." *The New York Times*, April 9, 1938.

"Neville Will Take Post as Marine Head." *The Evening Tribune*, February 8, 1929.

"Nicaragua Fuss Grows Serious." *The Anaconda Standard*, August 29, 1912.

"Nicaraguans Kill Yankee Marines." *Daily Herald*, October 11, 1912.

"No Indictments: No One Accused of Burning of Antonio Rodriguez at Rock Springs." *Advocate*, December 24, 1910.

"Offer Mahan $1000 Bail at Hearing Here." *The Abilene Daily Reporter*, September 1, 1936.

"Official Decree From Nicaragua Forbidding Vessels Enter Bluefield." *Lowell Sun*, June 2, 1910.

"150 Mexicans Slain in Seizure of Mexican Port." *Waterloo Evening Courier*, April 22, 1914.

"Philadelphia Mayor Fires Gen. Butler." *Logansport Pharos-Tribune*, December 22, 1925.

"Philadelphia Raids Close 973 Saloons." *The New York Times*, January 12, 1924.

"Pinchot Requests Coolidge to Grant Butler More Time." *New Castle News*, October 19, 1925.

"President Ordered Occupation to Prevent Landing of Munitions." *The New York Times*, April 22, 1914.

"President Refuses Butler More Leave." *The New York Times*, November 4, 1925.

"Public Hearing in Butler Case Heflin Demand." *Mason City Globe-Gazette*, February 4, 1931.

"Rally to Defense of Col. Williams." *The New York Times*, March 12, 1926.

"Rebels Crushed, Our Marines Die." *The New York Times*, October 6, 1912.

"The Relief Force Enters Tien-Tsin." *The New York Times*, June 26, 1900.

"Rush Work on Forts." *The Daily Times*, July 6, 1907.

"Scene Was Fearful." *Des Moines Daily News*, August 29, 1900.

"Smedley Butler Declares Wars Are 'International Rackets.'" *Frederick Post*, October 29, 1934.

"Smedley Butler Is Major General." *Kingsport Times*, July 14, 1929.

"Smedley Butler Joins Roosevelt Backers." *San Antonio Express*, July 8, 1932.

"Smedley Butler Leaves Marines." *Lowell Sun*, September 30, 1931.

"Smedley Butler of Marines Dead." *The New York Times*, June 22, 1940.

"Smedley Butler Organizes Oregon's New State Police." *Logansport Press*, April 25, 1931.

"Smedley Butler Quizzed About Dictatorship." *The Charleston Gazette*, November 21, 1934.

"Smedley Butler Tells Bonus Army Hang Together." *The Times Recorder*, July 20, 1932.

"Solace Sails from Manila," *The New York Times*, June 14, 1900.

"Spain to Use Privateers." *The New York Times*, April 25, 1898.

"Stand Taken: Americans Capture Fort Riviere Last Haytian Rebel Stronghold." *The Gleaner*, November 27, 1915.

"Sterling Clark, Art Patron, Dies." *The New York Times*, December 30, 1956.

"Still Fighting in Peking." *The New York Times*, August 20, 1900.

"Suspect Held For Attempt at Extortion." *Big Spring Daily Herald*, August 28, 1936.

"Taft Quits Zone for His Home." *Daily Gazette*, December 26, 1912.

"The Taku Fortifications." *The New York Times*, June 18, 1900.

"10,000,000 Suffer in Chinese Famine." *The New York Times*, January 12, 1928.

"Texas Auto Crash Toll 4." *The New York Times*, February 15, 1930.

"T.S. Butler Dies in Capital Hotel." *The New York Times*, May 27, 1928.

"Two Oil Men Shot to Death." *Evening Journal*, October 16, 1947.

"'Umbrella of Blessings' Conferred on Gen. Butler." *The New York Times*, October 21, 1928.

Untitled article. *The New York Times*, February 4, 1903.

"U.S. Apologizes to Italy for Gen. Butler's Remarks About Premier Mussolini." *Moberly Weekly Monitor*, January 29, 1931.

"Want General Butler as Keystone Governor." *The New York Times*, September 4, 1929.

"The War in Honduras: Bonilla's Forces Have Every Fort on East Coast." *Davenport Daily Republican*, March 28, 1903.

"Whether Colonel Was Drunk or Just Sick Subject of Inquiry." *Ogden Standard-Examiner*, April 16, 1926.

"Why Congress Should Rush Work on a Stronghold in the Philippines." *The Washington Post*, January 12, 1908, Magazine Section.

"Yankee Marines in Nicaragua Are Killed in a Battle." *Waterloo Reporter*, October 5, 1912.

Books, Documents and Manuscripts

Abshire, David M. *Saving the Reagan Presidency: Trust Is the Coin of the Realm.* College Station, TX: Texas A&M University Press, 2005.

Acker, Alison. *Honduras: The Making of a Banana Republic.* Boston: South End Press, 1988.

Aguinaldo, Emilio, with Vincent Albano Pacis. *A Second Look at America.* New York: Robert Speller & Sons, 1957.

Archer, Jules. *The Plot to Seize the White House: The Shocking True Story of the Conspiracy to Overthrow FDR.* New York: Hawthorn Books, 1973.

Asprey, Robert B. *Once a Marine: The Memoirs of General A.A. Vandegrift as Told to Robert B. Asprey.* New York: W.W. Norton, 1964.

Barbour, High, and J. William Frost. *The Quakers.* Westport, CT: Greenwood Press, 1988.

Bartlett, Marrill L., and Jack Sweetman. *Leathernecks: An Illustrated History of the U.S. Marine Corps.* Annapolis: Naval Institute Press, 2008.

Bayly, Edward H. "Journal entry, June 10, 1900." In *China 1900: The Eyewitnesses Speak: The Experience of Westerners in China During the Boxer Rebellion, as Described by Participants in Letters, Diaries and Photographs,* edited by Frederic A. Sharf and Peter Harrington. Mechanicsburg, PA: Stackpole Books, 2000.

Beede, Benjamin R., ed. *The War of 1898 and U.S. Interventions, 1989–1934.* "Battle of Guantánamo Bay, Cuba." "Philippe Sudre Dartiguenave (1863–1926)." New York & London: Garland, 1994.

Biggs, Chester M., Jr. *The United States Marines in North China, 1894–1942.* Jefferson, NC: McFarland, 2003.

Blow, Michael. *A Ship to Remember: The Maine and the Spanish-American War.* New York: William Morrow, 1992.

Blumenthal, Mark. *Images of America: Quantico.* Charleston, SC: Arcadia, 2003.

Butler Family Association. *The Butler Family: Noble Butler of Pennsylvania, Ancestors and Descendents.* Self-published, 1982.

Chenoweth, Avery, with Brooke Nihart. *Semper Fi: The Definitive Illustrated History of the U.S. Marines.* New York & London: Sterling, 2005.

Cohn, Jan. *Improbably Fiction: The Life of Mary Roberts Rinehart.* Pittsburgh: University of Pennsylvania, 1980.

Comfort, William Wistar. *Quakers in the Modern World.* New York: Macmillan, 1949.

Dorland's Illustrated Medical Guide. 31st ed. Philadelphia: Saunders Elsevier, 2007.

Douglas, Paul H. "The Political History of the Occupation." In *Occupied Haiti: Being The Report of a Committee of Six Disinterested Americans Representing Organizations Exclusively American, Who, Having Personally Studied Conditions in Haiti in 1926, Favor the Restoration of the Independence of the Negro Republic,* edited by Paul H. Douglas. New York: Writers, 1927.

Dudden, Arthur P. "The City Embraces 'Normalcy,' 1919–1929." In *Philadelphia: A 300-Year History,* edited by Russell F. Weigley. New York & London: W.W. Norton, 1982.

Espino, Ovidio Diaz. *How Wall Street Created a Nation: J.P. Morgan, Teddy Roosevelt, and the Panama Canal.* New York & London: Four Walls Eight Windows, 2001.

Fleming, Charles A., Robin L. Austin, and Charles A. Bradley. *Quantico: Crossroads of the Marine Corps.* Washington, D.C.: United States Marine Corps, History and Museums Division, 1978.

Franklin D. Roosevelt Papers. Franklin D. Roosevelt Presidential Library. Hyde Park, NY.

Garraty, John A., and Mark C. Carnes, ed. *American National Biography.* 24 vols. "John Archer Lejeune." "Hanford MacNider." "Lowell Thomas." New York: Oxford University Press, 1999.

Gobat, Michel. *Confronting the American Dream: Nicaragua under U.S. Imperial Rule.* Durham & London: Duke University Press, 2005.

Hamilton, Edith. *Mythology.* New York & Scarborough, Ontario: New American Library, 1940, 1942.

Hanks, Patrick, ed. *Dictionary of American Family Names O–Z.* Vol. 3. Oxford & New York: Oxford University Press, 2003.

Haw, Stephen. *A Traveller's History of China.* New York & Northampton: Interlink Books, 1995, 1998, 2001.

Heathcote, C.W., Sr., and Lucile Shenk, eds. *A History of Chester County, Pennsylvania.* Harrisburg, PA: National Historical Association, 1932.

Heinl, Robert Deb, Jr., and Nancy Gordon Heinl. Revised and expanded by Michael Heinl. *Written in Blood: The Story of the Haitian People 1492–1995.* Lanham, MD: University Press of America, 1996.

Hofmann, George F., and Donn A. Starry, eds. *The History of U.S. Armored Forces.* Lexington, KY: University of Kentucky, 1999.

Hooton, E.R. *The Greatest Tumult: The Chinese Civil War 1936–49.* London: Brassey's (UK), 1991.

Hoover, Herbert. *The Memoirs of Herbert*

Hoover: Years of Adventure, 1874–1920. London: Hollis & Carter, 1952.

Jaffe, Philip J. *The Rise and Fall of American Communism.* New York: Horizon Press, 1975.

Jeffreys-Jones, Rhodri. *The FBI: A History.* New Haven, CT: Yale University Press, 2007.

Jones, Richard Seelye. *A History of the American Legion.* Indianapolis: Bobbs-Merrill, 1946.

Karnow, Stanley. *In Our Image: America's Empire in the Philippines.* New York: Random House, 1989.

Keenman, Jerry. *Encyclopedia of the Spanish-American and Philippine-American Wars.* Santa Barbara, CA: ABC-CLIO, 2001.

Kimes, Beverly Rae. *Standard Catalog of American Cars, 1805–1942.* 3rd ed. Iola, WI: Krause, 1996.

Kinzer, Stephen. *Overthrow: America's Century of Regime Change from Hawaii to Iraq.* New York: Henry Holt, 2006.

Klag, Michael J., ed. *Johns Hopkins Family Health Book.* New York: HarperCollins, 1999.

Klein, Philip, and Ari Hoogenboom. *A History of Pennsylvania.* 2nd ed. University Park & London: Pennsylvania State University Press, 1980.

Krauze, Enrique. *Mexico, Biography of Power: A History of Modern Mexico, 1810–1996.* Translated by Hank Heifetz. New York: HarperCollins, 1997.

Linn, Brian McAllister. *The Philippine War, 1899–1902.* Lawrence: University Press of Kansas, 2000.

Lisio, Donald. *The President and Protest: Hoover, MacArthur, and the Bonus Riot.* New York: Fordham University Press, 1994.

Longe, Jacqueline L., ed. *The Gale Encyclopedia of Medicine: T–Z, Organizations General Index.* Vol 5., 3rd ed. Detroit: Thomas Gale, 2006.

Lyon, Eunice M. "The Unpublished Papers of Major General Smedley Darlington Butler, United States Marine Corps: A Calendar." PhD diss., Catholic University of America, 1962.

Lyons, Albert S., and R. Joseph Petrucelli. *Medicine: An Illustrated History.* New York: H.N. Abrams, 1978.

MacPherson, R.T. *John H. Russell, Jr., 1872–1947: Register of His Personal Papers.* Washington, D.C.: History and Museum Divisions, 1987.

Mosby's Medical Dictionary. 7th ed. St. Louis, MO: Mosby/Elsevier, 2006.

Murphy, Jack. *History of the US Marines.* North Dighton, MA: JG Press, 2002.

Musicant, Ivan. *Empire by Default: The Spanish-American War and the Dawn of the American Century.* New York: Henry Holt, 1998.

Offner, John L. *An Unwanted War: The Diplomacy of the United States and Spain over Cuba, 1895–1898.* Chapel Hill: University of North Carolina Press, 1992.

Pencak, William. *For God and Country: The American Legion, 1919–1941.* Boston: Northeastern University Press, 1989.

Perret, Geoffrey. *Old Soldiers Never Die: The Life of Douglas MacArthur.* Holbrook, MA: Adams Media, 1996.

Porter, Roy. *The Greatest Benefit to Mankind: A Medical History of Humanity.* New York: W.W. Norton, 1998.

Preston, Diana. *The Boxer Rebellion: The Dramatic Story of China's War on Foreigners That Shook the World in the Summer of 1900.* New York: Walker, 1999, 2000.

Price, Eva Jane. *China Journal, 1889–1900: An American Missionary Family During the Boxer Rebellion with the Letters and Diaries of Eva Jane Pierce,* edited by Robert H. Felsing. New York: Charles Scribner's Sons, 1989.

Renda, Mary A. *Taking Haiti: Military Occupation and the Culture of U.S. Imperialism, 1915–1940.* Chapel Hill: University of North Carolina Press, 2001.

Reppetto, Thomas A. *The Blue Parade.* New York: Free Press, 1978.

Rinehart, Mary Roberts. *My Story.* New York: Farrar & Rinehart, 1931.

Roberts, J.A.G. *A Concise History of China.* Cambridge, MA: Harvard University Press, 1999.

Schamel, Charles E., et al. *Guide to the Records of the United States House of Representatives at the National Archives, 1789–1989.* Bicentennial Edition. Washington, D.C.: National Archives and Records Administration, 1989.

Scheina, Robert L. *Latin America's Wars: The Age of the Professional Soldier, 1900–*

2001. Vol. 2. Washington, D.C.: Brassey's, Inc., 2003.

Schmidt, Hans. *Maverick Marine: General Smedley Darlington Butler and the Contradictions of American Military History.* Lexington: University of Kentucky Press, 1987.

Schoultz, Lars. *Beneath the United States: A History of U.S. Policy toward Latin America.* Cambridge, MA: Harvard University Press, 1998.

Silbey, David J. *A War of Frontier and Empire: The Philippine-American War, 1899–1902.* New York: Hill and Wang, 2007.

Smith, Charles. *Fire Creek: A New River Gorge Mining Community.* Glen Jean, WV: Gem, 1999.

Spence, Jonathan D. *The Search for Modern China.* New York & London: W.W. Norton, 1990.

Spivak, John L. *A Man in His Time.* New York: Horizon Press, 1967.

Tan, Chester C. *The Boxer Catastrophe.* New York: Columbia University Press, 1955.

Tebbel, John. *America's Great Patriotic War with Spain: Mixed Motives, Lies and Racism in Cuba and the Philippines, 1898–1915.* Manchester Center, VT: Marshall Jones, 1996.

Tugwell, Rexford G. *The Democratic Roosevelt: A Biography of Franklin D. Roosevelt.* Garden City, NY: Doubleday, 1957.

United States. Department of Commerce. *Historical Statistics of the United States: Colonial Times to 1970.* Bicentennial Edition, part 2. Washington, D.C.: U.S. Government Printing Office, 1976.

_____. Congress. House of Representatives. *Congressional Record.* 64th Cong., vol. 53, part 3, 1st sess., 1916.

_____. _____. _____. Special Committee on Un-American Activities. *Investigation of Nazi Propaganda Activities and Investigation of Certain Other Propaganda Activities.* Part 1, 73rd Cong., 2nd sess., 1935, No. 73-D, C-6.

_____. _____. _____. _____. *Investigation of Nazi Propaganda Activities and Investigation of Certain Other Propaganda Activities: Public Statement,* 73rd Cong., 2nd sess., 1935.

_____. _____. Congress. Senate. Senate Select Committee on Haiti and Santo Domingo. *Inquiry into Occupation and Administration of Haiti and Santo Domingo.* 60th Cong., 1st sess., 1921, S. Res.

_____. State Department. *Papers Relating to the Foreign Relations of the United States, 1931.* Vol. II. Washington, D.C.: Government Printing Office, 1946.

Vanderbilt, Cornelius, Jr. *Man of the World: My Life on Five Continents.* New York: Crown, 1959.

Venzon, Anne Cipriano. *Leaders of Men: Ten Marines Who Changed the Corps.* "Smedley Darlington Butler." "Henry Clay Cochrane." "Wendell Cushing Neville." "Littleton Waller Tazewell Waller." Lanham, MD: Scarecrow Press, 2008.

Walker, Samuel. *A Critical History of Police Reform: The Emergence of Professionalism.* Lexington, MA: Lexington Books, 1977.

Walker, Thomas. *Nicaragua: Land of the Sandino.* Boulder, CO: Westview Press, 1991.

Zinn, Howard. *A People's History of the United States: 1492–Present.* New York: Harper Perennial, 1980, 1995.

Index

Numbers in bold italics refer to photographs.